# ECONOMIC FOUNDATIONS OF STRATEGIC MANAGEMENT

*For Mihan*

# Economic Foundations of Strategic Management

MEHMET BARCA
*University of Sakarya, Turkey*

Routledge
Taylor & Francis Group
LONDON AND NEW YORK

First published 2003 by Ashgate Publishing

Published 2017 by Routledge
2 Park Square, Milton Park, Abingdon, Oxon, OX14 4RN
52 Vanderbilt Avenue, New York, NY 10017

*Routledge is an imprint of the Taylor & Francis Group, an informa business*



**British Library Cataloguing in Publication Data**
Barca, Mehmet
Economic foundations of strategic management
1.Strategic planning - Philosophy 2.Strategic planning - Economic aspects
I.Title
658.4'012'01

**Library of Congress Cataloging-in-Publication Data**
Barca, Mehmet.
Economic foundations of strategic management / Mehmet Barca.
p. cm.
Includes bibliographical references and index.
ISBN 0-7546-3001-3
1. Strategic planning--Economic aspects. 2. Managerial economics. I. Title.

HD30.28 .B3673 2003
658.4'012--dc21

2002034484

ISBN 13: 978-0-7546-3001-2 (hbk)

# Contents

# Preface

The subject area of this book - exploring the extent to which economic theory can be utilised to form the theoretical foundations of strategic management - has been the source of some discomfort throughout the 1980s and 1990s. The point of departure of the debate has been that the current approaches to strategy are 'atheoretical', and of little value to discipline building, or as bases for prediction. A common critique of business strategy scholarship is that it offers little more than astute descriptions of researchers' observations of business phenomena. While the study of business strategy is multidisciplinary in nature, a majority of researchers have been attracted to economics as a core building block of strategy theory. This is not surprising given the *prima facie* parallels between the economic theory of the firm and of the market, and a subject matter of interest to scholars of business strategy. However, from the point of view of these scholars, the work of economists is limited by some central assumptions in their theory - for example, that firms 'in the long run' cannot reap economic rents (i.e., profits beyond the competitive norm). Economists assume that competition in the product, labour, and capital markets, ultimately rein in these excess profits, independent of the best efforts of managers. Scholars of business strategy generally accept as a basic tenant that managers are not impotent against competition over any time frame. However, those strategic approaches such as Porter's positioning approach have been criticised on the ground that it draws on Industrial Organisation's Structure-Conduct-Performance paradigm, which gives a low profile to the managerial efforts in creating and sustaining superior profits.

This book proposes that, rather than dismiss any economic theory altogether because of some differences, there are legitimate uses of economic reasoning in the field of strategic management. In other words, the strengths and weaknesses of various theories of the firm and of the market in economics ought to be systematically explored. By undertaking this assessment, those theories of economic that are most likely to yield fruit in establishing a theoretical foundation for business strategy development can be identified. The book seeks to further this task of bridge building.

In clearer terms, one of the enduring problems facing researchers of strategic management is the lack of theoretical foundations available to describe, explain and predict the behaviour of firms and markets. Strategic management theory seems to be strongly focused on empirical issues rather than theoretical and methodological ones. By contrast, economics, which, like strategic management theory, is interested in firm and market behaviour, is particularly strong at theoretical and methodological issues. The present study develops the thesis that economic conceptualisations of the firm and of the market can help to further the development of strategic management theory. The study constructs theoretical linkages between basic propositions and assumptions of strategic management theory and those of economic theories of the market and of the firm. The study builds such conceptual bridges between strategic management theory and economics by assessing (1) neoclassical economics, economics of industrial organisation, Austrian economics, evolutionary economics, institutional economics, economics of the growth of the firm, behavioural economics, and (2) the strategic management theories, namely, the positioning approach (Porter) and resource-based approach (Wernerfelt, Rumelt, Barney, Hamel and Prahalad).

In so doing this book covers a wide range of subject matter ranging from the philosophy of science, microeconomics, and strategic management. This book begins by considering the basis upon which differing approaches of strategic management and of the firm/market should be examined and appraised. Here we identify two major criteria - problem orientation and core assumptions - given the notions of the Kuhnian 'paradigm' and the Lakatosian 'research programme'. If compared to some other criteria such as testability, unit of analysis, normative implications, dynamic-static distinctions, the notions of paradigms as world-views and research programmes as a group of world-views structured around a common set of hard core assumptions opened up a new avenue for us to examine essentials of economic and strategic management theories, such as their problem domain, situations to which they apply, hard core assumptions on which they are based and the institutional dimension of organisational behaviour. The notions of the paradigm and the research programme as analytical categories, thus, enabled us to examine the theories in their totality and essentiality, rather than in an *ad hoc* fashion, in order to make an informed judgement as to whether economic theories supply theoretical foundations on which strategic management may rely to explain and predict its phenomena of inquiry. It should be emphasised that the use of Kuhniann and Lakatosian frameworks was for identifying problem orientation in each economic theory, isolating hard core assumptions and comparing these to the strategic management field, not for the purpose of examining the nature of growth of scientific knowledge and assessing scientific contributions of each theory on various levels.

By examining research problem orientation and hard core assumptions, the study found that apart from neoclassical economics, other economic theories substantiate strategic management theory in economic terms. Specifically, this study explicated that a large overlap between economics and strategic management theory for explaining and predicting issues concerning (1) the sources of profit differentials (competitive advantage), (2) the reasons differentials are sustained despite competition, and (3) the conceptualisation of differentials as an outcome of strategy following the behaviour of firms under conditions of uncertainty.

Thus this book aims to make 'explicit' the connection between strategic and economic ways of thinking by demonstrating where and how the two bodies of knowledge produced within different frameworks substantiate each other. Readers-to-be are invited to understand and interpret strategic phenomena within the institutional context (market and firm) in which they take place. Moreover, we invite potential readers to see the fact that recommendations of each economic theory are not independent from their theoretical settings. Therefore, rather than imposing normative perspectives on readers, readers are invited to make their own choice between conflicting/complementing recommendations from alternative theories, depending on their problems at hand.

It should also be pointed out that I prepared and submitted this book as a PhD thesis to the University of Leicester in June 2000. Although not intended as a textbook, it seems useful for students in finding criteria for comparison between theories of economics and strategy (particularly, of course, those influenced by economics) and seeing this criteria developed. Therefore, this book can be used in teaching, particularly to management students with some economics background (not that a terrible lot of economics is required; the usual intermediate microeconomics course may well be sufficient). But this book is in particular projected to appeal to doctoral students (in Economics and Business Studies), MBA students, MA in business analysis students, advanced undergraduate students (both in Economics and Management Studies), students in executive programs and practicing managers. Yet the main target of the book is academics working in the areas of economics and management studies.

# Acknowledgements

I am grateful and indebted to many people who helped make this work possible. It is impossible to mention the names of everyone - academics, friends and relatives. I feel, however, that I owe special thanks to Sigmund Wagner, my PhD supervisor, for his invaluable comments, constructive criticism, and continuous encouragement. In particular, during the writing of this PhD, my own understanding of the nature and growth of scientific knowledge and of the scientific method has deepened considerably; for this I am profoundly grateful to S. Wagner. Besides, P. M. Jackson, my PhD co-supervisor, and Harry Scharbrough of University of Leicester read, commented and encouraged; therefore, they also deserve special thanks. I am also indebted to the University of Sakarya for funding this study, to Keith Taylor for proofreading, and to Remzi Altunışık, Hayrettin Zengin and Suayyip Calis for their assistance in preparing this PhD thesis as a book for publication.

I would also like to thank all the friends and relatives who helped me, in one way or another in the process of writing this book: Mehmet Bakır, Faruk Çakır, Zühtü Arslan, Muzaffer Emekçi, Abdulkadir Dere, Halit Öcal, Erdoğan Durkut, Meryem Fethi-Duygun, Sami Fethi-Duygun, Ali Egemen, İsmail Koş, İzzet Beyaz, Adem Çaylak, Hikmet Kırık, Metin Pişkin, Victoria Pişkin, Abuzer Pınar, Hamit Ersoy and Caner Asuman

This book has been some three years in the writing. Throughout that period Mihan, my wife and friend, has shared with me all the hardship of the study. For all the patience and encouragement she has shown, she has my heartfelt thanks. Last but not least, very special thanks to my parents, brothers and sisters, and my in-laws for always being ready to help us.

Chapter 1

# Introduction: Does Strategic Management Theory Need Economics?

## Introduction

The subject of strategic management analyses the firm's relationship with its market environment (Porter, 1980; Kay, 1993). Hence, researchers in the field of strategic management need conceptual frameworks regarding the firm and market on which they may rely to explain and predict strategic phenomena. Yet, one of the enduring problems facing the field of strategic management is the lack of theoretical foundations available to describe and predict the behaviour of firms and markets (Camerer, 1985; Levy, 1994). Economists have made many important advances in explaining and predicting the behaviour of firms and markets from a, primarily, public policy point of view. The aim of the present study is to examine the existing theories of the market and of the firm in economics for their potentialities to supply theoretical foundations on which strategic management theory may be based to explain and predict its phenomena of inquiry (Rumelt, 1984; Kay, 1991; Spulber, 1993; Seth, and Thomas, 1994).

Economics has already provided many of the building blocks upon which strategic thinking and research were constructed. Some authors go even so far as to say that 'a minor revolution' has been witnessed in strategic management research and writing due to the growing influence of economics (Rumelt, Schendel and Teece, 1991). Indeed, inspired by Porter in the beginning of 1980s, a new generation of strategic management scholars views economics as the base discipline for strategic thinking and research (Hirsch, Friedman, and Koza, 1990). In the last two decades, the economics and strategic management relationship has taken three forms: one group used economics for building approaches to strategy, another group critically assessed economics for identifying the kind of economics to improve existing approaches in the field, and a third group examined economics to improve the methodology of strategic inquiry. This study seeks to add another span to the theoretical bridge between strategic management and economics. In the following sections we argue that researchers working within the framework of strategic management theory need an associated theory of the firm and of the market to supply theoretical bases on which they may rely to explain their phenomena of inquiry. In this respect, the study aims to examine and assess whether economic theories of the firm and of the market provide perspectives for thinking about strategic issues and theoretical foundations for analysing significant strategic research problems.

In what follows, there will be three sections. The first section explicates the purpose of the study and the way that the economics and strategic management is related and to be examined. There, the studies having hitherto dealt with the relationship between the fields of strategic management and economics are also examined in order to locate the present study within existing literature, and to explicate the need for such an initiation. The second section sets the study's research agenda and method. The last section elucidates the organisation of the study.

## Purpose of Study

In this section, firstly, we attempt to identify various approaches to the economics and strategic management relationship in order to denote in which context the relations is to be examined, and, secondly, to explicate the need for such an initiation and its possible contributions.

### *Approaches to the Economics and Strategic Management Relationship*

Strategic management theory has drawn on a variety of academic disciplines in order to reach its conclusions: from political science, economics, organisational psychology, organisational sociology, military strategy, systems theory, even from biology. In fact, from the outset up to present-day, the hallmark of strategic management has been eclecticism and pragmatism.

But perhaps the most important discipline on which strategic management theory has drawn is likely to be economics (Pitt-Watson, 1992). As many scholars, for example, Camerer (1985), Montgomery, Wernerfelt and Balakrihnan (1989), Rumelt, Schendel and Teece (1991, 1994), have pointed out, the aim of making use of economics in the field of strategy is to further strategy thinking and research in different ways. Foss captures the ethos of this movement very well:

> Strategy scholars have increasingly turned towards economics because, among other things, they believe that economics may increase the problem-solving ability of strategy thinking, make strategy thinking more susceptible to confrontation with empirical reality, make concepts less ambiguous, and increase fruitful dialogue between strategy scholars (Foss, 1996a, p. 187-188).

There is a growing number of scholars who turn to economics in furthering strategy thinking and research. The usefulness of economic reasoning for strategic theorising and strategy research is virtually beyond dispute. But the treatment of the relationship between economics and strategic management is under strong scrutiny from different perspectives. Broadly speaking, in the recent debate in the strategy field over the economics-strategic management nexus, there have been three distinguishing sides.

The first group sees the role of economics in developing strategic thinking and research as significant and fruitful. They use economics to develop strategy theory or schools of thought in the field. The distinguishing character of this group is that they cross over between fields and disciplines, but in a systematic manner, and recognise and maintain their distinct strengths and weaknesses. The group can be classified as *recontructionists* due to their systematic utilisation of economic theories for theory development in the field of strategy. Reconstructionists do not necessarily deliver a body of ideas more or less as developed by its leading economic thinkers, but, instead, create new analytical categories where that seems only implicit in the original economic treatment, and sometimes deviates from them.

The best example in case for this group is Porter (1980, 1985). He developed the dominant approach, positioning approach, in the 1980s, by a careful treatment and extension of industrial organisation (IO). Porter's model basically turns the IO or, more specifically, the S-C-P paradigm, upside-down, by advising managers how to restrict competition to earn above-average profits (erecting various entry barriers), rather than to focus on how to increase competition to enhance consumer profits or welfare. A second example is Wernerfelt's (1984) development of the resource-based view by utilising the Penrosian theory of the growth of the firm, an alternative school of thought to the neoclassical school in economics, which looks at economic units or firms from their resource endowments viewpoint, rather than their reactions to market price signals. Another example in case is Jacobson's endeavour of reconstructing the ideas of the

Austrian School of economics which emphasises market process and entrepreneurial discovery to develop an alternative theory of strategic management (the 'Austrian' school of strategy) to the Porterian 'positioning theory of strategy' based on conceptual foundations of industrial organisation which focuses on market structure and barriers to competition (Jacobson, 1992).

The second group also believes that economic theories can offer a great deal to the still-developing strategic management theory, but is highly critical of using economics' ideas, concepts, reasoning, etc. They critically evaluate the legitimacy of schools of thought in economics from their assumptions, orientations, unit of analyses etc. point of view, in order to use them in furthering strategic thinking and research. In other words, they focus on identifying the *kind* of economics to further strategy thinking and research. Due to their legitimacy-centred viewpoint, they can be labelled *legitimists*.

An early example in case for this group is found in Porter's (1981) examination of 'the contributions of industrial organisation to strategic management'. In general, for him, there was 'increasingly clear evidence that much promise for cross-fertilisation existed' between the strategy field and the IO tradition (Porter, 1981, p. 609). He seemed to have been well aware of the unsuitability of such premises and limitations of the industrial organisation paradigm for strategic theorising as differing frames of reference (public v private), units of analysis (industry v firm), views of the decision maker (the firm as a single decision-making unit v the firm as a collections of individuals), the state of market structure (static v dynamic), causal relation (structural determinism v strategic choice), and other significant respects (Porter, 1981). In order to make industrial economics helpful for strategy theory and research, he made critical modifications.

On the other hand, McWilliams and Smart (1993) question the relatively uncritical transfer of theoretical concepts from the S-C-P paradigm in IO economics to the strategic management field by Porter and argue that this transfer has led to inappropriate or costly generalisations and predictions. In particular, they rationalise their argument on the grounds that the S-C-P paradigm and strategic management have a different level of analysis (industry v firm), kind of analysis (static v dynamic), and determinants of persistent competitive advantage (industry level entry barriers v firm level idiosyncratic barriers). Then, they offer an alternative paradigm in IO economics, referred to as the *efficiency paradigm*, or Chicago School, which does pose such translation problems.

Another example is Foss' (1996a) examination of economic theories for their potentialities to further the resource-based view in strategic management. He does not regard it as sensible for the resource-based view to draw extensively on widely different and even conflicting economic theories, such as the game theory of industrial organisation economics and evolutionary economics. Thus he expresses his disagreement with Mahoney and Pandian's (1992) extreme view of eclecticism that the resource-based view should draw freely on any kind of economics in order to further the conversation within the field of strategic management. He argues that choices have to be made to further the resource-based view. In this respect, he discusses the potentialities of new industrial organisation (game-theoretic studies of behaviour and performance in imperfectly competitive markets), Austrian economics and evolutionary economics. He observes that evolutionary perspectives are better able to further the resource-based view than new IO and Austrian economics, because they addresses more 'dynamic' as well as 'observable' issues.

There is yet another group who deals, quite differently from the first two groups, with the economics-strategic management nexus. They approach the relationship from a *methodological* vantage point. For example, to suggest the best way to answer (and ask) strategy questions, or to assess the usefulness of methodologies employed in economic disciplines for strategic management. Accordingly, this group can be categorised as *methodologists*. For example, Camerer (1985) criticises and rejects the strategic management's traditional method of inductive generalisations of case studies which result in theories being typically ambiguous and untested and not progressed swiftly. He proposes economics' method of deductive theorising. In his view, strategy research has 'symptoms of disease causing the queasy dissatisfaction' (Camerer, 1985, p. 2), which are the consequences of the *way* strategy research is typically done. Thus, he proposes a manifesto to call primarily for 'a *methodological* shift from induction to deduction' (Camerer, 1985, p. 2, emphasis in original) to remedy the disease. He argues that deductive theorising yields clear, often non-obvious conclusions that can be debated effectively and generalised slowly.

On the other hand, Mahoney considers the Camerer proposal as a rather narrow perspective for strategy studies, and possibly counterproductive to the future growth of strategy research. He argues that 'good science is good conversation' and, accordingly, strategy research should concern itself with continuing pluralistic and pragmatic conversation of the field rather than insisting upon a place for universal methodological criteria within that conversation, using both induction and deduction methods, which, he argues, are inextricably intertwined.

Broadly speaking, the present study can be essentially categorised within the legitimists group since it examines the economics-strategy nexus from the viewpoint of critically assessing the relevance of economic theories in order to identify the *kind* of economics for furthering strategic thinking and research. Yet, the study is also different from the above-mentioned studies within the category of the legitimists in terms of its purpose. Instead of using economic theories to further any approaches (positioning, resource-based, Austrian, etc.) in the field of strategic management in different respects (for instance, furthering their explanatory power by extending them to illuminate new issues, their predictability power, etc.), the study intends to find some *conceptual foundations* on which strategy theory, as a whole, may rely to explain its phenomena of inquiry with reference to the institutional context (firm and market) in which they take place and to the pertinent theoretical conceptions. As such, theories of the market and of the firm are examined as they are for their possible conceptual merits on which strategy theory may rely.

The foundational quest for strategy theory has hitherto been neglected. This study aims to make its chief contribution in this respect to existing knowledge produced around the debate over the economics and strategic management relationship from the different viewpoints. We hope that the study help to further the dialogue between the two neighbouring fields by bringing to the fore and shedding light on the hitherto neglected but requisite (foundational) relation.

An additional contribution that the study may make is to alleviate the debate over the economics strategic management relationship from the legitimists viewpoint. The state of the debate is no less than a state of 'legitimacy crisis'. As we have already implied by giving examples from conflicting viewpoints, the debate has hitherto demonstrated a number of significant disagreements rather than agreements over the legitimacy of economics in furthering strategy thinking and research. The number of scholars participating in the debate is still relatively small but certainly growing. And, over time, the debate is intensifying rather than fading away (Foss, 1996b).

What is the reason for such a growth of disparate views? The reasons for the growing conflict seem to be because that there are some significant inadequacies occupying all the studies done within the legitimist group. These are:

1. lack of justified criteria for the examination and evaluation,
2. lack of a comprehensive or complete examination of economic theories available for their potentialities, and

3. lack of a paradigmatic perspective of strategy (approaching the relationship from the viewpoint of a certain school of thought in the field of strategy).

This study aims to remedy all these deficiencies by developing and applying a standard (criteria) for examination and judgement, by examining all the theories of the firm and of the market being subject matter of the debate, and by approaching the economics/strategic management relationship from a paradigmatic viewpoint of strategy. In doing so, the study may help alleviate the debate and generate more light than heat.

*Towards a Foundational Quest for Strategic Management Theory*

In what follows we elucidate what we mean by a 'foundational quest for strategy theory' and what the expected contributions of such a quest may be. To elucidate the economics and strategic management relationship from a 'foundational' viewpoint, the opening sentence of Porter's well-known book *Competitive Strategy* seems to be a useful departing point: 'The essence of formulating competitive strategy is relating a company to its environment' (1980, p. 3).

Whether one agrees with Porter or not, his statement is interesting in this context because it can be broken down into three conceptual entities that clarify the economics and strategic management relationship:

1. strategy, which indicates a set of actions aimed at realising competitive advantage,
2. company, which indicates an organisation with unique characteristics, and
3. environment, which indicates the unique context in which the organisation operates.

Strategy, company and environment are not independent but strongly interdependent and interacting. Strategies are formulated/formed to suit and connect varying organisational and environmental contexts. In the wording of Porter's above-quoted statement, 'strategy is *relating* a company (firm) to its environment (market)'. In the same regard, a theory of strategic management must be *related* to a theory of the firm and of the market. More clearly, just as strategy making requires, in practice, information about characteristics of organisations and environments since the characteristics of the market and the firm severely constrain strategic decisions, their implementation and consequences, so the theory of strategic management requires, from a theoretical vantage point, a theory of the market and of the firm in order to explain and predict strategic phenomena.

In other words, the argument is that strategic phenomena cannot be studied independently of the firm and its market in which they take place. As Porter (1991) indicates, 'the reason why firms succeed or fail is perhaps the central question in strategy. ... Any effort to understand success must rest on an underlying theory of the firm [and, arguably, a theory of the market,] and an associated theory of strategy'. In the same regard, Rumelt, in examining the economics-strategy theory relationship, argues that 'it appears obvious that the study of business strategy must rest on the bedrock foundations of the economist's model of the firm [an economic theory of the firm] and the theory of industrial organisation [an economic theory of the market]' (1984, p. 557).

The idea that strategy theory must rest on the bedrock foundations of an economic theory of the firm and of the market can be approached as follows:

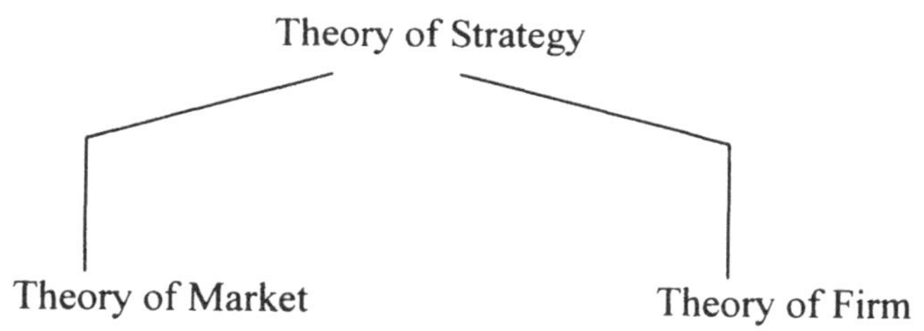


Why does strategy theory need an associated theory of the market and of the firm? Arguably, strategy theorists rely *inevitably* on some kind of conception of the firm and of the market when theorising and researching on firms' strategic behaviours and their consequences in competitive markets. In relying on economic analysis of the market and the firm, theorists of strategy may be able to build strategy theory on an explicit underlying general theory of the market and of the firm. In so doing, they may be able to build their theories of strategy from the ground up rather than the other way around.[1] In this respect, this study proposes to draw strategy theory on the conceptual foundations of economic theories of the firm and of the market. In so doing, it aims to further strategic management theory in the following respects, whatever other benefits may be obtained from such an initiation:

1. Benefits for a Grounded Perspective: First and foremost, a grounded perspective of strategic management onto theories of the firm and of the market is needed in order to construct the inferential linkage that connects basic propositions or explanations of strategy theory to those of economic theories of the firm and of the market, and thus save researchers from going back each time to find a relevant conception of the firm and of the market when conducting an inquiry about a strategic issue (i.e. the regress problem). In fact, it is difficult to imagine how strategic issues (e.g. why some firms perform better than others in the same market, do relatedly or unrelatedly diversified firms create more value and why?) could be addressed without an (implicit or explicit) associated theory of the firm and of the market which explains the context in which strategic phenomena occur. A grounded perspective makes it possible for investigators to accomplish their work without each involving in developing a suitable (implicit or explicit) conception of the market or of the firm. As such, the accumulation of the knowledge in the field might be faster and easier.
2. Benefits for a Systemic Perspective: A system-wide perspective links strategy theory to the explanations of the institutional context in which strategic phenomena occur. From a 'system' perspective, it can be asserted that every economic system consists of sub-systems and the basic sub-systems of a capitalist economic system are markets and firms. The domain concern of competitive strategy theory is, as Porter maintains, to explain reasons for *persistent performance differences* between individual *firms* operating in competitive *markets*. Strategy theory may be based on the foundations of the economist's theory of the firm and of the market in order to explain strategic phenomena in a wider context, i.e. in the context of the economic system constituting the institutions of markets and firms within which strategic phenomena occur. For strategic look involves not only a long-term perspective but also a system-wide (broad) perspective.
3. Benefits for a More Comprehensive Perspective: Economic theories of the firm and of the market may provide a fruitful basis for a more comprehensive understanding of strategic phenomena. Strategy theory does not address many key issues regarding the firm and the market. It is not principally concerned, for example, with the organisation of the market, with the evolution of the market, with the workings of the market, with the reason for the

existence of the firm, with employee motivation, with the reason and speed of the growth of the firm, with the nature of decision making in the firm, etc. Yet, these may influence the firm's strategy in practice, and shed light on strategic modes of explanation in theory.

A recognition of the 'foundational' significance raises the possibility that strategy theory as a 'specific' theory investigating the nature of *firm* differentials in competitive *markets* can be grounded in an explicit 'general' theory of the firm and of the market. Then, the research about the nature of firm differentials can be treated with reference to the workings and structuring of the firms and of the markets. In this respect, the goal of the present inquiry of the economic foundations of strategic management is to identify conceptual frameworks in economics of how firms and markets perform and are organised, and then assess whether which one of these conceptions provide best foundation for theoretically justifying strategic thinking and research.

## Research Agenda and Method

This study aims to examine theoretical bridges between economics and strategic management by drawing strategic management theory on economic theories of the firm and of the market for the purpose whether economic theories provide perspectives for thinking about strategic issues and theoretical foundations for analysing significant strategic research problems. In this regard, the overall question that we consider is, 'Can different economic theories of the market and of the firm supply theoretical foundations on which strategic management theory may be based to explain and predict its phenomena of inquiry at market and firm level of analyses? To put it in more specific terms, 'Can various economic conceptualisations of the firm and of the market be used to generate deductions about strategic phenomena or generalisations of propositions and assumptions from which strategic thinking and research proceeds?'

In order to approach the economics/strategic management relation in this respect, we also need to ask, 'In what respect should economic theories of the market and of the firm be examined and appraised, ontologically or methodologically?, 'What will be the unit of analysis for the appraisal of economic theories, hypotheses, individuated theories or research programmes?' and 'What kind of criteria should be adopted to examine and appraise or how to operationalise investigation into the relationship between economics and strategic management theory?'.

While the former questions set the research agenda for the study, the latter questions seek to find out how economic theories will be approached, what will be the unit of analysis for the appraisal of economic theories, and a standard against which the relevance of the theories will be ascertained. The former questions indicate multiple and/or competing conceptions of the market and of the firm present in the economics literature, and invite us to make a choice between them. The latter questions aim to find a relevant viewpoint from which we can evaluate economic theories, a relevant level of analysis, and a relevant standard of criticism that enables us to make the choice of the *kind* of economics of the firm and of the market on which strategy theory should rely.

As we see in detail later, there are various conceptions of the market and of the firm in the economics literature to illuminate the same reality (market and firm) but from different angles. For instance, the market is conceptualised as 'perfect competition' (neoclassical theory of the market), as an 'imperfectly performing organisation' (the structure-conduct-performance approach of industrial organisation), as a 'discovery process' (Austrian school of economics), as an 'evolutionary process of search and selection' (evolutionary theory); the firm is conceptualised as a 'production function' (neoclassical theory of the firm), as a 'governance structure' (transaction cost economics), as a 'nexus of contracts' (agency theory), as a 'repository of productive resources' (growth theory of the firm), as a 'coalition of interacting groups' (behavioural theory of the firm), and so on.

All these conceptions of the market and of the firm are developed to address different questions. For example, neoclassical economics questions how the price system coordinates the use of resources, industrial organisation economics questions how the way that markets are organised affects the performance of it, evolutionary economics questions what the dynamics of economic change are; transaction cost economics questions why firms emerge, behavioural theory of the firm questions the inner workings of firms, etc.

In this respect, the question is whether or not economic theories, constructed to address different questions regarding the market and the firm so that ended up with different conceptions of complex economic reality, address questions or problems of strategic management theory, although they are not meant to be applied to them, and, if any, which economic theory supply best theoretical foundations to address problems of interest to strategic management researchers? To put it more simply, in investigating into strategic phenomena and reaching their conclusions, can researchers of strategic management theory rely on the economists' conceptions of the firm and of the market, and which conceptions is most relevant among others for that purpose? As such, the study aims to demonstrate whether or not problems regarding the market and the firm on today's economic research agenda reflect or shed light on problems on the strategic management research agenda.

*How to Approach Economics, Ontologically or Methodologically?*

The appraisal of economic theories for their potential theoretical offerings to strategic management theory can be approached from two viewpoints: ontological and methodological. From an ontological viewpoint, economics reflects various ontic stances, for example mechanistic and evolutionary, from which economic reality is conceptualised. Different ontological stances, i.e. different conceptions of the nature of being (firm and market), can create drastic changes in the focus of theoretical thinking and research. For instance, the market is conceptualised as 'perfect competition' from a mechanistic viewpoint of being, and a 'discovery process' or 'evolutionary process of search and selection' from a processual, evolutionary viewpoint.

The most important point from an ontological viewpoint is that, as Dopfer points out, an ontic perspective not only profoundly influences the nature of economics as a science, it also influences the direction of theoretical efforts by determining what questions economists qua theoreticians are allowed to ask and what they are not (Dopfer, 1994). In other words, from different ontic stances, different theories of the firm and of the market in economics arise in response to explaining different problems. In dealing with different questions, for example, questions regarding structural or processual issues, as we see later, there come into existence various conceptions of economic reality or different conceptions ('world views') of the nature of being (market and firm). In the same line with Dopfer, O'Driscoll and Rizzo observes that point, although they do not use the term ontology:

> Proponents of different schools of economic thought have traditionally emphasised the conflicting answers that their respective schools have given the great economic questions. Recently, however, it has become evident that what really separates schools of thought is, in large part, the asking of different questions [from different ontic stances] (O'Driscoll, and Rizzo, 1985, p. 17).[2]

Economic theorising and research is driven in large part by an agenda that reflects researchers' ontic stances of what problems are tractable, significant and interesting. In other words, each ontic stance allows to view certain phenomena as significant and legitimate research problems and gives others a low profile and does not allow them to be investigated within its frame of reference. In this respect, an economic theory of the firm or of the market may or may not allow to investigate strategic phenomena as a legitimate problem from its ontic stance, or may contribute either little or, worse, confuse and obscure strategic phenomena. Therefore, the task from an ontic viewpoint is to evaluate the relevance of each economic theory of the market and of the firm with regard to whether its underlying conception of the market or of the firm or, more specifically, the question it sets to answer from its ontic viewpoint, allows us to investigate strategic phenomena within its frame of reference.

In contrast to ontological viewpoint, economics can also be approached from a methodological viewpoint. From a methodological viewpoint, economics is taken to be an 'approach', a 'method of analysis' or 'way of looking', in terms of Becker (1993, p. 385), underpinning all economic theories: 'what most distinguishes a discipline from other disciplines in the social sciences is not its subject matter but its approach.' (Becker, 1976, p. 5). This approach is the rational choice approach based on the homo economicus model of man behaving in the manner of self-interest and utility-maximising. Homo economicus model of man is only a 'heuristic' in the sense that it is not part of explanans or explanandum of economics but is only used for the purpose of model building (Popper, 1978; Lakatos, 1976; Wagner, 2000).

In other words, from methodological viewpoint, economics reflects a method, a mere way of looking rather than a subject matter or a set of questions set to answer. In this respect, economics appears to be a monolithic, homogeneous discipline rather than a discipline that is made up various theories constructed around certain problems. From a methodological viewpoint, the task is to simply evaluate economics on the basis of its potential application of its *analytical apparatus* (rational choice) to problems of strategic management decision making.

Apparently, approaching economics from a methodological viewpoint pre-empts the question of 'which conceptualisation(s)' of the firm or of the market in economics supply best theoretical foundations to strategic management theory. Indeed, in methodological respect, economics invades 'imperialistically' strategic management field by transferring its heuristic tools and assumptions to the field rather than supplies theoretical foundations on which strategic management may rely to explain its phenomena of inquiry at market and firm levels of analyses. Should the rational choice apparatus be applied to strategic problems, then, it would be hard to talk about strategic management theory since strategic management became economics or *vice versa*.[3]

### *Unit of Analysis and the Operationalisation of the Research Question*

While the ontological and methodological debate tells us how to approach the economics and strategic management relation, it does not, however, say anything explicitly about at which 'level' the assessment of economics should be conducted and how to 'operationalise' inquiry into the relationship. Arguably, the economics-strategic management relation can be treated at three different levels: hypotheses level, paradigms level, and research programmes level. At the hypotheses level the unit of analysis is single hypotheses, i.e. isolated statements (conjectures) of closely-specified relationship between two factors in a causal manner, as suggested by Popper in the context of the debate over the growth of scientific knowledge or, more specifically, over the demarcation criterion for distinguishing science from nonscience (Popper, 1959).[4] The examination of hypotheses as isolated constructs seems to be inappropriate in the context of the present study since not only is narrow isolation difficult; it is also because hypotheses about the social order cannot, in the nature of the case, be treated independent of the theoretical constructs to which they belong (Loasby, 1971). In other words, hypotheses do not stand alone; they are parts of larger theoretical constructs and links in chains of a logical argument. They require a system of ideas within which they can be interpreted (Cross, 1982; Hodgson, 1988).

At paradigms level, the unit of analysis is individuated theories, as suggested by Kuhn. Kuhn coins individuated theories as 'paradigms'. Paradigms as individuated theories are theoretical constructs, world views or shared values of a given scientific community which pre-define the relationships to be investigated (i.e. which problems to be solved), and the methods and abstractions which are to be regarded as being legitimate within their frame of references. Hence, from the Kuhnian viewpoint, economics seems to be ultimately a matter of competing 'world views' rather than an all purpose approach or methodology. To Kuhn, a paradigm pre-defines the nature and the range of questions that scientists can ask within its frame of reference.[5] We will call this 'problem area/problem orientation' By problem area we mean, in specific, which questions paradigms are designed to answer by a theory.[6] Note that the idea of problem area is consistent with the above-mentioned ontological argument that different theories arise in response to explaining different problems. In dealing with different questions they come up with different conceptions ('world views') of being (market and firm).

In this respect, what shall be done is to identify different problem areas of the market and firm theories in economics and then assess them from the viewpoint whether these different problem areas (conceptions) allow to investigate strategic phenomena within their frame of reference. In more operational terms, the question at paradigms level of analysis and appraisal of economic theories will be whether or not the following basic strategic problems or propositions are substantiated, interpreted, and illuminated within the theoretical system of each economic theory of the market and of the firm, given their problem area:

1. (why) firms differ in terms of their profit performances (?), and
2. (how) their differential profit performances persist for a long period of time despite of competitive equalisation (?).[7]

In so doing, we expect to be able to demonstrate whether or not the problems on today's economic research agenda regarding the market and firm analyses reflect those of strategic management theory.

At the research programmes level, the unit of analysis is a group of theories constructed around a set of common hard core assumptions. As Lakatos argues in the context of how to appraise the growth of scientific knowledge, 'the basic unit of appraisal must be not an isolated theory or conjunction of theories but a 'research programme' [i.e. a set of theories interrelated by a common set of presuppositions coined as the 'hard core assumptions']' (Lakatos, 1981, p. 116). As such, 'Lakatos demanded a theory that can be served as a hard core, not a mere methodology', as Latsis observes (Latsis, 1979, p. 318). Hence, the idea of hard core assumptions will also be consistent with an ontological inquiry into the economics and strategic management theory relation.

According to Lakatos, two kinds of assumptions constitute a research programme: hard core and auxiliary assumptions. To him, what differentiates one research programme from others is its hard core assumptions: 'research programmes may be characterised by their '*hard core*' ... [which is the rigid component of a research programme, thus ] 'irrefutable' by the methodological decision of its protagonists' (Lakatos, 1977, p. 133). The other component, auxiliary assumptions, 'form a *protective belt* around this core ... and get adjusted and re-adjusted, or even completely replaced, to defend the thus-hardened core' (Lakatos, 1977, p. 101). In other words, auxiliary assumptions are flexible and subject to change to protect the hard core from criticism and refutations. But, it is the hard core assumptions that constitute the identity and distinguishing character of a research programme.

The hard core assumptions distinguishing research programmes may be, primarily, motivational assumptions (e.g., maximising or satisficing), situational assumptions (e.g. environmental certainty or uncertainty), and cognitive assumptions (e.g. perfect/unbounded rationality or bounded rationality), as Latsis identifies when comparing from the Lakatosian viewpoint two research programmes (i.e. neoclassical situational determinism and the Simonian economic behaviouralism) in microeconomic theory (Latsis, 1972; Latsis, 1976). Hence, from the Lakatosian hard core assumptions of research programmes viewpoint, we should look at whether hard core assumptions of competing research programmes in economics and of strategic management theory are mutually consistent or exclusive. In more operational terms, the question at research programmes level of analyses and appraisal will be whether or not the following hard core assumptions of strategic management theory are supported by or consistent with those of economic theories:

1. firms have motivation to seek for and, if gained, sustain competitive advantages,
2. competitive advantages are phenomena of the world of uncertainty, and
3. of the world where management makes strategic decisions with limited knowledge, i.e. decision makers are boundedly rational.

It should also be pointed out that we believe that the paradigms and research programmes levels of analyses are complementary in providing us with a framework of regulative categories to assess the economic theories. While paradigms level of analysis provides us with the perspective that individuated theories can be assessed by looking at what problems they are designed to answer and what theoretical structures within which the problems are treated, research programmes level of analysis enriches and deepens our perspective by offering an analytical category which may enable us to penetrate into the internal logic of theories or to go beyond structural forms. In clearer terms, at paradigms level of analysis we ask whether or not the substance (content) of strategic management theory is interpreted, enriched and strengthened by that of each economic theory, at research programme level of analysis we ask whether the underlying assumptions governing content issues of strategic management theory are consistent with or supported by those of economic theories.

In summary, this study examines economic theories of the firm and of the market for their potential theoretical offerings to strategic management theory from an ontological viewpoint rather than applies economic approach to strategic issues from a methodological viewpoint. The unit of analysis will be individuated theories constructed around certain questions (paradigms) as well as a group of theories organised around a set of common hard core assumptions (research programmes). Hence, the task is to assess various paradigms and research programmes within economic discipline for their potentialities of theoretical illumination of strategic phenomena.

## Organisation of the Study

In order to proceed to examine and appraise economic theories of the market and of the firm for their potential theoretical foundations to strategic thinking and research, we have first to identify what the character-forming properties (problem area and hard core assumptions) of strategic thinking and research are. Thus, in Part I we ask, what are the character-forming properties of strategic management theory? Given the character-forming properties of strategic management theory, we embark upon the examination of economic theories.

In the second and third part we examine the economic theories of the market and of the firm by asking the following questions:

1. Do economic theories of the firm and of the market allow us to construct the inferential linkages that connect basic strategic explanations about performance differences between firms to the way that the market or the firm is conceptualised from the economics point of view?
2. Does the way that the market and the firm is conceptualised by economic theories allow us to treat the sustainability of performance differences between firms as a subject?
3. Do economic theories recognise that firms seek for, and if gained, sustain competitive advantages as motive force behind their behaviour?
4. Do economic theories assume some degree of uncertainty that leave room for management of firms to behave with discretion to create conditions of earning high profits or assume strong-form situational determinism (certainty) so that they deny the very

phenomena (i.e. discretionary behaviour of management) of interest that underlies the whole strategic thinking and research?

5. Do economic theories recognise some kind of constraints on the capacity of decision makers that force them to follow some kind of (imperfect) institutional guidelines (strategies, rules, operating procedures, etc.) as grounds for making choice so that end up with surprises (success as well as failure)?

In Part II we start with examining market theories, namely, neoclassical theory of perfect competition, (new and old) industrial organisation (the S-C-P approach, Chicago School, and game-theoretical approach), Austrian School of economics, and evolutionary theory. Market theories will be divided into 'structure' and 'process' theories, given their ontological orientation. Structure-oriented theories see the organisation or structure of markets as a primary factor in explaining market phenomena, whereas process-oriented theories give primacy to processual issues. Structure-oriented theories are developed within the neoclassical research programme, which are the neoclassical theory of perfect competition, the S-C-P paradigm of industrial organisation, Chicago School, and game theory. Process-oriented theories attempt to disassociate themselves from the neoclassical school. They are Austrian School of economics and evolutionary theory.

In Part III we examine economic theories of the firm. Given the same distinguishing orientations, firm theories are also divided into the two broad classes. In the first section structure-oriented theories of the firm, which are neoclassical theory of the firm and contractual theories of the firm (i.e., transaction cost economics and agency theory), are examined. In the second section process-oriented theories of the firm, namely the theory of the growth of the firm and behavioural theory, are examined.

It should be pointed out that all of the economic theories we are going to examine and appraise have achieved significant standing today because, at their core, they have groups (scientific communities) of dedicated researchers working within their frame of reference. Each theory or the set of theories may not refer to themselves as paradigms or research programmes, but they function as paradigms or research programmes in that they each have their own set of adherents, that is, distinct paradigm communities or organised around a common set of hard core assumptions.

Needless to repeat, the economic theories and strategy theory will be placed in the context of paradigms and research programmes. In the first section of each chapter we aim to identify, from a paradigmatic viewpoint, the problem area of each theory. Then, we attempt to find out whether their problem area allows us to treat the domain problems of strategic thinking and research (i.e. why firms differ in terms of their profitability, that is, what are the sources of firm differentials, and how firm differentials persist in spite of competition, that is, what is the mechanism that makes it possible for firms to sustain their differentials) within their frame of reference, although they are not designed to do so.

In the second section of each chapter, we try to identify the hard core assumptions of each theory and assess them from the viewpoint whether they are compatible with those of strategy theory.[8] In particular, we inquire whether the underlying motivational, situational and cognitive assumptions of each research programme recognise 1. strategic motivation of firms to seek and sustain competitive advantage, 2. strategic situation in which firms compete for advantage, and 3. cognitive properties of strategic decision makers.

In the concluding chapter we review the findings of the examination and evaluate the potentialities of the theories of the market and of the firm for their potential foundational service. There, we also ask, which theory of the market and/or of the firm supplies best foundational service? Furthermore, we ask, whether the economic theories compete or complement in explaining strategic phenomena? We also discuss the contributions that the study has made, and the implications for further research.

## Notes

1. It should be pointed out that in the field of strategic management, what comes closest to a theory of the market and of the firm are the positioning approach in its emphasis of market effects, and the resource-based view in its emphasis on firm specific effects, on strategic behaviours and performance differences of individual firms. According to the positioning approach a firm's competitive position is defined by its choice of market strategy (cost leadership or differentiation) and market forces, to the resource-based approach, by its bundle of unique resources and capabilities. And then, they prescribe general management to make constant improvements in the firm's market or resource positions as time, competition, and change diminish their competitive value. As Rumelt argues, 'this way of looking at the firm [and market] is *not* a theory; it is a set of constructs that have proved useful in describing and summarising the empirical studies of firm [and market] behaviour that form the core of the business policy literature.' For more details, see Rumelt (1984), in particular, pp. 557-558 (Towards a Strategic Theory of the Firm, in R.B. Lamb (eds) *Competitive Strategic Management*, Englewood Cliffs, NY: Prentice-Hall, pp. 556-570).
2. See also, Robinson, J. (1977), What are the Questions, *Journal of Economic Literature*, Vol. 15, pp. 1318-1339 and Foss, N.J. (1996), Whither the Competence Perspective?, in N.J. Foss and C. Knudsen (eds.) *Towards a Competence Theory of the Firm*, London: Routledge, pp. 175-200.

3. As Hirshleifer maintains, 'As economics "imperialistically" employs its tools of analysis over a wide range of social issues, it will *become* sociology and anthropology and political science. But correspondingly, as these other disciplines grow increasingly rigorous, they will not merely resemble but will *be* economics.' J. Hirshleifer (1977), Economics From a Biological Viewpoint, *Journal of Law and Economics*, Vol. 20, No. 1, pp. 1-52, pp. 3-4. It should also be pointed out that although we will not embark to extend the economic analysis of rational choice approach to strategic issues, we assess the usefulness of it when we deal with game-theoretical approach. Game theory is basically an application of rational choice approach to economic issues, thus underpins more or less all economic theories of the firm and of the market.
4. To Popper, the demarcation criterion between science and nonscience or pusedoscience is falsifiability: 'a statement ... has the status of belonging to empirical sciences is and only if it is falsifiable.' (Popper, K., 1983, *Realism and the Aim of Science. The Postscript to the Logic of Scientific Discovery*, Edited by W.W. Bartley III., Totowa, NJ: Rowman & Littlefield, p. xix.). Note that the objective of our analysis is not to 'prove' the scientific superiority of any of economic theories, as the philosopher of science, namely, Popper, Kuhn and Lakatos, as we see below, involved in. Our objective is to simply construct theoretical bridges between the two neighbouring fields of inquiry.
5. In the Lakatosian research programme explanation, the hard core contains also a 'positive heuristic' which is a set of suggestions or guideposts as to the directions in which work in the protective belt should proceed. The set of directives of the positive heuristic sets the agenda, i.e. the type of questions to be asked, and the mode of investigation to be followed, for a research programme.
6. Kuhn has been criticised for some inconsistencies and unclarities in the use of his notion of paradigm. For example, Masterman identified 21 different definitions of the notion of paradigm in Kuhn's book The Structure of Scientific Revolutions. See M. Masterman (1970), The Nature of a Paradigm, in I. Lakatos and A. Musgrave (eds.) *Criticism and the Growth of Knowledge*, Cambridge: Cambridge University Press, pp. 59-89.
7. The justification of the basic strategic explanations or propositions will be given in the next chapter.
8. We will not attempt to identify their auxiliary assumptions because they are likely to be less relevant for our purpose, i.e. finding stable economic foundations for strategic management. As we have pointed out above, auxiliary assumptions are subject to change to protect hard core assumptions. Moreover, they are irrelevant to some schools because they are not exposed to empirical practices due to schools' methodological orientation. For example, they play an insignificant role in the Austrian School of economics.

# PART I:

# SETTING CRITERIA TO APPRAISE AND JUDGE ECONOMIC THEORIES

The aim of this part is to identify criteria by which we can critically evaluate potential of economic theories of the firm and of the market to function as a useful theoretical foundation for strategic thinking and research. This requires identifying what strategy or strategic management is regarding its problem area and hard core assumptions. Identifying what strategic management is will then be expected to provide us a groundwork to examine and appraise the problem areas and hard core assumptions of economic theories of the firm and of the market with comparison to those of strategy theory in order to make an informed judgement about their offerings to strategy theory.

Chapter 2

# What are the Problem Area and Hard Core Assumptions of Strategic Management Theory?

## Introduction

The aim of this chapter is to identify the problem area and hard core assumptions of strategic theorising and research. In clearer terms, we attempt to identify what makes some studies categorised within 'strategy' paradigm or research programme. Towards this end, first, a brief historical evolution of the field of strategic management and various categorisations of approaches to strategy are introduced. There, we also discuss the scientific status of strategic management discipline. In the second and third sections, we attempt to identify the problem area of the field and the hard core assumptions of strategic thinking and research respectively. In the second section, we also raise the question whether the main approaches to strategy, positioning and resource-based, are competing or complementary?

## Strategic Management: Where it Comes and Where it Goes

### *A Brief History of Strategic Thinking*

Broadly speaking, it seems possible to identify two distinctive phases in the development of the field of strategic management. The year 1980 signifies the crossroad between the two phases. Prior to the year 1980, what characterised strategic management, then called business policy, was inductive reasoning and issue-centred organisation of the field. The origin of inductive reasoning in the field goes back to the Harvard Business School's case-study approach, which began in the 1920s. The case-studies revealed that firms within the same industry using the same technology differed in terms of their performances. The performance differentials were then attributed to the differences in policies such as different product approaches, organisational forms, marketing, and distributions.

From the 1960s up to 1980, many tools and techniques of strategic planning, such as product-portfolio analysis and experience curve, were developed. Common to all these endeavours was the idea that strategy theory is essentially a contingency theory, i.e. there is no best way to manage a firm or the best way to manage depends on the circumstances under which the firm operate. In this regard, up to 1980, the field was dominated by practical problems or issues, such as diversification, acquisition, innovation, revitalisation. Therefore, the field of strategic management research was organised by topics. Put it in other way, the field lacked a conceptual base.

On the contrary to the prior to 1980, 1980s were the decade of high theory. Michael Porter, in his well-known books *Competitive Strategy: Techniques for Analysing Industries and Competitors* published in 1980 and *Competitive Advantage: Creating and Sustaining Superior Performance* published in 1985, outlined a theory of competitive advantage with a set of tools for analysing industries, competitors and firms.

The importance of the Porter's Competitive Strategy Theory lies in its injection of the novel idea of generic strategies into strategy thinking and research, i.e. there are basically three generic strategies (cost leadership, differentiation and focus) that the firm can follow to achieve competitive advantage in any marketplace and time. The idea of generic strategies was deductive in character, and thereby having gone beyond the contingency arguments. It received a wide acceptance and dominated the field of strategy throughout 1980s.

A further significant development within the strategy field was of the resource-based view of strategy by Wernerfelt in 1984.[1] The approach is presented as a complementary explanation to the Porter's approach, drawing attention to the inside the firm, i.e. resources and capabilities, as much as outside the firm, i.e. competitive market or industry. The central thesis of this approach was that firms must establish strong *resource* positions, since strong *market* positions alone do not ensure persistent competitive advantage.

In the 1980s, there have been numerous notable contributions. For example, Teece (1980, 1982), Rumelt (1982, 1984, 1987), Wernerfelt (1984), Barney (1986b), Itami (1987), and Dierickx and Cool (1989), *inter alia*. However, the turning point for the resource approach was with the publication of Prahalad and Hamel's article 'The Core Competence of the Corporation' in *Harvard Business Review* in 1990. It was this article that drew practising managers' attention to the importance of the resources and capabilities, i.e. core competences in Prahalad and Hamel's term, within the firm.

The resource-based approach has gained significant momentum in 1990s, and it seems that it has been gaining dominance over the Porter's competitive strategy,[2] so far as some scholars of strategy have made the announcement of the arrival of a new paradigm.[3]

In short, as Montgomery and Porter observe, 'the 1980s were the decade during which strategy became a full-fledged management discipline' (Montgomery, and Porter, 1991, p. xi). Although Montgomery and Porter do not elucidate in what sense strategy is a discipline (ontologically or methodologically?), from their presentation it is understood that it has arrived a disciplinary standing in an ontological sense. In clearer terms, they imply that strategy theory now has an identifiable problem area. As we are to argue below, it concerns with the nature of firm differentials in terms of their profit performance. In doing so, it does not follow a certain method. Furthermore, it has arrived a disciplinary standing in the sense that it now has a conceptual base to investigate the nature of firm differentials. In 1980s the introduction of the Porter's competitive strategy and the resource-based view of strategy have brought about a disciplinary base, which has facilitated accumulation of knowledge, rendered a groundwork on which strategic thinking and research could be based.

### *Categorisations of Approaches in the Field of Strategic Management*

The production of knowledge within strategic management discipline, from the 1980s onwards, has been astounding. Yet, the field does not show a disciplinary purity. There are many schools of thought or approaches to strategy in the field. For example, Chaffee identifies three distinguishable models of strategy-making present in strategy literature: linear, adaptive, and interpretive (Chaffee, 1985). Linear model of strategy assumes that top managers follow a rational decision making process. In this respect strategy making is a sequential planning process. Adaptive model of strategy assumes that top managers assess external and internal conditions and align environmental opportunities and firm resources and capabilities in a simultaneous and continuous manner. Interpretive model takes a social contract view and portray the firm as a collection of cooperative agreements entered into by individuals with free will. It assumes that reality is not something objective and external to the perceiver, but, rather socially constructed, thereby defined through a process of social interchange in which perceptions are affirmed, modified, and replaced.

In a similar way, Whittington classifies approaches to strategy into four categories alongside two dimensions, namely, outcomes (the degree to which strategy either produces profit-maximising outcomes or deviates to allow other possibilities to intrude) and process (whether strategies are made through deliberate planning or emergent adapting): classical, evolutionary, processual, and systemic (Whittington, 1993).[4] Classical approach assumes that strategy is a rational process of deliberate calculation and analysis, designed to maximise long-term advantage; evolutionary approach assumes that strategies emerge in response to permanent environmental turbulence in order to maximise their chances of survival by aligning the firm with the environment; processual approach assumes that strategy emerges from a process of learning and compromise between divergent interest groups within the firm and the strategy needs not to be optimal; systemic approach assumes that strategies are always contingent on the social system such as Europe, Asia and Middle East in which strategy-making take place, and often deviate from the profit-maximising norm.

Mintzberg makes a more detailed classification of approaches to strategy according to the degree of rationality assumed in the process of strategy-making (formulation/formation) (Mintzberg, 1990). He identifies ten schools in strategy literature: design school (strategy-making as a conceptual process), planning school (strategy-making as a formal process), positioning school (strategy-making as an analytical process), entrepreneurial school (strategy-making as a visionary process), cognitive school (strategy-making as a mental process), learning school (strategy-making as an emergent process), political school (strategy-making as a power process), cultural school (strategy-making as an ideological process), environmental school (strategy-making as a passive process), and configurational school (strategy-making as an episodic process).

The above mentioned categorisations concern the 'how' of strategy, rather than the 'what' of strategy. In other words, they represent the 'process' of strategy-making, rather than the 'content' of strategy. Approaches to strategy content are concerned with the sources of sustainable performance differences. De Wit and Meyer (1994) classify approaches to strategy content into two categories: positioning approach and resource-based approach. While the former takes an 'outside-in' perspective and places most emphasis on various market structures and firms' positions within those structures as the decisive variables of firms' profitability, the latter takes an 'inside-out' perspective and places most emphasis on firms' specific resources and capabilities as the major factors of persistent firms' competitive advantages. We also follow, primarily, this categorisation. For the content, the strategy is essential for the examination of the relationship between economics and strategic management since the purpose is to find out whether economics provides a groundwork for thinking and researching about strategic *content* issues (i.e. the sources and mechanism of sustainable performance differences). Yet, we also concern to some extent the how of strategy when dealing with hard core assumptions of strategic thinking and research.

## Scientific State of Strategy Research

The above account should also have implied that there is yet no accepted 'mainstream' approach directing strategic studies or a 'dominant' framework to pull together all aspects or components of strategic studies and within which particular themes can be understood as specific applications. That is to say, the discipline of strategic management demonstrates a state of disciplinary fragmentation, rather than purity. As such, what is the scientific status of strategic management discipline? To use the Kuhnian terminology, is it a pre-paradigm or post-paradigm or, to use the Lakatosian's, is it an immature or a mature science?

In a Kuhnian model of science, the scientific status of strategic management should be considered as pre-paradigm, the period during which:

> ... there is a multiplicity of competing schools (but) ... evidence of progress, except within schools, is very hard to find. This is the period ... during which individuals practice science, but in which the results of their enterprise do not add up to science as we know it (Kuhn, 1970, p. 163).

In other words, according to Kuhn, the scientific status of strategic management corresponds to the 'early' rather than 'advanced' stage of scientific activity since no one paradigm or theoretical framework has yet established monopoly over the field. In the same respect, from the Lakatosian point of view, strategic management should not be considered as a 'mature' science since within a mature scientific research programme scientists consistently ignore both anomalous problems and outside criticism (intellectual and social), and focus, instead, primarily on the mathematical articulation of the research programme (Lakatos, 1970, p. 137). In short, to both philosophers of science, strategic management should not be seen as a genuinely scientific paradigm or research programme.

However, do these highly tight categorisations about the scientific status of a discipline have any correspondence in the history of science? Or, more simply, what are the examples of the other radically different types (post-paradigm or mature activity) of science? Laudan, another philosopher of science, observes that we cannot square that which Kuhn and Lakatos describe with what we know about the evolution of science:

> Kuhn can point no major science in which paradigm monopoly has been the rule, nor in which foundational debate has been questioned. Lakatos, for his part, has identified no (physical) science in which the disdain for anomaly and the indifference to extra-programmatic conceptual problems have been the prevailing features. As a result, it is extremely unclear whether the notion of a 'mature' science finds any exemplification whatsoever in the history of science (Laudan, 1977, p. 151).

That is to say, disciplinary fragmentation is the case for many, if not all disciplines. Therefore, it is rather difficult to label disciplines in this respect less genuinely scientific than their mature/post-paradigm counterparts. Nevertheless, disciplinary fragmentation has certainly presented a serious obstacle to scientific growth of the field of strategic management. Enormous effort has been wasted in interfamily disputes rather than put in search of a firm disciplinary base for the field.

There are some other obstacles to scientific growth of the field. As Camerer argues, the following three deficiencies originating in the *way* that strategic thinking and research is typically done also cause the slow accumulation of scientific knowledge in the field:

1. the field is plagued by confusion about its basic concepts which are often ambiguous and their definitions are not agreed upon,
2. theories and models in the field are rarely tested, and
3. theories in the field do not cumulate upon previous theories as they should (Camerer, 1985).

Camerer goes further and argues that the failure of knowledge to cumulate swiftly identifies strategy research as more an art than a science 'since most arts do not *need* to progress' (emphasis in origin) (1985, p. 4). But, the slow accumulation of scientific knowledge in the field should not be taken as a sign of the discipline being an art, but, rather of not being progressed towards the advance stage of scientific activity. Arguably, what makes it an art more than a science is its strong normative, practical/pragmatical orientation. The focus of strategy scholars is still on 'what ought to be' rather than 'what is'. Their major interest is in explaining persistent performance differentials between firms but the way they approach performance phenomena leads them into, primarily, discussion of implications for top management. They approach questions and problems relating performance phenomena in the practical/pragmatical way that they are asked and formulated by managers (for example, where to compete and how to compete to get competitive advantage?) rather than asked, formulated and answered by scientists.

Admittedly, all disciplines have a normative orientation. Yet, on the contrary to studies in other disciplines, studies in the discipline of strategic management often overlooks to make linkages from 'what is' to 'what ought to be'. This certainly relates its strong practical/pragmatical inclinations, i.e. to produce as much advises as and as much quickly as it can to sell, in the market of ideas (consultations, business schools, publications, etc.), people in or to be in the business world to overcome their (practical/pragmatical) problems.

Obviously, in order for strategic management to progress towards an 'advanced' stage of scientific status, it needs to ground its 'what ought to be' explanations onto 'what is' explanations. As we have implied in the previous chapter, one way of doing so is to connect practical/pragmatical strategic explanations to economics ones, such as connecting 'how markets are organised' to 'how the organisation of markets can influence the strategic behaviour and performance of firms' or connecting 'why firms are organised as they are' to 'how the organisations of firms can effect their competitive behaviour for advantage', etc. Thus, strategic thinking and research may proceed from 'what is' explanations to 'what ought to be' advises in a scientific manner. It is one of the purpose of this study is to find out whether such a connection is possible.

After this brief history of the emergence, development of strategic management discipline and its scientific status, it is time to deal with the question what constitutes its problem area and hard core assumptions or, to put it differently, what constitutes its disciplinary base?

## The Problem Area of Strategic Management Theory: Explaining Sources and Mechanism of Persistent Profit Differentials Among Firms

As we have already pointed out, Kuhn (1970) argues that what basically differentiates one paradigm from another or what constitutes a paradigm's distinctive character is its problem area, that is, which problems it attempts to solve. Which problems are more significant to solve or the choice of problem area constitutes a paradigm base within which research takes place. In this context, what is the problem area to which strategy research can attach importance and endeavour to tackle?

In his attempt. to define the field of strategic management, Teece observes that 'the field... is defined not by methodology, discipline-based theories, or paradigms, but a set of questions, the answers to which have tremendous implications for management practice' (1990, p. 42). He gives such examples: (1) what is the source of economic profits and performance differentials in profits between individual firms?, (2) how can the sources of these differential profits be protected from competitive equalisation? (3) can a firm's knowledge assets be managed strategically?, (4) how do the boundaries of the firm-lateral and vertical-affect performance?, (5) how much difference in performance does good strategic management really make?, etc.

He maintains that the strategy research focus on these issues separates the field from the related fields since no other field or discipline treat them as mainstream issues. However, a careful analysis of the all questions or issues makes it clear that all of them refer, in one way or another, to the identification of 'the sources and mechanism of *persistent firm differentials* in terms of profit performance'. In fact, Teece himself goes a bit further arguing that strategic management requires a dominant paradigm or research programme, and then suggests the 'study of rent-seeking by the enterprise' as discipline-base focus for strategy research:

> ... a key, if not *the* key, issue is one of how to position and manage the firm so as to generate, augment, and protect "economic rents". Economic rents are the returns above those necessary to keep the underlying assets available to the firm in the long run. ... It is ... what economists refer to as the "study of rent-seeking by the enterprise" (emphasis in origin) (Teece, 1990, pp. 45-46).

From Teece's viewpoint, if the strategy research deserves a name, it should be the 'rent-seeking paradigm/research programme'. In this respect the strategy field is a distinctive paradigm or research programme, not an extension of economic paradigm. As we see later, the mainstream economics, i.e. neoclassical theory, does not lack a *definition* of rent-seeking but it lacks a *theory* of rent-seeking.

Porter, the most celebrated theorist in the field, expresses the central problem of strategic thinking and research as follows: 'The reason why firms succeed or fail is perhaps the central question in strategy. It has preoccupied the strategy field since its inception ...' 1991, p. 95. The Porterian idea of 'firms' success and failure' as the central question is another way of expressing the idea of 'rent-seeking by enterprise', and to him it has been the unifying research question from the very outset up to now. For Porter the problem of firms' success and failure constitutes the base of strategy discipline in the sense that:

> the causes of firm success or failure encompass all the other questions that have been raised ... [in strategy work]. It is inextricably bound up in questions such as why firms differ, how they behave, how they choose strategies, and how they are managed (Porter, 1991, p. 95).

That is to say, according to Porter, the identification of the causes of firm success and failure is the problem area of strategic management, and all other questions must be considered the elaboration of this central problem. Lippman and Rumelt, accepting the rent-seeking behaviour of individual firms or firms success and failure as the research focus of strategic management, give a more precise and operational delineation of the problem area of any strategy-related endeavours. In their view, a theory explaining profit differentials (rent-seeking behaviour or success and failure) of individual firms must address 'both the origins of interfirm differences and the mechanism that impede their elimination through competition and entry' (Lippman and Rumelt, 1982, p. 419).

In other words, strategy theory does not deal with short-lived or temporary differentials, but 'persistent' profit differentials between firms. Therefore, alongside an explanation of the *sources* of firm differentials, there must also be an explanation of the *mechanism* of how the differentials persist over time. That is, business strategy deals with enduring competitive advantages in a competitive setting, and necessarily attempts to explain the sources of competitive advantage (success, etc.) as well as how they are sustained over time despite of competitive pressure, imitation or equilibrating market forces. If competition would erode profits, firms would find no incentive for 'strategic' investments and behaviours. Therefore, short-term advantages are not considered as a subject matter of strategic investigation.

Within the strategy discipline, there is, however, little agreement regarding the sources and mechanism of persistent firm differential. The answers given are quite diverse: the positioning of the firm relative to its market forces, the embodiment of the firm's visions, the firm's unique competencies, the firm's efficiency, the firm's critical success factors, the firm's learning ability, the firm's ability to innovate; barriers to entry and mobility, barriers to imitation and so forth. 'When reduced to their bare essentials, however, the diversity of views can be categorised into two fundamentally different approaches ... - the *positioning approach* and the *resources-based approach* ...' (De Wit and Meyer, 1994, p. 214). In order to give a more concrete idea of the strategic management's problem area, it seems necessary to introduce, at least briefly, the two approaches. They are first to be introduced in terms of their view on the sources of firm differentials, and then about the mechanism how the differentials are sustained.

## The Sources of Profit Differentials Between Firms

In any market there exist competitively advantageous and disadvantageous firms competing side by side. Some of them have competitive advantages in the sense that they outperform their rivals, and others have less advantages, earning lower rates of profit as compared with their market average. What are the sources of competitive advantages and disadvantages (success or failure)? The positioning approach, a name popularised by Mintzberg (1990), attempts to explain interfirm differences with regard to market phenomena, whereas the resource-based approach explains with internal organisational phenomena.

### *Positioning Approach*

According to the positioning approach, firm differences are the result of 'first ... the attractiveness of industries for long-term profitability and the factors that determine it ... second ... the determinants of relative competitive position within an industry' (Porter, 1985, pp. 1-2). To start with market attractiveness, the basic idea is that not all markets offer equal profit opportunities. Therefore, the average level of long-term profitability of firms varies according to markets in which they operate. Markets in which firms compete have characteristics which make them intrinsically more (or less) profitable. According to Porter, there are basically five competitive forces determine the ability of firms in a market to earn above-normal profits: 'the entry of new competitors, the threat of substitutes, the bargaining power of buyers, the bargaining power of suppliers, and the rivalry among existing competitors' (1985, p. 4). Markets with large barriers to entry, with a small number of firms, with a large degree of product differentiation, or low demand elasticity, are more profitable than markets with that of opposite features. In other words, in markets where the five forces are favourable, such as pharmaceuticals, printing and publishing, and chemicals, many competitors earn attractive returns. But in markets where one or more of the forces is intense, such as iron and steel or textile mill products, few firms earn attractive returns despite the best efforts of management. In short, the weaker the forces' collective power, the greater the potential of high profits, or *vice versa*.

Having explained five forces at the level of the market, Porter's positioning approach switches to competitors analysis to explain intra-market differences. According to the positioning approach, interfirm differences can be explained by firms' unique *positions* in their markets *vis-à-vis* the five competitive forces. The strength of their defence against the five forces determines whether they earn above- or below-average profits. Porter argues that there are in general three generic strategies available to firms to defend their positions against the market forces: firms may *position* themselves to outperform their rivals, by developing (1) a *cost* advantage or (2) *differentiation* advantage that somewhat insulates them from the five forces. Or, firms may identify (3) a market *niche* in which the five forces are less severe. The strategic positions refer also to strategic groups following the same strategy along the strategic dimensions (cost, quality, and focus). The profit differences of firms in strategic groups is often different because the five competitive forces do not have the same impact on different strategic groups.

Porter argues that those firms that successfully pursue one of these generic strategies earn above-average profits, and those firms that engage in each generic strategy but fail to achieve any of them are 'stuck-in-the-middle', i.e. in disadvantageous positions. This is because there is a trade off between the generic strategies, for example, the pursuit of differentiation advantage is usually incompatible with the pursuit of cost advantage, since they require a conflicting set of organisational arrangements, resources and capabilities, organisational culture, motivation system, etc.

### *Resource-Based Approach*

Contrary to the positioning approach's outside-in perspective (taking market as departing point to explain strategic phenomena), the resource-based approach to the economics of the firm differentials takes an inside-out organisational perspective to explain interfirm differentials (De Wit and Meyer, 1994).[5] For the theorists of the resource-based approach, firm differentials originate in firms resources. In other words, as Prahalad and Hamel argue, competitive advantages emerge through processes of resource accumulation, and deployment, so that a strategic position must be defined by the resources held by a given firm, not by market forces (Prahalad and Hamel, 1990).

Theorists of the resource-based approach assert that 'competitive advantage does not rest in industry structure or the firm's membership in a collective (e.g. strategic groups), but rather in its possession of unique difficult-to-imitate skills, knowledge, resources or competencies' (Rumelt, 1994, p. xvii). In other words, the argument is that being in an 'attractive' or 'unattractive' market is not the ultimate determinant of the firm performance in the long term. It is not difficult to find outperforming firms in markets lack of attractiveness or poorly performing firms in attractive markets. As Verdin and Williamson argue, 'industry is not destiny ... being in an 'attractive' industry is no guarantee for success, while lack of industry attractiveness is not a sentence to poor performance' (1994, p. 79). The ultimate determinant is, then, not the degree of market attractiveness, but the degree of productive resources and capabilities that firms possess. Therefore, firms differ along dimensions of their resources and capabilities that they have developed over time. If all firms have equal access to the resources and capabilities to reap or create benefits of market opportunities, then there will be no advantageous and disadvantageous firms.

What makes a firm different in terms of its profitability vis-à-vis its competitors is its position of some idiosyncratic resources and capabilities. Therefore, firm specific resources are crucial in explaining firm differentials. What are distinctive resources then? Wernerfelt broadly defines a resource as 'anything which could be thought of as a strength or weakness of a given firm' (1984, p. 172). Grant goes further and makes a distinction between resources and capabilities: 'Resources are inputs into the production process ... include items of capital equipment, skills of individual employees, patents, brand names, finance, and so on. ... Capabilities are what it can do as a result of teams of resources working together' (1991, pp. 118-120). In other words, resources are the individual assets of a firm, whereas capabilities are the working of resources together. Capabilities are firm-specific, and developed over time, through complex interactions among resources (Amit and Schoemaker, 1993).

As Barney (1991) points out, not all resources and capabilities are strategically important to create significant sustainable profit differentials between firms. Only does a *limited* number of resources and capabilities contribute to the firm long-term profit differentials. This means that, there are strategically 'core' and 'non-core' resources and capabilities in a firm, of which only core competences make significant persistent differences.

What makes a competence 'core'? Prahalad and Hamel (1990) and Hamel (1994) suggest five tests to identify core competencies in a firm:

1. a core competence provides potential access to a wide variety of markets - 'core competencies are the gateways to new markets' (Hamel, 1994, p. 15),
2. a core competence makes a disproportionate contribution to customer-perceived value-this distinction between core and non-core competencies rests partly on a distinction between core and non-core customer benefits, and
3. a core competence is difficult for rivals to imitate, i.e. it must be competitively unique (Prahalad and Hamel, 1990),
4. a core competence is an integration of skills, i.e. is a bundle of skills and technologies, rather than a single skill or technology, and
5. a competence is an accumulation of learning, an activity, not an 'asset' in the accounting sense, so competencies clusters of activities that a firm does especially well in comparison with other firms (Hamel, 1994).

The resource-based approach has not been fully developed because, as Grant points out (1991), first, the various contributions lack a single integrating framework, and second, little effort has been made to develop the practical implications of this theory. Grant attempted to make progress on both respects, proposing a framework for the resource approach. Nevertheless, the diversity of views within the approach has been continuing.

*The Mechanism that Impedes the Elimination of Firm Profit Differentials Through Competition or Sustainability of Competitive Advantage*

Perhaps the primary motive for the search for competitive advantages through strategy-following behaviour by firms is their expectation to be able to 'sustain' them after gaining. If advantages are to be nullified to the competitive level as competitors imitate successful practices easily and quickly, there is no point in behaving strategically to seek them. That is, temporary advantages have no strategic value.

But, empirical observation made by traditional strategy case research[6] as well as evidence from Western economies[7] show that competitive advantage does persist. So, what is the mechanism that impedes the elimination of firm profit differentials through competition even over a long period?

*Positioning Approach: Barriers to Entry and Mobility as Impediments to Competitive Erosion of Supernormal Profits*

The positioning approach assumes some barriers to competition, which make possible persistent differences. Barriers to competition are, simply, those factors that allow incumbent firms to earn positive economic profits, while making it unprofitable for newcomers to enter the market or the strategic group. Barriers to competition are categorised in barriers to entry and barriers to mobility. Barriers to entry refer to market-wide barriers, while barriers to mobility refer to intra-market mobility. Firms with first-mover advantages into an attractive market or strategic group erect barriers to entry from potential competitors into the market and barriers to mobility between strategic groups that restrict competition.

Porter lists six major sources of barriers to entry: economies of scale, product differentiation, capital requirements, switching costs, access to distribution channels, and government policy. For the positioning theorists, for example Caves and Porter, '...barriers are ... partly structural but at least partly endogenous' (Caves and Porter, 1977, p. 241). Caves and Porter treat barriers partly exogenous, depending upon structural variables determining demand, cost of production and cost of movement, and partly endogenous, resulting from strategic actions, for example, in the form of investments.

They also emphasise mobility barriers in addition to entry barriers. Mobility barriers are assumed created by the same sources which give rise to entry barriers. Mobility barriers help explain intra-market differences at strategic group level. In their view, differential protection offered by mobility barriers could allow some groups to consistently outperform others and enable its members to enjoy superior performance (Caves and Porter, 1977; Caves, 1984a).

*Resource-Based Approach: Barriers to Imitation as Buffers Protecting Supernormal Profits from Competitive Equalisation*

For the proponents of the resource-based approach, firms with resources and capabilities advantages cannot be easily imitated because of causal ambiguity attached to the source of competitive advantage, time compression diseconomies of creating them, nontradeablity, nonsubstitutability, and so on. They emphasise factor market imperfections, instead of product market imperfections emphasised by proponents of the positioning approach, in explaining the existence of barriers to competition. They argue that resource selection, deployment and development result in enduring differentials across firms due to factor market imperfections, defined as barriers to acquisition, imitation, and substitution of key resources and capabilities.

There is not agreement amongst theorists of the resource-based approach with regard to characteristics of resources and capabilities enhancing their sustainability.[8] Nevertheless, it is possible to classify the reasons mentioned for sustainability into three broad categories. That is, the reason why valuable resources cannot be readily imitated are because of (1) path dependencies (such as time compression diseconomies, asset mass economies, and interconnectedness that impede the accumulation of nontradeable factors that must be developed by the firm), (2) imperfect information (such as invisible assets, tacit collective knowledge and causal ambiguity, which arise in socially complex organisations and relations), and (3) idiosyncrasies (such as geographical immobility, immobility of firm-specific resources and capabilities that impede transferability of assets). Due to the above mentioned reasons, it is therefore assumed that firm resources and capabilities can, in principle, 'contribute to competitive advantage, and can be immune to the factor market threats of imitation, substitution, dissipation, and appropriation' (Collis, 1994, p. 146).

## Are the Positioning and Resource-based Approaches Competing or Complementing?

Although we have already identified the principal differences regarding the sources and mechanism of sustainable differentials among firms between the two main approaches in the field, we still need to dwell a bit more in elaborating their differences in order to get a better picture of strategic reasoning and research currently prevailing the field. More specifically, at this stage of the analysis, what should be addressed is whether these differences make the approaches competing or complementing paradigms. Although the resource-based view was put forward to complement the positioning view at the outset (Wernerfelt, 1984), an increasing number of scholars have been arguing that it is a rival paradigm to the positioning paradigm.[9] However, some other researchers maintain that they are complementary rather than rival paradigms (Barney, 1985; Porter, 1991; Mahoney and Pandian, 1992; Levinthal, 1996; Verdin and Williamson, 1994). In what follows, we first demonstrate the rationale underlying their differences, and then proceed to examine empirical findings supplied to support each approach, and finally attempt to answer whether they compete or complement.

One of the most important arguments put forward by the proponents of the resource-based approach is that product-market competition is merely the superficial expression of a deeper competition over resources and capabilities (Rumelt, 1994). An analysis of causality chain explains that product-market arena is just the last stage of a multiple-layered competitive game (Hamel, G., 1991). Moving back in the chain of causality highlights how competitive advantage or disadvantage is linked to firm-specific resources and capabilities which are basis of the value-creation process rather than structural market attractiveness.

For example, Grant (1991) argues that market attractiveness is based on resources and capabilities of individual firms rather than in and of itself. Structural sources of market attractiveness such as barriers to entry, monopolistic price-setting power or vertical bargaining power are all, in the final analysis, the consequences of individual firm resources and capabilities. For instance, barriers to entry are results of individual firms' patents, brands, and retaliatory capability; monopolistic price-setting power stems from market share which is a consequence of cost efficiency, financial strength or some other resources and capabilities; vertical bargaining power depends upon individual firm size and financial resources, etc. Therefore, not market attractiveness but individual firms' resources and capabilities are the primary basis for inter-firm profit differentials.

To Grant, moving back in the chain of causality highlights also how the Porterian generic strategies are linked to firm-specific resources and capabilities which are basis of the value-creation process. For example, cost advantage is based upon such firms' resources and capabilities as process technology, size of plants, and access to low-cost inputs, while differentiation advantage comes from brands, product technology, and marketing, distribution and service capabilities. Therefore, the resources and capabilities of a firm are primary constraints in formulating its strategy and creating high/low performance.

On the other hand, Porter (1991) argues the ultimate sources of competitive advantage originates in the structural forces that shape a market. To him, there are logically two answers to the sources of competitive advantages. The first is, as the proponents of the resources and capabilities approach argue, resources and capabilities conditions, which Porter calls *initial conditions*. As a result of their history, firms may have pre-existing reputations, skills, service capabilities, etc. influencing choices as well as constrain them. The second is that competitive advantage may be through pure *managerial choices*, independent of initial conditions. Then, he argues that lying behind all initial conditions and managerial choices are external market conditions:

> Earlier choices, which have led to the current pool of internal skills and assets, are a reflection of the external environment surrounding the firm at the time. The earlier one pushes back in the chain of causality, the more it seems that successive managerial choices and initial conditions *external* to the firm govern outcomes (emphasis in original) (Porter, 1991, p. 106).

In other words, to Porter, we have to push back in the chain of causality a step further than the proponents of the resource-based view propose in order to find out the ultimate source of competitive advantage between firms. Yet, moving back the chain of causality does not stop there. The proponents of resource-based view may propose even a further step back in the chain, i.e. what made them choose, at the first place, where to compete (the choice of market). To them, there must be some kind of internal factors made them believe that they were capable of doing business better in a particular market. From a Porterian viewpoint, having capability of doing business is not in and of itself sufficient for the choice; they must have believed that the market was promising in terms of its profit offerings, so on and so forth.

In this respect, the debate turns out to be finding out the origins of the origins ..., or, to put it differently, which one comes first, chicken or egg? The debate becomes, as such, fruitless. Even worse, it is impossible to put an end to the debate since it turns over an empirically unjustifiable causal reasoning. It is empirically unjustifiable because, as Hume argued long ago (1967), causality is not an empirical category. All the causal reasoning can only be rationally justified on the basis of the assumption of an immutable causal order but cannot be justified by reference to evidence by empirical investigation.

Although the causal reasoning cannot be established or even made probable by factual enquiry, there have been a number of significant empirical studies to identify the relative importance of market effects and firm effects in accounting for firm differentials. Most notable, researches by Schmalensee, Wernerfelt and Mongomery, and Rumelt examined this issue and have produced consistent findings:

**Table 2.1: Profit Differentials Across Firms: Comparison Between Schmalensee (1985), Wernerfelt and Montgomery (1988), and Rumelt (1991)**

| Source | Schmalensee | Wernerfelt and Montgomery | Rumelt |
|---|---|---|---|
| Corporate | x | 2.65 | 0.80 |
| Market | x | x | 8.28 |
| Market-Year | x | x | 7.84 |
| ALL MARKET | 19.46 | 19.48 | 16.12 |
| Share | 0.63 | -.18 | x |
| Share-Market Covariance | -0.62 | x | x |
| Business-Unit | x | x | 46.38 |
| Business-Unit Year | x | x | 36.70 |
| ALL INTRA-MARKET | 80.54 | 80.52 | 83.54 |
| Total | 100. | 100. | 100 |

x: Component not estimated.

Schmalensee investigated systematically the extent to which market factors as a whole explained overall performance variance among firms. Using 1975 data from the Line of Business Program of the U.S. Federal Trade Commission (FTC), Schmalensee reported that *market effect* accounted for 19.46 percent of observed variance in business unit returns. In a follow-up study using 1976 FTC data and Tobin's $q$ as a performance measure, Wernerfelt and Montgomery arrived almost the same result, with 19.48 percent market effect. Using and extending the same data base for 1974-77, Rumelt found that market effect explained 17 percent of business unit returns, but that only about half this proportion was stable from year to year, with long-term market effect accounting for 8 percent of overall variance.

Schmalensee, and Wernerfelt and Montgomery concluded that their findings supported market-centred economic view. Nonetheless, the remaining 80 percent of unexplained performance variance suggested the existence of nonmarket variables not explored in their researches. Rumelt carried out a longitudinal approach to explain the remainder. He found 46 percent of 83 percent unexplained variance in the 4-year FTC data attributable to stable *firm effect*. Rumelt concluded that 'stable business-unit effects are six times more important than stable industry effects' (Rumelt, 1991, p. 168). Note that not all of the 80 percent of unexplained performance variance is attributable to firm idiosyncratic resources and capabilities, since some will also be attributable to shared generic strategies, chance, etc.

Using a sample of 1000 firms, Hansen and Wernerfelt (1989) found that the market effect accounted for 18.50 percent and the firm-specific effect accounted for 37.78 percent of overall performance variance, i.e. firm specific effect explains about twice as much variance in profit rates as market effect. Also, using an alternative sample and methodology based on executives' perceptions, Power (1996) derived findings supporting those reported in previous studies, with industry factors explaining about 20 percent of overall performance variance. In a recent study, using recently compiled data from the Compustat Business Segment Reports for 1981 through 1994, McGahan and Porter (1997) found variations in year effects, stable market effects, stable corporate-parent effects, and stable segment-specific effects account for 2 percent, 19 percent, 4 percent, and 32 percent, respectively, of the aggregate variance in business-segment profits. They argued that studies (Schmalensee, 1985; Wernerfelt and Motgomery, 1989; and McGahan and Porter, 1997) repeatedly show that average market profitability is, by far, the most significant predictor of firm performance and 'called into question Rumelt's finding that stable industry effects have low influence' (McGahan and Porter, 1997, p. 29).

Empirical evidence notwithstanding, the debate on the relative importance of market effects and firm effects in accounting for firm differentials has also not been conclusive and, as such, '... will continue to prove fruitless', as Henderson and Mitchell argue (Henderson and Mitchell, 1997, p. 6). There seem to be two reasons for this, they cite: (1) 'in the first place, both organisation [firm effect] and competition [market effect] are clearly important in shaping strategy and performance' (2) in the second place, there seems to be a reciprocal interaction between these elements, that is, 'reciprocal interactions at multiple levels of analysis between the market environment and firm capabilities shape business strategy and performance, in turn, shape both organisational capabilities and competitive environments' (Henderson and Mitchell, 1997, p. 6). In other words, market effects and firm effects explain interdependently firm differentials across markets and across firms.

In fact, while easy in theory to discuss the role of each market and firm factors independently, in practice it is very difficult to separate the impact of market and firm specific effects on performance differentials. Although their relative importance varies from study to study, obviously, as empirical evidence suggests, firm effects and market effects are together of paramount importance in explaining observed variance in business unit returns.

In this respect, given the debate over which one is decisive (i.e. the problem of the origin), market or firm-specific factors, and the relative merit of each, it can be argued that they complement rather than compete, and they complement interdependently in explaining profit differentials across firms. This can be demonstrated diagramatically as follows:

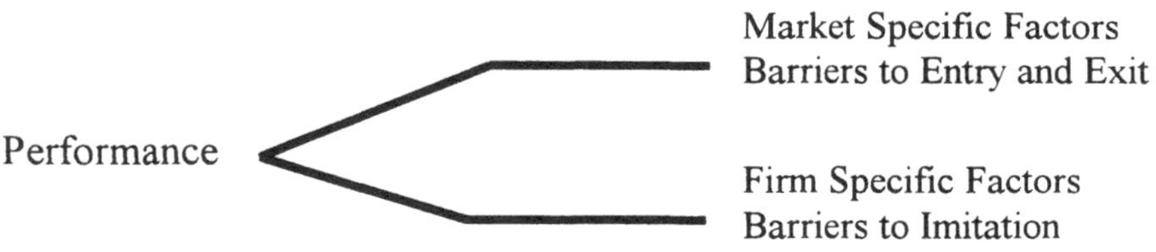


In other word, competitive advantage typically reflects some combination of market-specific and firm-specific factors. Arguably, the balance between each factor varies from company to company and from market to market, depending firm and market attributes, but it is always a repercussion of external and internal factors which are strongly interrelated, in particular, when considered over a long period of time. As Henderson and Mitchell maintain:

> firms develop organisational capabilities as they act in competitive, institutional, and cognitive environment ... The capabilities, managers' understanding of the capabilities, and the historical context that surrounds them then condition firms' reactions to changes in their environment. The reactions and firm performance in turn affect the structure of industry, and all these changes generate new information which in turn creates new learning opportunities. Thus, ... strategy and performance as an ongoing sequence of capabilities-conditioned adaptations by firms which in turn become exogenous events in the environments of the managers of other firms (Henderson and Mitchell, 1997, p. 5).

Researchers who maintain that they are rival paradigms put forward the argument that they ask different questions and suggest different policy recommendations. For example, Hamel and Heene mention the following questions to exemplify the divergence of opinions in the field, which represent contrasting and competing paradigmatic bases:

> Is strategy about 'positioning' within an extant industry structure or about redrawing industry boundaries for one's own advantage? Is the essence of strategic management the creation of sustainable advantage or the continuous discovery of new sources of advantages as old advantages lose their potency? Does the dynamic of strategy derive from the search for 'fit' between the firm and its environment or from a 'deliberately created misfit' between resources and aspirations? (Hamel and Heene, 1994, pp. 1-2).

Arguably, all these questions indicate not contrasting and competing paradigms but intra-paradigm conflicts. What unites them is the same paradigmatic base: to identify the sources and mechanism of persistent firm differentials. In other words, both share an identifiable problem area. Within this problem area they approach the phenomena of inquiry from different angels: market position and resource position. Yet, as Porter argues, 'stress on resources must complement, not substitute for, stress on market positions' (Porter, 1991, p. 108).

To Porter, the rationale behind the view that the conceptions of market position and resource position complement rather than compete in explaining persistent firm differentials is that resources are only meaningful if they allow firms to perform activities to achieve certain competitive advantages in particular markets. The founder of the resource-based view, Wernerfelt, also shares the same idea and maintain that 'for the firm, resources [position] and products [market position] are two sides of the same coin.' Therefore, what underlies every product market position is a pool of firm-specific resource position, that is, product market positions (cost or differentiation) require the service of certain resources and capabilities (such as brand names, in-house knowledge of technology and efficient procedures). Then, the firm-specific resources and capabilities can be used to diversify in different markets

Finally, it should be pointed out that the field of strategic management lacks, for the time being, a 'grand theory of strategy' to unify the diversity and variety of views in the field, which is the case for all social sciences. Yet, as we have demonstrated, it has an identifiable disciplinary base in explaining why firms differ from one another in terms of their profit performance, despite of equilibrating competition. In this respect, for an economic theory of the market or of the firm to be considered as potentially promising for its foundational service to strategy theory, it must present an explanation about the sources and mechanism of persistent firm differentials.

## Hard Core Assumptions of Strategic Management: Reconstructing Strategic Management Theory to Identify Assumptions Governing All Strategic Thinking and Research

The point of this section is to make explicit the hard core assumptions that underlie strategic thinking and research. This requires a rational reformulation of the body of ideas expounded by leading thinkers in the field. Rational reformulation is basically to create new analytical categories, or more simply, to unearth the hidden assumptions implicit in strategic theorising and research. These assumptions are assumed to govern all strategic thinking and research. The identification of the hard core assumptions of strategic thinking and research is a subsequent endeavour to that of identifying its problem area, and is expected to shed more light on the nature of reasoning and research carried out within this frame of reference.

The fundamental presupposition of strategy research programme is that every firm is assumed to follow some kind of strategy. For example, as Henderson puts it, 'since the beginning of business, all firms have had plans and all firms have followed some kind of strategy' (Henderson, 1984, p. 2). Strategy-following behaviour simply means that each firm walks through life with some (strong) opinions of what is the best, whether it be their views about how to run a firm (management philosophy), how to organise the firm, where to compete and how to compete, etc. The strategy-less firm is thus not assumed to exist and is not seen as an area of interest for strategy research.[10]

As we have pointed out in the first section of this chapter, strategic thinking and research originated in the observation that that firms within the same industry using the same technology differed in terms of their performances. The performance differentials were then attributed to the differences in strategy-following behaviour of firms such as different product approaches, organisational forms, marketing, and distributions.

Strategy-following behaviour of firms are often assumed to be implicit in the patterns of decisions (for example in the decisions regarding the choice of which resources to be developed and deployed, pricing or product design, etc.).[11] Note that strategy-following behaviour is assumed to appear even the firm does not have a 'declaratory/articulated',[12] and/or 'grand/overall' strategy.[13] Strategy-following behaviour (actions) can be an outcome of an articulated/grand strategy from very outset, lead over time to an articulated/grand strategy, or never produce an articulated/grand strategy.

For the presupposition, the presupposition of the strategy-following behaviour, to be operational, several important conditions must exist. These conditions relate to the motivation and cognitive nature of decision makers and the situation under which the decisions are assumed to be taken. In this respect, the following set of conditions are assumed to be at work to make possible for firms to follow some kind of strategy.

1. *Firms (Management) Have Motivation to Compete to Seek for and Sustain, if Gained, Advantages:* In a competitive market, firms are assumed

to compete for advantages; this is the meaning attached to 'competition' in strategic thinking and research. Approaches to strategy in the field may disagree over sources of sustained competitive advantage (market position, resource position, visionary leadership, discoveries/innovations, etc.), but have the common belief that the motivation of firms is to seek for and sustain, if gained, competitive advantage.

Hence all strategic thinking and research is based on the assumption that, from the very outset, firms have intended to create conditions of earning high profits or gaining and sustaining competitive advantage, which is a manifestation of that firm implementing or following some kind of strategy (Barney, 1985). In other words, the reason for following strategy is the driving motive of seeking for and sustaining competitive advantage.

Competitive advantage describes an edge that a firm has over its rival in external market competition in terms of high profit performance. Therefore, competitive advantage indicates, not an absolute (optimal, maximum), but a relative notion of profit performance. A firm can enjoy a competitive advantage only relative to its rivals in the same market or in the same strategic group. Sustainability means that competitive advantage can persist over a long period of time since disadvantageous firms are unlikely to do equally well in a short period of time what advantageous firms do for long. Yet, the length of time does not correspond to an observed reality; it could be from five years to fifty years.

Hence, competition for advantage indicates a 'process' rather than a 'state' or 'one-off' action. In the face of change (demand, social, political, and so on conditions) and competitive pressure (entry to profitable markets and exit from unprofitable markets, discoveries/innovations, imitative actions, etc.), new sources of competitive advantage must be developed, and the existing ones need to be consistently nurtured. For example, Porter suggests that in order for a firm to sustain its competitive advantage, it must offer a 'moving target to its competitors by reinvesting in order to continually improve its position' (Porter, 1985, p. 20). In the same respect, Grant suggests that 'commitment to upgrading the firm's pool of resources and capabilities ... will form the basis of the firm's future competitive advantage' (Grant, 1991, p. 124).

Motivation for competitive advantage also indicates that top management focuses on some of decisions which are considerably more important (having more impact on performance) than others (i.e., the distinction between strategic and non-strategic decisions) (Rumelt, 1984). Therefore, they have strategic value (having firm-wide, long-term and considerable effect in terms of creating competitive advantage), and need to be treated differently from that of non-strategic ones. However, the distinction between strategic and non-strategic decisions is not clear-cut. In fact, the distinction between them is one of degree rather than of kind (Karlof, 1993). Strategic decisions are assumed to be concerned with a firm's long-term and broad direction, and thus constrain the operational/day-to-day, or tactical/administrative issues. Yet, it should be noted that this does not mean that what is going on within the firm and overall outcomes are determined solely by strategic decisions, but strategic decisions are assumed to represent 'the pinnacle of a hierarchical system of decision-making' (Cowling, and Sugden, 1993, p. 68), and are critical determinants of the firm's competitive advantage. However, operational and administrative gains can also be translated into sustainable profitability or competitive advantage (Peters, and Waterman, 1982). But it is still assumed to be the task of strategic management to translate them into competitive advantage (Porter, 1996).

2. *Strategic Decisions are Made in a World of Uncertainty:* Strategic decisions are taken in conditions of widespread, irreducible uncertainty regarding future outcomes, future contingencies, rivals' behaviour, consumers' behaviour, best means to achieve competitive advantage, etc. With uncertainty prevailing, firms need to be strategically governed, that is, in an uncertain world firms are forced to rely on institutional guidelines and standard patters of action to deal with unanticipated events, to avoid launching themselves each time afresh into overcoming new problems, to ensure consistent coordination between departments and actions, to achieve some kind of stability, etc.

Under the conditions of irreducible and widespread uncertainty, strategic guidelines, by establishing more or less fixed patterns of constraints upon firm behaviour, supply information to management about how to deal with problems. Thus strategic guidelines enable the conscious decision-making over time. Whereas if constraints did not exist the behaviour of the firm could change with every perturbation in the business world, and such frequent adjustments to behaviour, and thereby the resultant profit performance, might be perceived as random. In assuming the informational function of strategy-following behaviour strategy scholars imply non-random firm differentials, despite uncertainty, complexity and information overload surrounding business environment. Yet, they also recognise that the strategic process necessarily leads to outcomes with an unavoidable degree of uncertainty. They assume that there is some possibility of predicting the consequences of strategic choices (for example, predictions based on structural market analysis), but no prediction can be perfect. Therefore, the goodness or the betterness of strategies as projections of some future outcomes will never be known for sure until they have been tried. In this sense, strategy-following behaviours are experimentally organised behaviours in the face of uncertainty.

A second function of strategy-following behaviour is to create 'stability' in the face of uncertainty. The reason for obtaining stability in the face of uncertainty is the need of management for continuity and sameness in all they are doing. They obtain stability by adopting the practice of basing their actions on long-lasting opinions, guidelines, or projections about what is good for them to do in all contingencies and modifying them only to the extent that there exist more or less definite reasons for a change. Another function of strategy-following behaviour in the face of uncertainty is to create 'consistency' between departmental activities, and 'consistency' between actions taking place in different times, when viewed from either the perspective of a grand strategy or any single set of reasons (e.g., to achieve cost leadership or differentiation). Any strategy theorising and research postulates some consistent pattern that is to be found in strategic decision makers' choices, or put it another way, that decision makers act consistently with some kind of the patterned actions to seek for persistent advantages.

In fact, strategy-following behaviour in a world of uncertainty can, overall, be understood as a process of rationalisation of firm behaviour in the sense that it works to reduce uncertainty by providing consistency, facilitating action, bringing stability, providing guidelines to save to launch each time afresh to overcome new problems, giving direction, etc., and thereby rationalising success and failure.

3. *Strategy-Following Behaviour is a Boundedly Rational Behaviour:* Strategy-following is assumed to be a 'rational' behaviour. Strategic decision makers are assumed to behave rationally in the sense that when they make strategic decisions they are assumed to have some good reasons to make choices among alternatives. To put it in another way, rationality - whether we are speaking about rational strategic actions or rational strategic believes, opinions or perspectives - consists in believing in, and acting on those ways of managing the firm that they (managers) have good personal reasons (e.g., based on market analysis or resource and capability analysis, visions, experience) for doing so to obtain competitive advantage.[14]

It should be emphasised that a way of managing the firm that would count as good reasons for one firm cannot constitute good reasons for another firm. Managers make strategic decisions with limited knowledge, foresight, time, capacity of processing and interpreting data, etc., with different suppositions, expectations, routines and criteria, under different conditions and pressures, and in the face of different problems, so that they believe in and act on different personal reasons. In other words, firms specific bundle of resources, path-dependencies, previous choices, constraints on the perception and capabilities of decision makers, etc., do not allow to make the best choice 'universally' open to them, but make best choice 'specifically' available (given its history, resource bundles, perception of opportunities and threats, future expectations, etc.) to them. In this respect, strategic decision makers are only 'boundedly' rational. Boundedly rational decision makers are neither conscious of the whole set of alternatives (opportunities) that lie before them and what will follow from their actions, nor they know the complete set of means to exploit them. In addition, they are not capable of calculating the probability of outcomes in order to maximise the expected value of their actions. That is, strategy-following behaviour does not solve problems optimally.

It should also be noted that the notion of strategic rationality does not necessarily mean a highly-structured rational decision making procedure in the sense that the general management identify techno-economic opportunities and problems, systematically search for and weigh alternatives, and make choices that maximise organisational performance. Strategic rationality can be structured, analytical and systematic in the above sense (Porter, 1980, 1985; Ansof, 1965), as well as manifest itself in a processual trial and error learning fashion (Mintzberg and Waters, 1985) or in a logical incrementalist way (a process in which each action step is logical given the information at that step, without assuming a grand logic that derives action within firms) (Quinn, 1980).

As the above analysis shows, at the heart of strategy research programme lies the notion of strategy-following behaviour. It attempts to explain why some firms do well and others poorly in market economies. It presupposes that firm differentials is not a matter of chance, although it may play some role, but the consequence of firms intentional actions. Furthermore, it hints that firms with good strategies outperform firms with bad strategies.[15] Therefore, it suggests that good strategies explain a substantive deal of success. Yet, it recognises that there are severe difficulties as to the assessment of what is 'good', especially in situations of uncertainty and in a world where decision makers are boundedly rational and decisions are made through time.

Given the hard core assumptions, the notion of strategy-following behaviour implies a situation in which the existence of some significant room for strategic choice, discretion, or intentionality of actions in seeking persistent high profits prevails. The notion of strategic situation in which discretional choices are assumed to be made to affect outcomes constitutes the very basis of strategic theorising and research. The implication is, then, that theories which assume a situation of 'strong-form economic determinism' are unlikely to function as a useful foundation for research in strategy as they assume away the very phenomena, i.e. intentional profit-seeking behaviour [in the face of environmental uncertainty and limited cognitive capacity of decision makers], of interest to strategy researchers (Seth and Thomas, 1994). In other words, firm differentials in profits should not be considered as results of situational factors (accidents, luck, random or pre-determined) altogether, but of intentional firm strategic actions at least to some extent. They must recognise some grounds for making strategic choices.

Strategy-following behaviour denotes not only the carrier of persistent firm differentials but also an institutionalised behaviour. At its core, strategy-following behaviour is a historical and social behaviour that marshals and expends its energies in the pursuit of high profits in a competitive capitalist social order. Like other social and historical entities such as society, state, and civic organisations that follow some kind of rules, the firm as a social and historical category is also assumed to follow some kind of strategies as rules to govern its activities.

Until recently strategy theorists have not explicitly dealt with the institutional (social, historical) side of strategy making. Rhetoric- and prescription-laden literature approached strategy phenomena as if strategies are made with one-off decisions, formulated through a purely universal 'decision logic' or 'logic of choice'. Resource-based approach and process oriented studies of strategy seem to have remedied, at least partly, the institutional deficiency by furthering the theory into human behaviour in a socially interactive order. Thus, they have helped to make clearer the conceptual starting points (bounded rationality, uncertainty, path-dependency, organisational failure, etc.) and the method of inquiry (social science perspective, rather than, a-historical, a-social analytical models).

In this respect, for the economic theories of the market and of the firm to be considered as legitimate foundations for strategy theory, they must recognise, or at least, be suitable to accommodate, the presupposition that every firm follows some kind of strategies. The presupposition of strategy-following behaviour is fundamental to all strategic thinking and research. In fact, all the hard core assumptions render rationalisation for it. In other words, the assumptions give existence or meaning to the presupposition of strategy-following behaviour. They are rendered irrefutable by the methodological decision of the researchers that are working within the strategy research programme. Therefore, for the economic theories of the market and of the firm to be considered as the legitimate bases for strategic thinking and research, they need to recognise all the hard core assumptions.

Arguably, the hard core assumptions, namely, the motivational assumption (seeking and sustaining competitive advantage), the situational assumption (strategic decisions are made in a world of uncertainty), and cognitive assumption (strategic decision makers are boundedly rational), can easily be applied to any social context. In other words, they are not specific to strategic context, but, rather can be generalised to any social setting in which social individuals are in an interdependent situation (i.e. in competition with each other). The economic theories regarding the social settings under considerations, i.e. markets and firms, can thus be examined in this respect.

## Conclusions

Although after two decades in which an increasing number of researches have been done in the field of strategic management, the present study has revealed that the field of strategic management faces a number of significant obstacles to scientific growth of the field. These are, primarily, the lack of a dominant paradigm governing strategic research, much intra-disciplinary conflicts, confusion about concepts, failure to cumulate upon previous theories in the field through theory testing, strong pragmatical (normative) orientation, etc. One way of progressing towards an 'advance' stage of scientific activity in which the accumulation of scientific knowledge will be swift seems to be drawing strategic thinking and research upon a common conception of the firm and of the market. For this purpose, we turn to economics because in the field of economics there have already been significant advances in conceptualising the firm and the market.

Although there is no one 'theory' of strategy, there is what might be considered to be 'mainstream' approaches to strategy. These mainstream approaches are the positioning approach, which takes market structure, and resources-based approach, which takes firm-specific resources and capabilities, as their decisive factors in explaining and predicting strategic phenomena. In examining strategy literature broadly and the two approaches specifically, we find out that the field has an identifiable problem area. Research in this area concentrates on why firms differ from each other in terms of their profit performance and why profit differentials between them seem to be persistent despite struggling for entry to profitable markets and strategic groups, and imitative competition to equalise the differentials.

The field has also an identifiable set of hard core assumptions governing strategic thinking and research. The central presupposition on which all strategic theorising and research turn is that every firm follows some kind of strategy. For the presupposition to be viable the following hard core assumptions are made: firms have motivation to seek for, and if gained, to sustain advantages over each others in a capitalist competitive setting, the situation in which strategic decisions are made is inherently uncertain which is irreducible and widespread, and strategic decision makers behave rationally in their choices (make their choices on good grounds) but are cognitively bounded to do so.

Given the problem area and hard core assumptions, for the economic theories of the firm and of the market to be considered as a legitimate basis for strategy theory, they need satisfy the following criteria:

1. an explanation concerning sources or causes of profit differentials between firms,
2. an explanation concerning the mechanism or reason(s) why the differentials are not equalised by competition, and
3. a recognition of strategy-following behaviour, as an boundedly rational (cognitive assumptions) to seek and sustain competitive advantage (motivational assumption), under the condition of uncertainty (situational assumption).

The set of criteria seems to be necessary and sufficient to demarcate strategic from non-strategic theorising and research, thereby enabling us to evaluate and judge whether the economic theories of the market and of the firm can be potentially treated as 'strategic' in order to draw strategic thinking and research on their conceptual frameworks, although they are not designed to do so. In other words, these criteria constitute the acid test for the potential foundational role of economic theories to strategic management discipline.

## Notes

1. Wernerfelt, B. (1984), A Resource-based View of the Firm, *Strategic Management Journal*, Vol. 5, pp. 171-180. In the 1960s, at University of Chicago, academics criticised the traditional market or entry barriers theory and put forward the alternative view that high profits were returns to specialised, high-quality resources and capabilities. This becomes an important inspiration for the resources and capabilities approach, which has been highly popular in the 1990s. The Chicago School offered

'efficiency' based explanations for a number of practices such as firm size, advertising, as opposed to the Mason/Bain-type Industrial Organisation (IO) tradition view of monopoly power centred explanations. The work of Penrose (1959) *The Theory of the Growth of the Firm*, has had a significant effect on the resource approach. She attempted to explain the growth of the firm *from within* the firm. She accepted the key role of the entrepreneur and the competence of management, but gave detailed attention to the bundle of resources in explaining the growth of the firm. Nowadays, the resource-based approach has fed from evolutionary theory, put forward by Nelson and Winter (1982).

2. For example, Segal-Horn declares the resource-based view 'as the dominant strategy paradigm of the 1990s.' Segal-Horn, S. (1998) The Resource-Based View of Strategy. Introduction, in S. Segal-Horn (eds.) *The Strategy Reader*, Oxford: Basil Blackwell, pp. 177-178.
3. For example, Conner, K.R. (1991) A Historical Comparison of Resource-Based Theory and Five Schools of Thought Within Industrial Organisation Economics: Do We Have A New Theory of the Firm?, *Journal of Management*, Vol. 17, pp. 121-154; Teece, D.J., Pisano, G. and Shuen, A. (1990) Firm Capabilities, Resources and the Concept of Strategy, CCC Working Paper No. 90-8, University of California at Berkeley; Peteraf, M.A. (1993) The Cornerstones of Competitive Advantage: A Resource-based View, *Strategic Management Journal*, Vol. 14, pp. 179-191.
4. See, in particular, pp. 2-41.
5. For a comparison between the two approaches, see Chapter 5 (De Wit, B. and Meyer, R., 1994), in particular pp. 214-217.
6. See Porter (1980); Peters and Waterman (1982).
7. See H. Odigari, and H. Yamawaki (1990) The Persistence of Profits: International Comparison, in D.C. Mueller (eds.) *The Dynamics of Company Profits*, Cambridge University Press; J. Cubbin, and P. Geroski (1987) The Convergence of Profits in the Long Run: Inter-firm and Inter-Industry Comparisons, *Journal of Industrial Economics*, Vol. 35, pp. 427-442.
8. For example, Barney (1986a, 1991) mentions four characteristics, that is, resources must be valuable, rare, imperfectly imitable (because of unique historical conditions, causal ambiguity, social complexity), and limitedly substitutable in order to be the sources of persistent supernormal profits; Dierickx and Cool (1989) mention three characteristics, namely, nontradeability, nonimitability (because of time compression economies, asset mass efficiencies, interconnectedness of asset stocks, asset erosion, causal ambiguity), and nonsubstitutablity; Amit and Schomaker (1993) mention three characteristics as difficult to buy, sell, imitate or substitute, complementarity, and firm specificity, durability, and scarcity; and Grant (1991) mentions four imperfections with regard to durability, transparency, transferability (due to geographical immobility, imperfect information, firm-specific resources, immobility of capabilities), and replicability, as the characteristics of resources to be sources of sustainable high performance.
9. For example, Conner (1991); Grant (1991); Teece, Pisano, and Shuen (1990); Peteraf (1993); Stalk, Evans, and Shulman (1992); Hamel and Heene (1994), and so on.
10. Inkpen and Choudhury (1995) and Inkpen (1996) argue that strategy absence should also be viewed as a legitimate phenomenon of interest. In fact, what they mean by strategy absence is not the absence of a strategy but the absence of an *articulated* strategy. But they acknowledge that 'from a strategy content perspective, every firm has a strategy because every firm has products, markets, channels of distribution, and so on' (Inkpen, 1996, p. 669) and from a process point of view, if the strategy is taken as a pattern in a stream of decisions, strategy absence does not apply. For a discussion

see A. Inkpen and N. Choudhury (1995) The Seeking of Strategy Where It is Not: Towards a theory of Strategy Absence, *Strategic Management Journal*, Vol. 16, pp. 313-323; A. Inkpen (1996) The Seeking of Strategy Where It is Not: Towards a Theory of Strategy Absence: A Reply to Bauerschmidt, *Strategic Management Journal*, Vol. 17, pp. 669-670; A.D. Bauerschmidt (1996) Speaking of Strategy: A Comment on Inkpen and Choudhury (1995), *Strategic Management Journal*, Vol. 17, pp. 665-667.

11. For strategy making process and whether strategies are deliberate and emergent, see H. Minzberg, D. Raisinghani and A Theoret (1976) The Structure of "Unstructured" Decisions, *Administrative Science Quarterly*, Vol. 21, pp. 246-275; H. Mintzberg and J.A. Waters, 1985, Of Strategies, Deliberate and Emergent, *Strategic Management Journal*, Vol. 6, pp. 257-272; H. Mintzberg (1987b) Crafting Strategy, *Harvard Business Review*, Vol. 65, No. 4, pp. 66-75.
12. Porter, for example, states 'every firm competing in an industry has a strategy, whether explicit or implicit' (1980, p. xiii).
13. Declaratory and grand strategy can be emergent rather than intended as consequence of strategy-following behaviour.
14. Personal reasons are not based on 'objective' but 'subjective' knowledge, no matter whether they are based on analysis, vision, experience or intuition.
15. However, there is no accepted criteria to judge what a good strategy is. The criteria for the betterness or goodness of strategies change from one school of thought to another in the field, such as an explicit choice between the generic strategies, commitment, superior visions, the capacity of developing and deploying core competences, the capability of learning fast than rivals, etc.

# PART II: MARKET THEORIES

In the first chapter, we maintained that every theory aims to investigate certain phenomena as significant and legitimate research problems and gives others a low profile and does not allow them to be investigated within its frame of reference. Given this argument, we raised the question 'whether or not economic theories of the firm or of the market allow us to investigate strategic phenomena as a significant and legitimate problem within their research scope, despite the fact that they are not constructed for that purpose'. To embark on answering the question, we needed, first, to know what strategic phenomena are. In the second chapter, we attempted to find out how strategic phenomena are understood or interpreted within strategic management theory. In the theory, strategic phenomena is taken to be observed (1) *persistent* (2) *firm differentials in profits as outcome variables of firms* (3) *strategy-following behaviours* (4) *due to the limited knowledge of decision makers* (5) *under the conditions of uncertainty*.

## Questions to be Raised for the Appraisal of Economic Theories

Now, we are ready to embark on evaluating and judging economic theories from the viewpoint whether they recognise strategic phenomena as a legitimate and significant research problem. In clearer and more operational terms, for an economic theory to function as a useful theoretical foundation for strategic thinking and research, it must satisfy the following five criteria:

1. An economic theory of the firm or of the market must offer an explanation concerning sources or causes of profit differentials between firms or, more generally, why some firms succeed and others fail. The explanation of the causes of firm success or competitive advantage underlies the whole strategic thinking and research so that the strategic way of thinking can not be thought of without such an implicit or explicit explanation. Therefore, we ask, 'Do economic theories of the firm and of the market allow us to construct the inferential linkages that connect basic strategic

explanations about performance differences between firms to the way that the market or the firm is conceptualised from the economics point of view?'

2. An economic theory of the firm or of the market must also offer an explanation concerning the mechanism or reasons why profit differentials are not levelled away by competition in long term. If a firm' success or competitive advantage can be replicated easily and quickly by its rivals, so that the success or advantage is temporary rather than sustainable, it does not have a 'strategic' significance. Therefore, we also ask, 'Does the way that the market and the firm is conceptualised by economic theories allow us to raise the possibility of dealing implicitly or explicitly with the reasons or mechanism of persistent performance differences between firms?'
3. An economic theory of the firm or of the market must recognise that firms compete with each other over gaining and securing advantages in competitive markets (i.e. they have intention to outperform each other). In order to outperform each other firms need to create some favourable conditions in markets in which they operate. Therefore, we ask, 'Do economic theories recognise that firms seek for, and if gained, sustain competitive advantages as motive force behind their behaviour in competitive markets?'
4. An economic theory of the firm or of the market must assume some degree of uncertainty regarding future contingencies, rivals or consumers' behaviours, best way of doing business, etc. that makes it possible for firms to behave with discretion to create favourable conditions of earning high profits. If future, rivals and consumers' behaviour, best way of doing business, etc. is certain or pre-known, there would be no grounds for making strategic choice. Therefore, we ask, 'Do economic theories assume some degree of uncertainty that leave room for firms to behave strategically to create conditions of earning high profits or assume strong-form situational determinism (certainty) so that deny the very phenomena (i.e. discretionary behaviour of management) of interest that underlies the whole strategic thinking and research?'
5. An economic theory of the firm or of the market must also recognise some bounds on decision makers' cognitive, computational, predictive etc. capacity that pave the way to firms' success as well as failure. Strategy is about choice, and strategic decision makers behave rationally in the sense that they have some grounds or reasons for choosing. Yet, their capacity in finding reasons (for example, based on their analyses of markets and

> idiosyncratic resources, predictions, visions, etc.) for creating conditions of earning sustainable high profits must be limited or imperfect. With bounds to their capacity of being globally or perfectly rational, decision makers are forced to rely on (imperfect) institutional guidelines (strategies, rules, routines, standard operating procedures, etc.) as substitutes for global or perfect rationality. Therefore, we ask, 'Do economic theories recognise some kind of constraints on the capacity of decision makers that force them to follow some kind of (imperfect) institutional guidelines for making choice so that end up with surprises (success as well as failure)?'

To answer the questions, the economic theories of the market and of the firm are placed, as it has been applied to strategy theory, in the context of the Kuhnian paradigms to identify their problem areas, and of the Lakatosian scientific research programmes to unearth their hard core assumptions. In the first sections of each of the following chapters in Part II and III, we deal with the problem areas of economic theories, i.e. the types of questions they set to answer, in order to evaluate the relevance of each economic theory of the market and of the firm with regard to how the underlying various *conceptualisations* of the market and of the firm in economics allow us to investigate strategic phenomena. More specifically, we are to look at whether economic theories supply an explanation about the basic strategic propositions regarding sources and sustainability of competitive profit differentials between firms (the first two criteria). In the second sections, we try to find out whether the assumptions underlying economic theories are compatible with those of strategy theory. More specifically, we are to conduct a situational analysis of each theory in order to see whether the situations that economic theories are designed to apply or explain can be considered strategic situations in which firms follow some kind of strategies to obtain and sustain competitive advantages under the conditions of uncertainty and limited capacity of decision makers (last three criteria). We expect that utilising both the Kuhnian paradigm and the Lakatosian research programme as analytical concepts will enable us to examine the theories in their totality and essentiality, thereby saving us from committing the fallacy of looking for their possible partial and *ad hoc* contributions.

## Classification of Economic Theories

Economic theories can be categorised into two broad classes: 'structure-oriented' and 'process-oriented'. The rationale behind this classification is the observation that the development of the modern economic discipline can be characterised by two ontological stances that seem to compete each other. As we pointed out in Chapter 1, arguably, there are, in economic discipline, two different ontic conceptions of the nature of economic reality, based on the analogies borrowed from classical mechanics and biology. Although the ontological standpoint from which economic reality is conceptualised is often implicit, they create drastic changes in the focus of theoretical thinking and research. While the former focuses on the structure (organisation) of economic reality (markets and firms), the latter turns attention to the process (dynamics) of economic reality (i.e. to the basic nature of economic interaction and economic change).

The use of mechanistic and biological analogies in economics is an old tradition. For example, Jevons and Walras, the two prominent founding fathers of neoclassical schools of economics, make an explicit statement of how they construct their theory of economics in analogy to mechanics. Jevons relates economics very closely 'to the science of Statical Mechanics' (1924, p. xvii) and states that 'economics, if it is to be a science at all, must be a mathematical science' (1924, p. 3). For him, the fundamental principles of economics are so general in character that they can be rightfully compared to the principles of natural sciences whose 'basis more or less obviously in the general principles of mechanics' (1924, p. xvii). From the same ontic stand, Walras maintains in his preface to the fourth edition of his Elements: 'if the pure theory of economics ... is a physico-mathematical science like mechanics or hydrodynamics, then economists should not be afraid to use the methods and language of mathematics' (1977, p. 71). As we have seen, his general equilibrium theory is a consequent repercussion of the mechanistic approach.

Yet, some neoclassical economists, for instance Marshall, do not seem to be satisfied with studying the purely mechanical operation of abstract economic forces. 'The Mecca of the economist lies in economic biology rather than in economic dynamics' (1924, p. xiv) argues Marshall and sees that 'Economics is a branch of biology, broadly interpreted' (1924, p. 772). But he also makes the excuse that we have no other choice than to start with economic dynamics since biological conceptions are more complex than those of mechanics. He intended to write later a volume on dynamics which would proceed with an evolutionary and biological analogy but never materialised his intention or in Hodgson's (1993) terms, never reached his Mecca.

However, some other researchers working within the neoclassical paradigm or research programme did use biological analogies in their work. The first systematic endeavour in developing an economic theory in analogy to biology seems to have been Alchian's (1950) famous article in 1950, *Uncertainty, Evolution and Economic Theory*. Alchian made use of the natural selection metaphor in order to legitimate continuing use of the neoclassical theory of the firm at a time when it was under severe attack. Alchian, unhappy with maximising assumption, argued that 'profit maximisation' can be replaced with the weaker assumption of 'positive realised profits' with no loss of predictive content. Suffice to say here that Alchian's evolutionary theory was a social Darwinist theory, according to which the internal workings of the firm are irrelevant, since the behaviour of the firm is determined by the long term environmental pressure to survive.[1] Despite the fact that he approached economic reality from an evolutionary standpoint, the way he treated social, economic reality (strong-form environmental determinism) did not break up with mechanistic modes of thinking which do not allow to inquire social interaction and social change based on discreational individual units (economic agents and institutions).

In contrast, some economists have challenged the mechanistic world-view, and promoted an organicist alternative. For example, Veblen (1919) was so influenced by Darwin that he was to ask 'Why Is Economics Not An Evolutionary Science?' in his famous 1898 essay, and resolved to transform economics into an 'evolutionary science'. His endeavours gave rise to the dissenting school of (old) institutionalism offering an explanation of the historical progression of social forms, habits and beliefs. Another dissenting school, the Austrian, criticised the mechanistic approach on the basis that economics set in timeless logic could not be construed as scientific in any practical sense. Hayek (1979; 1988) invoked evolutionary arguments in his work, and offered a theoretical conception of the development of rules and institutions, or, in Hayek's terms, the notion of *cultural evolution*, and of the relation between the character of a spontaneous social order and the kinds of rules (genetic and cultural) governing human behaviour. Yet, it is the seminal work of Nelson and Winter, *An Evolutionary Theory of Economic Change* (1982) which has brought about the modern revival of an evolutionary approach to economic phenomena as an alternative theory of economics to the mainstream neoclassical scheme of the mechanistic approach.

The boundaries between mechanistic and organistic standpoints are not, in fact, as clear-cut as they seem to be at first glance. For example, the Williamsonian version of 'transaction cost economics' within the researech programme of institutional economics shows signs of both ontic conceptions. On the one hand, Williamson (1991) uses a mechanical metaphor to define transaction costs,[2] and, on the other hand, he uses evolutionary metaphor to explain the coordination of investment.[3] Similarly, although the focus of theories of industrial organisation is on the 'structural' issues, they also accommodate time dimension, in contrast to rigid mechanistic stance of neoclassical theory, in their analyses.

Yet, it is still possible to classify economic theories around these broad trends, given their 'central' interest: the 'structure' and 'process' of social and economic existence. Theories within the first trend pertain to neoclassical or neoclassically-inclined paradigms or research programmes, and approach their phenomena from an 'equilibrium-structure standpoint'. Theories within the second trend stem from an increasing desire to analyse their phenomena from a 'disequilibrium-process standpoint'. The structure-oriented theories have generally been concerned with consequences, and have tended to jettison process 'details' in order to concentrate on 'structural' impacts; in contrast, the process-oriented theories have generally tended to go beyond the apparent structural consequences or impacts, and tended to find out the dynamic forces that have led to the current state of the market and of the firm.

Given these considerations, in this part, first, structure-oriented (neoclassical theory of perfect competition and theories of industrial organisation), and then, process-oriented (Austrian economics and evolutionary economics) market theories are going to be assessed. In the following part, we turn, with the same considerations, to firm theories.

Before proceeding, a cautionary note should also be made. As we have pointed out in Chapter 1, theories as conceptual frameworks are 'constructed' in order to illuminate a 'specific' aspect of reality under consideration (problem dependency), that is, theories are not descriptions of the total complex reality. In the process of developing a theory or model to examine a specific part of or variables of reality, it is unavoidable to make 'unrealistic' assumptions in order to isolate particular problems with which researchers may be concerned (Friedman, 1953). In this respect, the realism or unrealism of scientific theories is not or should not be an issue for debate.

Yet, it must be highlighted that, in some places, the debate on the realism or unrealism of theories is indicated, *not as our own view*, but rather, to give the rationale or reasons of successive theorists initiating a new conceptual framework. In so doing, besides the benefit of being able to follow the developmental chain of theories one after the other in the context of the growth of scientific knowledge, we may also be able to point out differences between them in terms of their implications for strategic management thinking and research.

As we see, all successive economic theories in question emerge to distance themselves from neoclassical theory of the market and of the firm in one way or another. Hence, we also start our examination with neoclassical theory, and then proceed to examining other theories, tracing back their departing points and implications for strategic thinking and research.

## Notes

1. This, therefore, seems not to be useful for strategic thinking and research since it presupposes a strong-form situational determinism and down plays individual firms' discreational behaviour in determining their performance outcomes.
2. 'A transaction occurs when a good or service is transferred across a technologically separable interface. One stage of activity terminates and another begins. With a well-working interface, as with a well-working machine, these transfers occur smoothly. In mechanical systems we look for friction: do the gears mesh, are the parts lubricated, is there needless slippage or other loss of energy? The economic counterpart of friction is transaction cost: do the parties to the exchange operate harmoniously, or are there frequent breakdowns, and other malfunctions?' Williamson, O.E. (1985) *The Economic Institutions of Capitalism: Firms, Markets, Relational Contracting*, London: Free Press, pp. 1-2.
3. See Williamson, O.E. (1991) Strategizing, Economizing, and Economic Organization, *Strategic Management Journal*, Vol. 12, pp.75-94.

# 'Structure-Oriented' Theories of the Market: Perfect Competition and Industrial Organisation

The neoclassical school of economics has been the dominant school of economics almost for a century. Neoclassical principles are taught in university courses as the foundations of economic science, without even mentioning alternative schools of thought in economics discipline. As Gee observes, 'in fact, the orthodox economist would regard the type of economics taught as being definitive, rather than as belonging to a particular school among alternative equally valid schools' (1990, p. 71).

Gee likens the neoclassical school to a broad church, offering a methodology and paradigm embracing many sects. In this respect, neoclassical market theories can be categorised into two identifiable sects: theory of perfect competition and theories of industrial organisation (the S-C-P paradigm, Chicago School, and Game Theory). In general, while the former has a strong theoretical, the latter has an empirical tendency. Yet, what really differentiates them is that they focus on opposing end of the same spectrum: the former deals with perfectly organised highly competitive markets, whereas the latter concentrates on imperfectly organised (oligopolistic/concentrated) markets. They are perfect or imperfect in terms of the number and power of individual firms competing in the market, that is, the situation of an infinite number of firms with no market power (perfect competition), and that of a few firms with some kind of market power (imperfect competition). First, the neoclassical theory of perfect competition, and then the theories of industrial organisation, will be examined.

## Chapter 3

# Neoclassical Perfect Competition

### Introduction

In what follows, we examine the most renowned sect, the theory of perfect competition, from the viewpoint that whether strategic phenomena can be treated as a legitimate research problem within the theory in taking its problem area and hard core assumptions as given.

Many of the issues in this area of economics date back to Adam Smith in the eighteenth century, whose work must be deemed as important in the history of economic thought in terms of the nature of what is studied in the subject called 'microeconomics' today. The neoclassical theory of perfect competition emerged between 1870 and 1900. During this period a transformation from classical economics to neoclassical economics occurred. This transformation gave shape to modern microeconomics theory. The foundations of this new paradigm were based on the works of W.S. Jevons' *Theory of Political Economy* (1871), C. Menger's *Principles of Economics* (1871), L. Walras's *Elements of Pure Economics* (1874), and A. Marshall's work, *Principles of Economics* (1890).

### Problem Area: Conceptualising the Market as a Perfectly Running Machine

The problem area for research regarding capitalist market institution in the neoclassical paradigm was to solve the mystery of order in the world of business, which is not imposed from above, i.e. from an administrative/hierarchical structure which ensures that the actions of individual agents are coordinated, but somehow the consequence of the exchange transactions between economic agents, who seek to maximise their own gain. In terms of Hahn,

> the central question ... [is] how do decentralised choices interact and perhaps get coordinated in favour of a theory according to which an economy is to be understood as the outcome of the maximisation of a representative agent's utility over an infinite future? (Hahn, 1991, p. 49).

In other words, the problem central to neoclassics was to explain, by the means of 'equilibrium' notion, the consequences of decentralisation of a capitalist economic system based on market transactions of individual economic agents (Blaug, 1985; Demsetz, 1982). In this respect, they endeavoured to deal with the same problem as classics did before them. For example, Adam Smith attempted to explain market order through his conception of 'invisible-hand'. For him the economic problem is the coordination of economic activities, and coordination is needed since specialisation is more productive than self-sufficiency.

The problem of the mystery of market order remained as a link between classics and neoclassics. Nevertheless, what led neoclassics to bring about a new paradigm was the principal criticism of the classical theory of value on the basis that it had been inadequate to explain market forces determining market order and to lack generality. Instead of seeking the ultimate explanation of value in labour, they put forward the argument that the value, or price, of a commodity depends upon the marginal utility of the commodity to the consumer. Then they assumed that in a competitive 'free market' economy, economic activities are related to one another through a system of prices, which are determined by the interaction of the marginal adjustment (maximising) behaviour of economic agents, in allocating scarce resources between their alternative uses, through which market coordination obtains. In general, the introduction of marginal analysis, among other analytical tools such as equilibrium and optimality, into explaining the economics of the firm, the behaviour of the household and price determination in the market revolutionised the theory of economics into a new paradigm.

More precisely, the focus of economic analysis in the hands of neoclassics shifted from the great question on wealth growth, as in the Smith's seminal work *the Nature and Causes of the Wealth of Nations*, to exclusively on resource allocation. In other words, as Dasgupta observes,

> The advent of marginalism marks a decisive shift in the nature of economic theory. Economic theory ceases to be an inquiry into the causes and implications of the growth of wealth; it becomes an inquiry into the problem of allocation of *given* resources among competing lines of production. (emphasis in original) (Dasgupta, 1985, p. 77).

Thus, the research area of neoclassical paradigm, which distinguishes it from that of classical paradigm, substituted the problem of resource allocation as economic problem for the problem of wealth accumulation. The application of marginal analysis was principally to the way in which competitive markets allocate scarce resources among alternative uses, that is, to move resources from uses yielding lower rates of returns to uses yielding higher returns. The regulator of resource allocation is assumed to be relative prices: if 'too much' of some commodity is available, or 'not enough' of another is produced, the only way requisite proportions can be restored is by a change in prices which now encourages agents to reallocate resources in appropriate ways. Thus, the equilibrium is assumed to be obtained.

However, in practice, the most important research question in neoclassical paradigm has been the question of what conditions will suffice to ensure that such an equilibrium is possible. In other words, from a normative point of view, the economic problem envisaged was one of how to secure an 'efficient' allocation of scarce resources in free (competitive) markets. As Arrow observes, this is the best developed part of the theory: 'The best developed part of the theory relates to only a single question: the statement of a set of conditions, as weak as possible, which insure that a competitive equilibrium exists and is Pareto-efficient' (1970, p. 67). Because of the huge intellectual energy spent dealing with this level of analysis in the paradigm as well as its importance for our purpose, it seems essential to spend some time in its examination.

In order to identify the necessary and sufficient conditions for competitive equilibrium to yield an optimal allocation of resources, the focus of the neoclassical paradigm has been on 'competition', or more precisely 'perfect competition', which can deliver them. Historically contemplated,[1] conditions of competition were first loosely conjectured by Smith in the sense of rivalry in a race. Jevon merged the concepts of competition and market, and characterised perfect market by two conditions:

1. a market is theoretically perfect when all traders have perfect knowledge of conditions of supply and demand, and
2. there must be perfectly free competition, so that anyone will exchange with anyone else (Jevon, 1871, pp. 87-86).

Walras develops his analysis of general equilibrium for a hypothetical regime of perfect competition: 'we shall suppose that the market is perfectly competitive, just as in pure mechanics we suppose, to start with, that machines are perfectly frictionless' (1954, p. 84). For Walras the key requirements for competition resulting in an equilibrium being reached are:

1. supply and demand be equal in all markets, and
2. the price of every commodity equals its cost of production.

That is, the requirements are that markets clear at equilibrium prices and producers make neither profit nor loss. What are characteristics of Walras' perfectly organised market are first, that, as Dasgupta points out (1985, pp. 78-79), decisions taken by economic agents are *reversible* in the sense that agents as consumers or producers make experimental (and hence reversible) decisions. The only way the market can establish equilibrium prices is by a process of trial and error, that is, by a process of *tatonnement*. Therefore, the time dimension in the Walrasian analysis is not considered to be irreversible historical time, but reversible spatial time. Second, in perfectly organised markets, no transactions are concluded until a price is determined at which effective demand is equal to effective supply for the commodity concerned. That is, Walrasian economic agents enter actively his economy only at a particular point in time. In this particular point in time equilibrium 'will be established effectively through the reciprocal exchange between services employed and products manufactured within a given period of time during which no change in the data is allowed' (Walras, 1954, p. 242). Therefore, equilibrium is a stationary phase.

In developing the new paradigm, it was Edgeworth who was the first to attempt to examine systematically and define 'perfect competition' (Edgeworth, 1881). For him the necessary and sufficient conditions of perfect competition were (1) indefinitely large number of suppliers and consumers, (2) complete absence of limitations upon individuals self-seeking behaviour, and (3) complete divisibility of the commodities traded. Clark added two new elements to the Edgewort conditions: the mobility of resources and the model of the stationary economy (Clark, 1899). Furthermore, Knight attempted to establish an economic model to explain the impact of uncertainty (Knight, 1921). He took complete knowledge as a preliminary step in the analysis to establish the precise nature of an economy. For him to achieve complete competitive equilibrium requires full knowledge of all relevant circumstances, which realistically can be reached only when these circumstances do not change, that is, when the economy is stationary. He argued that if we wish to have the concept of perfect competition denote only equilibrium which is not affected by the actions of individual suppliers and consumers, then large numbers and complete knowledge are sufficient to eliminate monopoly power.

The historical development of the concept, as Stigler notes, resulted in the increasing recognition of the stringency of the conditions that appeared to be necessary and/or sufficient for perfect competition. Together they are: large numbers, full information and negligible search costs, product homogeneity and divisibility, free entry and exit, lack of collusion, and absence of externalities and of increasing returns to scale. To have explained the 'existence' and 'optimality' of competitive equilibrium, the concept of perfect competition in the sense of its modern usage was thus reached. The theory of perfect competition about which Stigler wrote still largely corresponds to the way most economists think about perfect competition when doing applied work.

## Can Strategic Phenomena be Investigated Within the Neoclassical Perfect Competition Paradigm?

Then, given the notion of perfect competition as well as those of equilibrium, optimality, maximising behaviour in order to explain efficient resource allocation, can strategic phenomena (persistent firm differentials) observed in business markets be taken as a legitimate problem of inquiry within the theory of perfectly organised markets?

On the face of it, the problem of resource allocation seems to be very significant for strategic inquiry into firm differentials. For resource allocation is, in essence, a behavioural choice problem, which is at the centre of strategy theory. It may illuminate answering such strategic questions as where to allocate resources: to this market or that, to this market position or that, to this department or that, to this product or that, etc., which one is better for my business, what quantity of a product should be produced? And, thus it may enable us to understand differentials through different resource allocation decisions or choices.

For neoclassics, a market system offers a way for economic agents to reach decisions about how to use their resources. The system works through market prices. Prices are assigned to goods and resources in markets so that each economic agent can make his/her own choices at those prices, on a decentralised basis. Some assumptions that the argument is based on are: prices reflect all information that economic agents need to make decisions; costs of information gathering are negligible; economic agents make decisions independently (atomistic behaviour); prices for all markets, including future markets for goods, are known; all decision makers use the same decision making procedure, that is, profit maximising or cost minimising, and so on.

Given these assumptions, resource allocation problem envisaged in the theory is not a real decision problem, certainly not a strategic one, but reduced to one of simple calculation. Because, first of all, strategic decisions are taken under uncertainty; if there is certainty, there is no need for a 'strategic' decision. Second, business firms are not atomistic units independent of the behaviours of other firms. The behaviours and activities of other firms in the same and prospective markets will have great importance for, and influence on, each firm's decisions. Third, strategic behaviours in resource allocation such as building barriers to competition (advertising, differentiating, etc.) are routinely condemned as 'monopolistic' and, thus, as resource 'misallocating'. The list can be enlarged. In short, the problem of resource allocation through market prices does not help to illuminate strategic choice, and accordingly, persistent firm differentials.

At the heart of the theory of perfect competition lies the notion of equilibrium.[2] However, equilibrium explanations of, or approaches to, market coordination has a variety of meanings. For example, if 'no tendency to change exists, [the] system may be said 'to be in equilibrium'' (Frisch, 1936, p. 100); 'a market is in equilibrium, statistically considered, if every person [firm] is acting in such a way as to reach his most preferred position, subject to the opportunities open to him [it]. This implies that the actions of different persons [firms] trading must be consistent' (Hicks, 1939, p. 58). From a decision making point of view, 'an economy is in equilibrium when it generates messages which do not cause agents to change the theories which they hold or the policies which they pursue' (Hahn, 1973, p. 25) or from strategy-following behaviour of firms in seeking competitive advantages, equilibrium is 'a state in which no agent [firm] can improve himself [itself] by any action' (Hahn, 1984a, p. 79) and so on.

Common to these definitions is that the equilibrium position is, from an individual firms' point of view, a state of rest for them, and of harmony with one another. In this state of rest and harmony, all possible gains from trade are assumed, by definition, to be already exhausted, and all firms in all industries earn the same rate of return. The equilibrium state has obtained, since each firm has correctly expected (estimated) the strategy of the others and hence optimised relative to those correct expectations. Therefore, there is no 'endogenous' tendency to change their positions, strategies or plans. Moreover, if any 'exogenous' disturbance moves the economy out of the equilibrium state of firms' rest and harmony, giving rise to firm or industry profitability differentials, equilibrating forces swiftly bring them into the state of rest and harmony, without being subject at any time to interference from market participants' (i.e. firms) obstacles. In this respect, the theory is 'designed to explain why people [firms] do not move' (Loasby, 1991, p. 53), not why they do move to create sustainable advantageous positions.

The theory of perfect competition, which seems, on the face of it, to explain the nature of competition among economic agents, thereby shedding light on strategic competition, unfortunately, suggests that there should be no competition at all in its everyday and strategic usage sense. First of all, it should be remembered that the idea of perfect competition is used as a tool to explain efficient resource allocation with relation to market price mechanism. In this respect, the aim is not to understand competition *qua* competition but to explain all the market phenomena through competition or more clearly exchange/transaction. More specifically, the focus is not on competitive behaviour between individual firms but on competition as a mechanism of resource allocation at market level.

In the theory excessive attention is given to only one kind of competition, namely price competition. Yet, price competition is also not used in its daily usage, i.e. price wars or competition based on price discrimination. But, as Arrow defines it, competition 'refers to the assumption that each household or firm takes prices as given and independent of its decision' (1983, p. 118). In other words, all economic agents participating markets behave competitively when each acts as if they cannot affect prices, and given prices, as if they follow optimising behaviour since they are so small and powerless relative to market to enforce a strategy affecting market supply, aggregate demand, and/or market price. This is the basis of the explanation of how market equilibrium and efficient resource allocation are achieved.

Apart from price competition, all other kinds of more strategic competition such as competition from new commodity, the new technology, new types of organisation (Schumpeter, 1962), or, competition which commands a cost or quality advantage (Porter, 1985), competition for better resource and capabilities (Prahalad and Hamel, 1990), and competition for profitable markets and market niches, which are seen as the essence of competition in the real world of business and lies at the heart of the notion of competitive strategy, have been ignored, if not denied. In general, in neoclassical perfect competition theory, competition is taken to be characterised by the absence of rivalry. This is clearly a denial of a strategic view of competition in the sense of active rivalry, or more clearly, struggle with others to get ahead (competitive advantage). As Morgestern argues, in neoclassical perfect competition theory,

> there is nothing of this true kind of competition: there are only individuals, firms or consumers, facing *given* prices, *fixed* conditions, each firm or consumer for convenience *insignificantly* small and having no *influence* whatsoever upon the existing conditions of the market (rather mysteriously) formed by tatonnement [the process of equilibrium formation, or tentative proceedings] and therefore solely concerned with maximising *sure* utility or profit - the latter then being exactly zero (emphasis in original) (Morgenstern, 1972, p. 1164).

Obviously, strategic phenomena, i.e. persistent firm differentials, cannot be taken as a legitimate research problem in neoclassical theory of market. On the contrary, they are denied by the theory. Firms are assumed to have identical technology, resource and capability endowments, market niches, decision making rules (maximising behaviour), etc. Therefore they have at least none of these sources for differentiating themselves by engaging in strategic competition. Nor have they any incentive to engage in competitive advantage since they have no reason to change their strategies or plans. As Hicks (1976) points out, when an economy is in a state of equilibrium, no firm is learning, no development takes place other than replication, no growth is possible, and the data of current and future markets remain the same, etc. Thus, firms do not need to make strategies to yield sustainable above-equilibrium rates of return given the market conditions.

Apparently, taking this framework for granted, strategic phenomena is not only a matter of irrelevance but also of illegitimacy as a research problem. Given the above-mentioned assumption, the only way that firms achieve a competitively advantageous position is, in a negative sense, when they can affect the values of equilibrium prices, i.e. cause higher prices, thus violating the state of rest and harmony and make themselves better off. Yet, can this advantageous position be sustained?

Neoclassical theorists argue that monopoly or monopolistic prices cannot last very long, because other agents soon perceive an opportunity, enter the market, and force prices back into equilibrium. In other words, once a market equilibrium is violated, prices quickly, smoothly and predictably change until demand and supply are back in balance, as Marshall states:

> When demand and supply are in stable equilibrium, if any accident should move the scale of production from its equilibrium position, there will be instantly brought into play forces tending to push back to that position; just as, if a stone hanging by a string is displaced from its equilibrium position, the force of gravity will at once tend to bring it back to its equilibrium position (Marshall, 1961, p. 346).

Walras is even stricter than Marshal in his view of the swiftness of convergence to equilibrium as it is implied in his analogy of auctioneering. Moreover, he assumes 'no disequilibrium trading'.

To put it differently, in the neoclassical world of competitive equilibra, the market mechanism has property of 'self-correction' of 'random and temporary deviations' from equilibrium values. The state of equilibrium is assumed to be not only stable but also permanent, i.e. economy is always either in equilibrium or nearing it. Therefore, disequilibrium positions are only 'transient'. For the market power other than state regulations on which they are based, is temporary.[3] They are temporary because they are not structurally stable. Therefore, diequilibrium positions cannot be prolonged, and disequilibrium behaviours are unimportant, and not worthy of inquiry. In Machlup's terms, 'just as equilibrium may by design take no account of adjustments that go beyond ... a certain time, equilibrium may also by design overlook certain short-term oscillations or fluctuations' (Machlup, 1963, pp.53-54). Thus, the theory is only concerned with the inquiry of equilibrium (non-strategic) state.

In this respect, persistent above-equilibrium profits can only be assumed when market forces are weak, i.e. they operate slowly and imperfectly, so that profits can persist out of equilibrium for long periods of time. In general, as the analysis shows, 'imperfections' or 'failures' of the competitive market seem to be necessary conditions for supranormal profits and their persistency. Therefore, the most pressing strategic questions lie outside the 'perfect' competition frame of reference. But the theory may help us to understand strategic phenomena by being, in a negative sense, a benchmark. In fact, as we see, the following theories are developed as such, i.e. as deviations from the ideal perfect competition to explain the real world.

## Hard Core Assumptions: Single-exit Situational Determinism

It is more than one hundred years since neoclassical research programme has been developed. Following the publication of Marshall's *Principles of Economics* in 1891, it has also been the dominant research programme in microeconomics. Throughout this time, probably, hundreds of books and articles have been written about neoclassical price theory, each with somewhat different characterisations of its assumptions and implications. However, Latsis identifies, taking the Lakatosian research programme framework as an analytical tool, four hard core assumptions of neoclassical research programme:

1. decision-makers have correct knowledge of the relevant features of their economic situation,
2. decision-makers *prefer* the best available alternative given their knowledge of the situation and of the means at their disposal,
3. given (1) and (2), situations generate their internal 'logic' and decision-makers *act appropriately to the logic of their situation*, and
4. economic units and structures display stable, coordinated behaviour (Latsis, 1976, p. 22).

There are some other researchers who also identify slightly different and more detailed hard core assumptions of neoclassical research programme.[4] Given the hard core assumptions, Latsis sees neoclassical school of economics as a whole, a research programme of 'Situational Determinism'. By this he means that in the research programme decision making is seen, in essence, as the behaviour of rational economic agents acting appropriately to the 'logic of the situation' in which they work.

The situational logic and the strategic behaviour, which is defined in the previous chapter, are not opposites but 'heuristic twins', at least at the level of the initial assumptions. Both the situational logic and the strategic behaviour imply rational behaviour in the sense of behaving/making decisions by taking into consideration the environmental conditions to influence obtainable results. From a research point of view, they imply 'situational necessity' - historical, current or future - leading agents to behave in the way they behave, given their knowledge -no matter whether it is objective or interpretative- about the situation in which they operate. Indeed, without the assumption of situational logic, it is hard to see how general theoretical statements could be made about any social processes.

In this respect, what becomes crucial is then to classify different situations or to identify initial conditions characterising different decision making situations in order to assess whether they allow strategy-following behaviours to appear and develop. In other words, the four hard core assumptions form the common ground from which proponents of neoclassical school proceed. Needless to say, within the research programme there are a number of theories or subdisciplines. In order to assess directly the theory of perfect competition from the viewpoint that whether the situation it characterises is strategic or not, it is then necessary to examine it within the context of its subdisciplinary specialisation.[5]

In this respect, what are the subdisciplinary hard core assumptions of perfect competition theory? Latsis also identifies hard-core postulates of the perfectly competitive model, as a paradigm case for the application of neoclassical research programme, as follows (Latsis, 1976, p. 23; 1972, p. 209):

1. Profit maximisation: The goal of all firms is profit maximisation; no other goals (non-profit objectives) are pursued. Maximising profits simply means arranging matters so that the difference between the future inflowing stream of revenue and the future outflowing stream of costs is bigger than the difference that could be secured by any alternative arrangement (Towsend, 1995, p. 32). The assumption of profit maximisation is not, *per se*, inconsistent with that of competitive advantage as the motive force behind the behaviour of firms assumed in strategic management theory. Yet, maximisation of profits under certainty and complete information means that firms have no choice but accept normal profits, rather than compete for sustainable high profits. Moreover, the assumption implies that the firm is as a unitary actor so that there is no process and implementation problems to be managed. However, strategic management theory is grounded on the idea that process and implementation issues need to be managed, and managed strategically, to achieve competitively advantageous positions *vis-à-vis* rivals.
2. Perfect knowledge: It is assumed that all sellers and buyers have complete, objective and identical knowledge of the conditions of the market, production possibilities and marketable opportunities available to them. This knowledge refers not only to the prevailing conditions in the current period but in all future periods as well. Under these conditions uncertainty about future developments in the market is ruled out. Note that the assumption of perfect knowledge is necessary for the assumption of maximising profits to render determinate results. The assumption also renders no grounds for making genuine choice since, given perfect knowledge, choice is predetermined. Needless to say, under condition of perfect knowledge, there is no need for firms to follow some kind of institutional guidelines (strategies, rules, etc.) to overcome uncertainty, to rationalise their behaviour, to create conditions of earning high profits such as erecting barriers to imitation, etc.

3. Independence of decisions: The assumption implies that 'in an economy with very many agents the market environment of any one of these is independent of the market actions he decides upon' (Hahn, 1989, p. 98). In other words, since the number of suppliers in each market is so large that any one individual firm has only a negligible effect on market price, they do not need to take into considerations the influence of other firms when making decisions. This assumption debases any consideration about strategic rivalry for advantages among firms (i.e. firms compete against nature, not each other). In a perfectly competitive market, only does the price system, in conjunction with supply and demand considerations, determine what to produce and in what quantity to produce (i.e. firms are price-takers). Moreover, the assumption implies that no collusive action on the part of either buyers or sellers which might empower them collectively to control market prices is permitted.
4. Perfect markets: Perfect competition is attained if a market is made up of firms with identical (cost) conditions, and if the number of firms is sufficiently large for firms' demand curve to be completely elastic (i.e. the firm can sell any amount of output at the prevailing market price).

For markets to be perfectly workable, three additional (auxiliary) assumptions are also needed:

1. Product homogeneity: The firms in a given market deal in a perfectly homogeneous commodity. Thus the market is defined as a group of firms producing a homogeneous commodity. Products are assumed to be homogeneous in every dimensions (technical characteristics and services associated with its sale and delivery), so that there is no way in which a buyer could differentiate among the products of different firms. If the product were differentiated the firm would have some discretion in setting its price (possibility for strategic behaviour).
2. Large number of sellers: The market is made up of a large number of firms, so that each individual firm, however large, supplies only a small part of the total quantity offered in the market. As a result, no firm has power to affect the working of the market strategically in its favour.
3. Free entry and exit of firms, and perfect mobility of factors of production: Firms have freedom of movement in and out of the market if any firm thinks that it can earn higher profits by moving

> from its current market to some other market or, if it is incurring losses, it will be free to go out of business. If barriers exist, the number of firms in the market may be reduced so that each one of them may acquire power to affect the price in the market. Moreover, the factors of production are free to move from one firm to another throughout the economy; that is, production factors are not monopolised. As a result, there is perfect competition in factor markets.[6] The assumption of perfect markets (product as well as factor) debases any consideration of institutional constraints or barriers causing competitive differentials to persist between firms since firms are assumed to compete wherever they want (no protected attractive markets or free to move) and to buy whatever they want (no idiosyncratic resources and capabilities or free to imitate good ways of doing business).

These are initial conditions for perfect competition to be workable to render resource allocation fully and efficiently, as we explained in the first section of this chapter. In a perfectly competitive situation, all necessary data for decision making is assumed to be given, and given objectively (perfect knowledge). Decision makers do not have any problem of gathering, processing and interpreting information, learning, discovering or creating new possibilities of doing things, making errors, etc. Having full and objective knowledge of the relevant circumstances of their economic situation as well as decision making rule (profit maximisation), economic agents are assumed to act rationally to find (calculate) the optimal solution for resource allocation (maximise profits or minimise costs). In other words, decision makers are assumed to have always a unique choice (one best solution) which is pre-determined by the given conditions.

> In terms of Latsis, under the conditions economic agents' discretion in choosing among alternative courses of action is reduced to a predetermined single choice, which he calls 'single exit' situations: 'I shall call situations, where the obvious course of action ... is determined uniquely by objective conditions ... "*single exit*" or "*straightjacket*" situations' (1972, p. 211). Under the conditions of single-exit situations managerial decision making becomes simply a calculation of the best choice, leaving no room for real strategic 'discretion'.

As such, the situations envisaged and behavioural assumptions about how to deal with the situations do not seem suitable at all for the investigation of strategic decision making. For in strategic situations decision makers follow a variety of patterns of rational behaviours to seek superior profits and to sustain them if obtained, with the possibility of missing or hitting right opportunities for their advantages.

What is amiss in neoclassical perfect competition theory is not that it is false but that it deals only with an extremely special or rare, if it exists at all, sort of decision making situation. In order to think out the question of how to achieve ideal efficient resources allocation at the market level, theorists of perfect competition construct a highly specialised model of the market. In that model, no element of strategy-following behaviour could develop in order to obtain and sustain competitive advantages (such as differentiating products, influencing rivals' decisions in their favour, monopolising valuable resources and capabilities of production). In this respect, then, the investigation of strategy-following behaviour is that of a theory of the situation which is not perfectly competitive.

So far, it must have been realised that, the principal difference between neoclassical perfect competition assumptions and that of strategy concerning decision making is not so much about the 'logic' of decision making but about 'situations' or 'initial conditions' in which decisions are made. It should also be pointed out that in the process of the study more detailed analysis of perfect competition theory will be introduced since all the other theories to be examined are deviations from perfect competition theory, and thus need to be understood with reference to it.

## Conclusions

The problem area of neoclassical perfectly competitive market theory turns around the following question: 'how can scarce resources be allocated efficiently?' The theory, like any theoretical construct, asserts that if certain conditions, i.e. initial conditions in terms of Lakatos, are met, then necessarily particular subsequent conditions will be met. In other word, the theory focuses on the *specification* of the market coordination problem which allows economists to prove the *notional existence and stability* of a perfectly competitive equilibrium in which the *optimal* resource allocation is attainable. The conditions assumed to be necessary and sufficient for efficient allocation are, for example, rational economic calculations, independence of decision-making, perfect knowledge, perfect certainty, perfect mobility of factors, and so on. With all these assumptions, the theory conceptualises the market like a perfectly working machine, allocating resource factors spontaneously and frictionlessly, having been set once, rather than as a social, historical institution. Within this mechanistic construct there seems to be no room for investigating strategic phenomena.

Yet, from the standpoint of logic, it is impossible to argue that the theory is wrong. But, it is perfectly possible to argue that if the conditions for perfect competition held, there would be no strategic phenomena possible. For the conditions for perfect competition and for strategic competition cannot be assumed to exist at the same time as they are mutually exclusive (perfect v imperfect knowledge, profit maximising v profit seeking, atomistic decision making v strategic-interdependent decision making, etc.) and, consequently, the problem of efficient resource allocation at market level does not shed light on the problem of strategic phenomena.

Therefore the theory is not a useful basis for investigating strategic phenomena within its frame of reference. In contrast, far from being able to 'predict', or tell us anything meaningful concerning strategic phenomena from the market competition viewpoint, it denies the existence of persistent firm differentials in profitability within its notional existence and stability of competitive equilibrium. Perfect competition can only describe what things would be like if the world of business is 'non-strategic' in the sense that it contained 'consumers with homogeneous tastes, atomistically structured firms identical in every important respect, with no locational advantages, no advertising, no entrepreneurship, and no rivalry whatever' (Armentano, 1978, pp. 96-97).

## Notes

1. See for a good historical analysis of the evolution of the concept of perfect competition as uniqueness of competitive equilibrium and stationary conditions, G.J. Stigler (1957), Perfect Competition, Historically Contemplated, *The Journal of Political Economy*, Vol. 65, pp. 1-16. Stigler has traced the historical development of the idea of perfect competition essentially through the 'imperfect competition revolution' of the 1930s.
2. As we see in the following chapters, the idea of 'equilibrium' is a heuristic convention of all economics but in different formats and meanings.
3. In perfect competition theory sustained above-normal profits are suggested to be the result of government interference, for example, in the form of regulation or other protection, without of which this protection there is suggested to be no persistent economic profits. Clearly, this protective kind of monopolistic above-average earnings are fundamentally different from that of the outcomes of firms own competitive behaviours.
4. For example, Futon (1984, *Research Programmes in Economics, History of Political Economy*, Vol. 16, No. 2, pp. 187-205) suggests a longer and more comprehensive list of hard core assumptions: (i) the central economic problem is that of allocating scarce resources among alternative uses; (ii) economic theories are abstract, general theories based on deductive models; (iii) economic theory is based on individual entities such

as the consumer, the firm, the worker, each of these acts independently of other like units; (iv) these individuals have full knowledge of the relevant circumstances of their economic situation; (v) each individual acts rationally; (vi) each individual is a maximising agent, either profit maximisation or cost minimisation; (vii) economic theory is essentially static in the sense that it is concerned with equilibrium states and movements between these states; (viii) economic theory is within the tradition of positive science; (ix) theories should, if possible, be presented in mathematical form. Futon argues that these assumptions are not hard core assumptions but 'presuppositions', which are statements that are prior to hard core. I think that this definition of 'presupposition' itself can be considered as a definition of 'hard core' since the definition indicates the metaphysical or unfalsifiable part of a theory. Apart from that, some of presuppositions given, for example, economic theories are abstract, general theories based on deductive models, and theories should, if possible, be presented in mathematical form, are not hard core assumptions, but are the maxims of the positive heuristic of the programme.

5. Remenyi (1979, Core Demi-core Interaction: Toward a General Theory of Disciplinary and Subdisciplinary Growth, *History of Political Economy*, Vol. 11, No. 1, pp. 30-63) also identifies the following eight propositions as the hard core assumptions of neoclassical economics: (i) consumers or producers can legitimately be assumed to be rational decision makers who know their wants; (ii) economic activity is motivated by individual self-interest; (iii) more is better than less; (iv) given perfect knowledge and good government, economic welfare is maximised by free competition; (v) although welfare and economic welfare are not synonymous, the latter is a good approximation for the former; (vi) stable Pareto-efficient equilibrium solutions can be defined for any and all markets relevant to economic research and analysis; (vii) everything has its opportunity cost; and (viii) abstract, reduced-form models and simplifying assumptions are valid tools of economic analysis. In his analysis Rumeyni brought welfare considerations to fore.

   For the interaction between disciplinary and subdisciplinary hard core and auxiliary assumptions, see J.V. Remenyi (1979), Core Demi-core Interaction: Toward a General Theory of Disciplinary and Subdisciplinary Growth, *History of Political Economy*, Vol. 11, No. 1, pp. 30-63.

6. Most authors would agree on the basic assumptions that underlie neoclassical perfect competition. For example, for Blaug, 'the 'hard core' or metaphysical part of this programme consists of weak versions of what is otherwise known as the 'assumptions' of competitive theory, namely, rational economic calculations, constant tastes, independence of decision-making, perfect knowledge, perfect certainty, perfect mobility of factors, et cetera' (Blaug, 1976, p. 161).

## Chapter 4

# Theories of Industrial Organisation

### Introduction

In the previous chapter it was demonstrated that the concept of the market is employed in the development of the neoclassical theory of perfect competition essentially as an *heuristic* device to specify the conditions under which efficient allocation of resources is attainable. In so doing the market was stripped of all its usual characteristics (rivalry, structure, product homogeneity, etc.). Bain, one of the central architectures of industrial organisation,[1] while supporting the main presupposition of neoclassical perfect theory, namely, the way that the market is organised affects how it performs (for example, in allocating resources efficiently or inefficiently), argued that the neoclassical price determination analyses lack realism by not considering the actual characteristics of industrial organisation in contemporary economies. To him, a more appropriate market (price) theory has to take into account the relationship between the market and forces constituting its structure in explaining market performance (Bain, 1952).

This was particularly necessary after the emergence of the large modern manufacturing corporations around the turn of the century (Chandler, 1977). The large corporations could not be examined with reference to atomistic firms envisioned within the neoclassical perfect competition paradigm since its constructions were 'irrelevant to the real problems' (Mason, 1939, p. 62). Thus another line of inquiry under the title of Industrial Organisation emerged during the 1950s and 1960s essentially as an empirical field to address real world problems, and in turn, as a guide to action (a guide to the formulation of public policy objectives towards antitrust behaviours).

Like most applied disciplines, industrial organisation has taken many forms in different hands so that there is no widely accepted approach to be characterised by a single label (McKie, 1970). The recent works on strategic competition, and the works on the strategic management/economics nexus refer to three paradigms in the field of industrial organisation: the structure-conduct-performance (SCP), the

Chicago School (efficiency paradigm), and new industrial organisation (game theory).

So, given its problem area and hard core assumptions, what are the promises of industrial organisation in explaining persistent firm differentials in profits as consequences of strategy-following behaviour of firms?

## Problem Area: Conceptualising the Market as an Imperfectly Working Organisation

When describing, almost three decades ago, the boundaries of industrial organisation, Stigler argued that industrial organisation does not really exist as a separate discipline, that it is simply differentiated neoclassical microeconomics:

> ... there is no such subject as industrial organisation. The courses taught under this heading have for their purpose the understanding of the structure and behaviour of the industries ... of an economy. ... But this is precisely the content of economic theory - price or resource allocation theory (Stigler, 1968, p. 1).

Ferguson and Ferguson argue that Stigler missed the point, and draw the distinguishing line between them as such: 'the distinction arises from the overriding emphasis, in industrial economics, on empirical work and on implications for policy' (Ferguson, and Ferguson, 1988, p. 2). In fact, the distinguishing line mentioned does not give a precise definition of the field; frontiers sound rather fuzzy yet. For many years industrial organisation was generally viewed as an empirical field, nevertheless, in the last three decades much of the significant work in industrial organisation has been theoretical (Schmalensee, 1988, p. 643).

Tirole, when discussing why one should be interested in industrial organisation, points out the problem area of the discipline and its relation with microeconomics: 'to study industrial organisation is to study the functioning of markets, a central concept in microeconomics' (1988, p. 1). Schmalensee gives a more accurate description: 'industrial economics is the study of the supply side of the economy, particularly those markets in which business firms are sellers' (1988, p. 643).

In fact, none of these definitions gives a precise description of the problem area of industrial organisation. Nonetheless, common to all is the observation that industrial organisation is, in essence, a discipline of applied neoclassical economics. As Auerbach argues: 'the literature of industrial economics has developed as a dutiful application of the research programme implied by standard microeconomic theory' (1988, p. 2). That is to say, all the three paradigms (SCP, efficiency, and game theoretical) to the economics of industries in market economies take neoclassical theory as their background explanation, but attempt to operationalise it.

Yet, we can identify the problem area of industrial organisation much easier with comparison to neoclassical perfect competition theory. The focus of industrial organisation studies changes from one on the functioning of firms in a *particular* market structure (perfectly organised market) to one on the functioning of firms within *various* market structures (perfectly, or imperfectly organised such as monopoly, monopolistic or oligopolistic markets), implied by neoclassical theory. As Mason, probably the pioneer of the field, wrote in retrospect,

> I had some hand in this [in developing the field of industrial organisation] along with younger colleagues and graduate students [of Harvard University Economics' Department] of whom Donald H. Wallace and Joe S. Bain deserve particular mention. ... we had some hope of developing an *operational classification of market structures* that would not only go far *toward explaining the behaviour of firms* but also provide normative standards of performance of use to antitrust policy (emphasis added) (Mason, 1982, pp. 423-424).

Leaving aside the normative side of the field, i.e. providing standards of performance of use to antitrust policy, the general orientation for investigation was to understand *why firms perform as they do in various market structures*.[2] This point needs some elaboration due to its importance for defining the problem area of industrial organisation.

To begin with, the central problem of perfect competition theory was to explain how the organisation of the market affects the behaviour of economic agents in allocating their resources. Nevertheless theorists working within its frame of reference approached the market not from what it *is* but what it *should* be. The focus was then on the identification of the 'form' of competition that can deliver efficient allocation. Thus the notion of perfect competition has come to denote a *special form* of the market, i.e. a perfectly organised market in which competition takes place among infinite number of small suppliers of the same product, having no power to influence market structure in their favour, thereby allocating resources efficiently, taking market prices as parameters for decisions.

In this respect, playing a central role as a hallmark also implies *other forms* of the market, that is, imperfectly organised markets in forms of monopoly (only one producer constituting the whole market) and oligopoly (competition among few producers with some kind of power to influence the market in which they operate in their favour).[3]

Therefore, the focus in industrial organisation shifts from the efficient market explanation of optimal allocation of resources to the explanations of why markets are imperfect or inefficient in allowing some firms to earn substantial profits. In other words, the overriding emphasis in industrial organisation is on seeking *empirically,* at least at the beginning, to understand and evaluate, for their public policy implications, *why industries perform differently*, rather than on explaining *hypothetically how efficient allocation of resources is attainable.*

More specifically, although it has rarely been explicitly stated, the general orientation of investigation in industrial organisation studies has been towards imperfectly competitive[4] or oligopolistic (concentrated) markets, that is, most real markets fall somewhere between extremes of perfectly competitive markets and monopoly markets.

Yet note that although different explanatory frameworks have been developed to analyse each category (perfect competition, monopoly and oligopoly) though, the underlying logic common to all the three is the same: the market environment of firms is generally described explicitly or implicitly in terms of the *structural* characteristics (number of firms in the market, the ease or difficulty in entering markets,..) of markets regardless of the particular concept of *market environment* under analysis. In diagrammatic form, it can be demonstrated as follows:[5]

| ***Structure*** | ***Conduct*** | ***Performance*** |
|---|---|---|
| Perfect competition | Marginal cost pricing | Allocative efficiency and equity |
| Monopoly | Marginal cost pricing | Inefficiency and monopoly profits |
| Imperfect competition | Departures from marginal cost pricing | Inefficiency and possible monopolistic/supernormal profits |

In perfect competition, firms are so numerous and small that none can affect market price and each takes market price as given, and in the long-run market equilibrium price equals marginal cost, and also equals average cost, and profits are at a 'normal' level. Under monopoly, the outcome of market structure with one firm and high barriers to entry is that marginal cost is equated with marginal revenue, price is above marginal cost and there are 'super-normal' profits. In between these two extremes, as we move through the spectrum from markets with a large number of firms to markets with only a few firms, it is assumed that profitability will rise from a normal level towards the super-normal level of monopoly.

The logic underlying the theoretical apparatus of each model that offers predictions about the behaviour of firms in each of the market structures is the same. They are thus considered within neoclassical paradigm. But the focus of interest and the results of each model are different. In this regard, concern turns, at this stage of the analysis, to the relevance of the conceptualisation of the market as an imperfectly competitive organisation with strategic management theory.

## Can Strategic Phenomena be Investigated as a Legitimate and Significant Research Subject Within the Frame of Reference of Imperfectly Competitive Markets?

With regards to strategic management, the significance of imperfectly competitive markets stems not only from their real and prevalent existence in the world of business, but also from being only 'competitive' markets in the everyday sense of the concept of competition. For there can be, in a practical sense, no competition assumed to be taking place in perfectly competitive markets where there is no interdependency between powerless and infinite number of firms (atomistic competition), or, in monopoly markets, where there is only one power. On the contrary, in imperfectly competitive markets firms are assumed to be in a state of competition among finite or few, and can exercise an appreciable effect over the market and each other, such as building up entry barriers to block newcomers into the market, advertising, differentiating their products, strategic behaviours that they follow and so on. Therefore, the focal area of inquiry of industrial organisation, from a market environment point of view, overlaps with the research area of the theory of 'competitive' strategy.

Moreover, in the theory of imperfectly organised markets it is assumed that 'supernormal profits' arise between firms in various degrees, depending on the degree of market power and efficiency-building abilities that firms possess. In other words, performance is not assumed to be 'optimal' by definition, but variable according to the unique characteristics of the particular market in which a particular firm competes, or the unique conduct of the firm, or both. In this respect, market and conduct are considered to be 'strategic' variables in the sense that they have decisive impact on performance. Therefore, the theory of imperfect competition of industrial organisation seems to provide a framework in which firm differentials in profit performance can be investigated.

There have been three approaches or paradigms investigating the economics of the market in the area of industrial organisation, namely, SCP, efficiency and game theory. Now it seems necessary to look, to some details, at the approaches respectively for their explanations about the sources and mechanisms of sustainable firm differentials.

## Structure-Conduct-Performance Paradigm (Harvard School of Industrial Economics)

Most analyses of industries have been conducted according to the linear relationship prevailing in the well-known, dominant paradigm of structure-conduct-performance (Mason, Bain, Caves, Porter). To the paradigm, 'market structure affects the character and intensity of competition among firms in the same industry, and thus the conduct and performance of these firms' (Bain, 1959, pp. 27-28). Structure describes such market aspects as number of sellers and buyers, the height of barriers to potential competition, rate of growth, product differentiation, vertical integration, and so on.[6] Conduct, refers to strategies of firms that they follow, which Bain defines, as the 'patterns of behaviour which enterprises follow in adapting or adjusting to the markets in which they sell (or buy)' (Bain, 1959, p. 9). Performance relates to the level of profits earned, the relationship between prices and costs, and welfare considerations (productive efficiency, i.e. avoiding wasteful use of available factors of production, and allocative efficiency, i.e. producing the 'right' goods in the 'right' quantities - Ferguson and Ferguson, 1994).

The paradigm is concerned with identifying properties of industries contributing to above-normal profitability. Within the general framework of the relationship between market structure, conduct, and performance, the specific aim of the approach is to investigate:

> Why do enterprises perform as they do, and in particular why do some perform differently, or better or worse, than others? To answer these questions is to identify the determinants of enterprise performance, and to learn how variation in these determinants leads to corresponding variations in performance. This sort of knowledge is desirable because of its scholarly or scientific interest. It is also essential for the formulation of ... public regulatory policy ... (Bain, 1968, pp. 2-3).

Leaving aside the normative orientations of the S-C-P paradigm and strategic management for opposite purposes (prescribing policy makers how to improve competition, where market performance is the extent to which the profitability of firms in the industry departs from the Paretian allocative efficiency ideal, or, prescribing businessmen how to gain and sustain supra-competitive profits), the grand problem, i.e. why firms perform differently - better or worse - that both attempt to tackle is identical. In essence, both provide a paradigm for explaining firms success and failure but from different angles. As Caves maintains, when discussing the reasons for the absorption of the S-C-P research paradigm into the study of business strategy in the 1980s, 'after all, the manager who wishes to obtain or preserve rents and the policy-maker who wants to check these efforts need the same information about the mechanisms that are involved' (1994, p. 11).

According to Bain, there are two sources of the determinants or variations of market performance of enterprises:

> First, the organisation or structure of an industry ... . That is, market structure constraints and canalises enterprise activities and their results; and variations in structure may lead to associated variations in performance. Second, the market conduct of enterprises-by which we mean policies, practices, and devices they employ in arriving at adjustments to the market in which they participate-also influences performance (Bain, 1968, p. 3).

In fact, to Bain, the ultimate determinant of performance is market structure, as is apparent in his linear view of the unidirectional causal flows operating from structure to conduct, from conduct to performance. Yet, the element of conduct, which is the most important one for strategy theory, is usually ignored in statistical studies, especially in early ones. This was because the numerous attempts to relate market structure to market performance were unsuccessful due to measurement problems. As Bain points out,

> Actual patterns of market cannot be fully enough measured to permit us to establish empirically a meaningful association either between market conduct and performance, or between structure and market conduct. It thus becomes expedient to test directly for net associations of market structure to market performance ... (Bain, 1968, p. 329).

Therefore, the primary reason for the ignorance of conduct element in the linkage does not seem to constitute the essential part of the paradigm. Later studies attempted to remedy this deficiency.[7] Moreover, some others have made significant modifications and improvements in the framework of the assumed relationship. For example, Needham argues that in the real world the causal flows operating from structure to conduct is not unidirectional, but,

> run both ways, not only from structure to conduct but also from current conduct to resulting implications for structure at a point in time. If so, two simultaneous relationships will exist between structure and conduct; moreover, the resulting relationship between these factors will then be dynamic in character, implying a process which involves changes in structure and conduct through time. There may also be causal flows running from economic performance to conduct, structure, or both ... (Needham, 1978, p. 2).

The hypothesis of unidirectional flows of causation has been challenged on both theoretical and empirical grounds in favour of the belief that there are simultaneous relationships.[8] Moreover, some researchers take the idea of a more proactive view of behaviours of firms to alter market structure in their favour and have found empirical evidence for support. For example, Encaoua, Geroski and Jacquemin argue:

> In the struggle to create, maintain and expand favourable market positions, firms' actions are intended not only to affect the current conduct of rivals directly, but also to have an indirect effect by altering market structure in a way which constrains the rival's subsequent actions. In this dynamic process, market strategies or conduct ... interact with market structure; and current conduct can become embedded in future market structure through strategic investments made by firms to bar entry and reduce intra-industry mobility (Encaoua, Geroski, and Jacquemin, 1986, p. 55).

The argument for the two ways direction of causality is, in essence, a significant departure from static explanations of the relationship between structure and performance that are to be found in the neoclassical theories of perfect competition and monopoly. Recognising a more dynamic conception of the behaviour of firms is of significance because it not only rejects the idea of static market *exogeneously* given, but also that of *marginal calculation in decision making in certain and static environments*, and an *equilibrium relationship* between the variables assumed in the neoclassical theory of perfect competition.

Bain identifies four elements, which are the 'primary characteristics of market structure, in the sense that they are the aspects of market organisation which most clearly and systematically influence market conduct and performance throughout all industries' (1968, p. 7):

1. the *concentration of sellers* - described by the number and the size distribution of sellers in the market,

2. the *concentration of buyers* - described in parallel fashion,
3. the degree of *product differentiation* as among the products of various suppliers in the market that are perceived nonidentical by buyers, and
4. the *condition of entry* to the market-referring to the relative ease or difficulty with which newcomers may enter the market, which may give advantages to established firms over potential newcomer.

The last characteristic, namely, barriers to entry, is also the reason given for the sustainability of firm differentials. Bain observes that barriers to entry indeed do exist and vary from industry to industry. Correspondingly, industries may be classified, for example, according to whether the condition of entry is 'easy' (no barriers to entry), 'moderately difficult' (some barriers), or 'blockaded'. He classifies entry barriers into four broad groups:

1. absolute cost advantage - when incumbent firms experience lower costs at every level of output than would potential newcomers,
2. economies of scale,
3. capital requirements, in particular in those industries where minimum efficient scale is quite large, where vertical integration is essential, and where the production process is highly capital intensive, and
4. product differentiation (buyers preference for established products that have been promoted for long periods of time (Bain, 1956, 1968).

These barriers are expected to influence conduct and performance by placing limits on the price obtaining, either because incumbent firms deliberately limit price or because the supply of new entrants depresses price if incumbents do not. Moreover, Caves and Porter (1977) introduced the notion of barriers to mobility/strategic group in addition to the barriers to entry to explain sustainable differentials *within* markets. The circumstances that give rise to mobility barriers are, in general, assumed to be the same

In Bain's (1956) view, both high concentration and high barriers to entry are necessary to produce excess profits in the long-run. Non-perfect competition is not a sufficient condition for monopoly profits due to entry, and unless entry is controlled, price-fixing will increase the number of firms instead of the profits of existing firms. He found support for this interactive hypothesis using data on leading U.S. firms in 1936-40 and

1947-51. However, it was Brozen (1971) who first explicitly addressed in 1970 the question of the persistence of high profit rates over time. Brozen argued that if there is successful explicit or implicit collusion in concentrated industries then the above-average profits flowing from the collusion should persist over time, other things being equal.

Before proceeding to examine the other approaches, it should also be pointed out that some scholars, such as McWilliams and Smart (1993), and Foss (1996a), argue that market or strategic group as a unit of analysis is not suitable for strategic management studies, because they do not focus on individual firms. In fact, Bain deliberately and explicitly chose to use industry as the unit of analysis:

> I am concerned with the environmental settings within which enterprises operate and in how they behave in these settings ... By contrast, I do not take an internal approach, more appropriate to the field of management science ... Correspondingly, my primary unit of analysis is the industry or competing group of firms, rather than either the individual firm or the economywide aggregate of enterprises (Bain, 1959, pp. vii-viii).

Nevertheless, arguing that the market as a unit of analysis is not suitable for strategic analysis of firm differences is to commit the 'fallacy of misplaced correctedness' since it is not designed for the purpose of individual firm analysis. From the foundational approach viewpoint, we do not have to commit the fallacy, because we examine the SCP as a market theory as such, not as a theory of strategy to explain and predict individual firm differences in profitability. The approach seems to be, as we have demonstrated, highly promising for its foundational service as a market theory in explaining *firm differentials at market level*.

## Efficiency Paradigm (Chicago School of Industrial Economics)

The conflicting results of the numerous tests carried out on the causal relationship underlying the S-C-P paradigm, as well as the need to deepen the theoretical base of industrial economics, have paved the way to what has become known as the efficiency paradigm[9] and new industrial economics. On the contrary to the S-C-P, the efficiency paradigm (Stigler, Demsetz, Peltzman, and Brozen) offered an alternative explanation for the observed market differences by the S-C-P researchers. It associated performance differences to efficiency differences between firms, rather than to market structure.

Stigler, in 1963, observed that the relationship between market concentration and market performance was weak and unstable over time. In 1971, Brozen studied Bain's work in detail and found similar results to Stigler's. He claimed that the industries examined had become less concentrated over time which may simply indicate that new entry reduces profitability confirming the view that barriers to entry have a bearing on profits. Brozen discovered that larger firms earned more than smaller ones in seven out of nine concentrated industries. And Demsetz, in 1973 and 1974, argued that if above-average profits do not persist, barriers to entry must be generally insignificant, and market power is generally a transitory phenomenon. Therefore, a positive association between concentration and profits is no proof of profit enhancing collusive behaviour among firms with the aid of artificial barriers to competition, but as an indication of a firm's ability to lower costs or to improve product quality that increases its profits and size. Thus, only leading firms, with efficiency advantages, should earn persistent supra-normal profits in concentrated industries (Demsetz, 1973).

Given the pressure of competitive rivalry and the absence of effective barriers to entry, the intriguing problems facing the efficiency paradigm's adherents have been:

> Does the market concentration doctrine [of the S-C-P approach], *unaided by this "efficient structure"* explanation [of competitive markets], adequately explain the pattern of profit rates and market concentration? Do higher profits in concentrated industries reflect only monopoly [power of anti-competitive behaviours of firms]? Or are they in whole or part brought about by the efficiency of large firms in these industries? (italics in original) (Demsetz, 1974, p. 104).

Note that both approaches, the SCP and efficiency-based, share the same problem area, i.e. the identification of the sources and mechanism of profit differentials in performance. Nevertheless, not only do they approach the phenomenon of inquiry from different positions, that is, structuralist explanations vs. efficiency explanations, but they also take different conceptions of market competition.

Proponents of the efficiency paradigm argued that high profits could simply be the result of efficiency differences between firms, and thereby high levels of concentration could simply be the incidental result of market share becoming concentrated in the hands of firms which are more efficient, not because of collusive behaviours between firms. In other words, results of market performance are associated with inherent, natural (competitive) requirements, such as cost and quality advantages, for individual firms to increase efficiency rather than with artificial entry barriers as results of anti-competitive collusive behaviours between few firms in a market. Therefore, efficiency affects structure rather than the other way round. Thus, it essentially reverses the direction of causality assumed by the S-C-P proponents.

Studies within the S-C-P framework linked market performance and market concentration by postulating that fewness in the number of firms in the market facilitates collusion to restrict output and raise price. Above-average profitability of these concentrated oligopolistic markets was assumed to be protected by restrictive behaviours of incumbents erecting entry barriers to competition from potential entrants. This was an expression of highly concentrated and closed-entry oligopolistic market competition conception.

However, it was claimed within the Chicago circles that there is no necessary relationship between the number of sellers and market profitability. For example, Demsetz (1968) argued 'that the asserted relationship between market concentration and competition cannot be derived from existing theoretical considerations and that it is based on an incorrect understanding of the concept of competition and rivalry'. He even gave the example of natural monopoly to illustrate the point: size economies in some markets may require natural monopoly, that is, there is room in the market for only one efficient producer at a time, nevertheless, the point is that there could still be *rivalry to determine which firm will serve that market*.

To elaborate the argument, it is maintained that even under natural monopoly, let alone other competitive markets, the kind of competition differs from unregulated monopoly described by the S-C-P proponents. Rivalry to determine which firm (the most efficient and the next-most-efficient) will serve the market can produce essentially perfectly competitive results even in the face of high concentration. In other words, 'results are competitive no matter how many sellers are in the market at any given time' (McGee, 1988, p. 91). Thus, competition is not regarded as a particular type of market structure and market efficiency as a resultant. On the contrary, they maintain that competition in a market economy is prevalent in all markets no matter the kind of structure that they have. To the adherents of the efficiency paradigm, as Singleton observes, 'competition should be understood as a process that can result in a variety of structures - some unconcentrated, others highly concentrated - each yielding efficient industry performance' (1986, p. 43).

The importance of the high degree of active competition assumed by the efficiency paradigm lies in its resultant diversion of attention from the market as a whole to individual firms as the unit of analysis to explain and predict market differences in performance. In other words, under competitive pressure, concentration and performance differences among markets are likely to come from individual firms' competitive behaviours, such as cost and quality improvements, rather than collusive behaviours or barriers to entry common to all firms established in an industry.

For the purpose of the current study, the most important argument put forward by the proponents of the efficiency paradigm is that market structure is merely the superficial expression of a deeper competitive process over ownership of competitively valuable resources such as patents, company reputation, licensure, etc. or efficiency-creating capabilities (Demsetz, 1982). Demsetz points out, for example, that an analysis of causality chain explains that market structure is the manifestation of competitive struggle between firms. Moving back in the chain of causality highlights how market performance and individual firm performance are linked to firm-specific resources which are basis of the efficiency-creation process:

> an industry will become more concentrated under competitive conditions only a differential advantage in expanding output develops in some firms. Such expansion will increase the degree of concentration at the same time that it increases the rate of return that these firms earn. The cost advantage that give rise to increased concentration may be reflected in scale economies or in downward shifts in positively sloped marginal cost curves, or it may be reflected in better products which satisfy demand at a lower cost (Demsetz, 1973, p. 1).

In clearer terms, to the adherents of the efficiency paradigm, the market characteristics that are assumed by the S-C-P paradigm's proponents to give rise to inter-industry performance differentials, originate in individual firm specificities. For example, differentiation is based on brands, product technology, marketing, distribution, and service capabilities, while cost advantage is based on process technology, size of plants and economics of learning. All these are firm-specific resources in creating efficiencies. Therefore, not market structure but individual firms' idiosyncratic resources or efficiency-creating abilities are the primary basis for inter-firm and -market profit differentials.

In the same vein, regarding the mechanism that makes it possible for firm differentials to persist in the long run in spite of active competition, the efficiency paradigm breaks the analysis of monopolistic competition free from the S-C-P perspective that pits insiders against outsiders or first-movers against late-comers, which indicates the presence of a barrier to entering the profitable market. Proponents of the paradigm argue that it is not the possibility of holding some firms outside competition that generates sustainable advantages for established firms in a competitive economy but the superior ability of the firms participating in competition in building-up efficiencies better than potential entrants or current rivals in the market that determines the longevity of competitive advantages. Accordingly, to them, cost, quality and scale advantages should not be viewed as barriers to entry. Such advantages are consequences of individual firms competition for offering better services to consumers and improving efficiency due to learning, technical efficiency, better business decisions, etc. (Densetz, 1982; 1997).

Taking the efficacy of market mechanism for granted, the question, then, is why competition fails to equalise firms differences in performance. To answer, Demsetz argues:

> Such profits need not be eliminated soon by competition. It may well be that superior competitive performance is unique to the firm... It may be very difficult for these firms to understand the reasons for this difference in performance or to know to which inputs to attribute the performance of the successful firm (Demsetz, 1973, p. 2).

In other words, even under the pressure of competitive rivalry, and in the apparent absence of effective barriers to entry, 'since information is costly to obtain and techniques are difficult to duplicate, the firm may enjoy growth and a superior rate of return for some time' (Demsetz, 1973, p. 3). In other words, the reason for the persistency is because of barriers to imitation. As Demsetz forcefully argues, in a competitive setting it is the barriers to imitation, not barriers to entry, that create sustainable competitive advantages, and these barriers are desirable since they are in nature competitive. And, in this respect, if the association between high profits and concentration is attributed to efficiency rather than collusion, then there is no need for government intervention at deconcentrating markets since this may bring about inefficiencies (sacrifice scale economies) and remove the incentive for progress (competition for cost and quality advantages), etc.

In sum, the efficiency paradigm's kind of market competition conception seems not only to recognise persistent differences (advantages) in efficiency between markets and individual firms as a norm of the real economic world rather than an exception, but also to view them as consequences of a 'competitive' struggle between firms for betterness, and thereby desirable and unavoidable (if market mechanism is considered to be competitive in the everyday sense). Such a conception seems a highly productive basis for a competitive strategy theory since it makes it possible to assume that strategic competition for seeking and sustaining profit advantages over rivals prevails in all markets, no matter whether it is organised perfectly or imperfectly, nor how many sellers compete in one market. In this respect, strategic behaviours are considered to be, in essence, 'competitive' rather than 'anti-competitive' initiations, and thereby socially desirable rather than would-be punished actions. Overall, the efficiency conception of market competition provides a constructive basis for competitive strategy theory. Also, note that there is a clear parallel between the arguments of positioning approach of strategic management theory and S-C-P paradigm of industrial organisation on the one hand, and of resource-based approach of strategic management theory and efficiency paradigm of industrial organisation on the other hand.

## Game Theoretical Approach to Industrial Economics

From the 1980s onwards the field of industrial organisation has been experiencing a significant change from empirical to theoretical oriented studies towards the development of new approach to the organisational phenomena with the emphasis on behaviour of economic players in imperfectly competitive markets. This new current of studies is called 'new industrial organisation' (Spence, Dixit, Stiglitz, Cowling, Clarke, Kreps and Waterson).[10] This new current of studies has been almost exclusively devoted to applying game-theoretic techniques to the modelling of issues in industrial organisation.[11] New industrial organisation sharpened the SCP approach by relating it more rigorously to neoclassical theory in the sense that it shifted attention from industry structure to individual firms and their strategic behaviour as factors in requiring explanation. Game-theoretic techniques not only have been applied to industrial organisation but also to other subfields of economics such as micro and macro economics, international trade and labour economics. The application of the language, concepts, and techniques of game theory to economics is even seen as a mild revolution in methodology (Kreps, 1990).

It must be emphasised, at the very outset, that the new industrial organisation in form of game theory is not a fully-fledged market theory. Rather, it makes use of the existing theories of industrial organisation. Kreps states this point very well when discussing the standard for judging the usefulness of game theory in economics:

> Game theory *by itself* is not meant to improve anyone's understanding of economic phenomena. Game theory ... is a tool of economic analysis, and the

> proper test is whether economic analyses that use the concepts and language of game theory have improved our understanding. Of course, there is an identification problem here. Without the concepts and language of game theory, essentially the same economic analyses may well have been carried out; game theory may be nothing more than window-dressing. Hence improvements in understanding that I may attribute in part to game theory may in fact have little or nothing to do with the theory (Kreps, 1990, p. 6).

In this respect, the new industrial organisation should not be judged by its market view, but rather by its ability to facilitate comprehension of economic (as well as strategic) phenomena under study. Game theory provides a framework for analysing economics of markets on the basis of single issues such as product differentiation, tacit collusion, price discrimination, advertising, first mover advantages, etc. This is the uniqueness of game theory, which makes it different from all other theories we examine, as Aumann and Hart observe:

> unlike other approaches to disciplines like economics ..., Game theory does not use different, ad-hoc constructs to deal with various specific issues ... Rather, it develops methodologies that apply in principle to *all* interactive situations, then sees where these methodologies lead in each specific application. (emphasis in original) (Aumann and Hart, 1992, pp. xi-xii).

It classifies interactive decision situations, identifying common features of each situation separately. Then, economic or socially interactive issues are treated as applications of the theories of the different classes of games. Therefore, game theory, or more properly game-theoretical approach, is an instrument to facilitate analysis of, rather than a theory to put forward new ideas about, economic phenomena. Yet, every instrument *does* also carry implicit or explicit assumptions about the phenomena on which it aims at shedding light. In other words, there is no objective analytical instrument; every instrument is a subjective manifestation of a background theory of perceiving reality. If so, what are the problem area of the background frame of reference of game-theoretical instrument? And, can strategic phenomena be illuminated by using game theoretical approach?

What is, then, game theory? 'Game theory is,' Colman defines, 'a branch of mathematics devoted to the logic of decision making in social interactions' (1995, p. 1). This is a useful definition because it implies, first, that game theory is a branch of mathematics, which is not directed to a single question about reality, second, that it can be applied to any decision making situation where decision-makers affect each other in a socially interactive context, and third, that it concerns with logical analysis of games rather than psychological analysis of participants (players), that is, it is a normative model of an idealised decision maker, not a description of the behaviour of real people.

Thus, Game theory promises to apply to any social interaction where individuals' interdependent actions have an impact on outcomes in a variety of situations from marriage to politics, crossing the road in traffic, and to decisions to disarm. Since many industrial organisation issues involve interdependent outcomes, game theory has been successfully and intensively applied to industrial organisation. For example, the oligopoly pricing problem reflects all the characteristics of a game. The firms are the players. Each firm recognises that its profit depends directly on the strategies of its rivals. Therefore, the logic of such competitive interaction falls within the domain of game theory.

The oligopolistic nature of the firm's competitive environment is explicitly recognised in new industrial organisation. Large firms in concentrated markets are analysed with regard not only to their decisions regarding pricing policies, but also investments, inventories, product choice, marketing, and distribution. In new industrial organisation, most modern oligopoly models are treated using the tools of game theory, in particular of non-cooperative games.[12] For instance, discriminatory pricing practices, barriers to entry initiations, and product differentiation policies are all examples of non-cooperative games, and of strategic moves in oligopolistic markets.

A strategic move is an action, as Schelling defines, 'that influences the other person's choice in a manner favourable to one's self, by affecting the other person's expectations on how one's self will behave' (1960, p. 160). In more general terms, if actions call forth reactions from rivals and the likely reactions are taken into account initially, given different 'environmental' scenarios, then these actions are considered in strategic terms. In game-theoretical language, the situation of oligopolistic markets is a game situation in which firms are *players*, their behaviour is *strategic*, and their rewards - the effects of their actions on outcomes (profits, sales, market share, etc.) - are *payoffs*.

In other words, firms are presumed to be in a competitive situation of strategic interdependence, in which '*the outcome for a given firm depends not just on what strategy it chooses, but also on what strategies its competitors choose*.' (emphasis in original) (Gardner, 1995, p. 4). From a market performance point of view, the outcome depends on strategies that firms in the market choose. For example, in a mature market, competition can be modelled as a zero-sum game, where one firm gains at the expense of the other. In this situation, the more intense the rivalry in terms of, for example, aggressive penetration into the market via advertising or competition on market share via cut-throat price wars, the more likely competition will deteriorate into a negative-sum game due to the process of competition imposing costs on all the players, and subsequent low market performance.

The above-mentioned presumptions have already been either central or implicit to the previous theories of industrial organisation. As we have argued above, the problem areas of the theories of old industrial organisation and strategic management share significant commonalties, and as a consequence, so does the new industrial organisation.

Yet, from a strategic management viewpoint, new industrial organisation differs in some significant respects from the S-C-P paradigm and Chicago of old industrial organisation as well as from neoclassical price theory. To start with the latter, what is amiss in neoclassical price or perfect competition theory is not that it is false but it deals only with an extremely rare situation of market competition in which firms are too small or known too little to measure their impact on others and the impact of others on them. As we discussed earlier, in this setting there is no place for any strategic decision-making or action. Instead, the new industrial organisation approach focuses explicitly upon strategic decision-making by firms that are capable of exercising at least some degree of market power in complex situations of interdependence.

As to the former, in the Bain-type S-C-P paradigm, many of the aspects of the firm's market environment, such as market structure and barriers to entry were taken largely as given and exogenous. In fact, neoclassical perfect competition theory also takes market variables (market prices, market structure, etc.) as exogenous. However, in the new industrial organisation, the aspects of the firm's economic environment:

> are now treated as endogenous and capable of being influenced directly by the firm's behaviour: they are part of each firm's strategy space. The strategy space of a firm is undoubtedly affected by the market structure within which the firm operates but the strategies chosen by the firm also have the potential to influence market structure in important ways (Gee and Norman, 1992, p. 1).

Thus, the new industrial organisation has shifted the focus of inquiry away from market structure to market conduct, 'arguing that conduct is the key element, interacting both with structure ... and performance' (Ferguson and Ferguson, 1994, p. 19). The view of the endogeneity of market variables is, as we have seen, also one of the distinctive characteristics of the Chicago School. However, the new industrial organisation differs from the Chicago School in terms of its focus on *strategic behaviours* of firms, rather than on their *efficiency abilities*, since 'advantages' are then contemplated as consequences of their strategic behaviour.

From the above comparison it must be clear that the problem area of the new industrial organisation based on game theory is to examine situations of strategic interdependence. Put differently, 'game theory is not useful when decisions are made that ignore the reactions of others or treat them as impersonal market forces' (Rasmusen, 1994, p. 9). And, the problem area is also to examine situations whose fundamentals (market structure, barriers to entry, product differentiation, market prices, etc.) are endogenous to market players decision-making processes.

The situations of strategic interdependence and of, at least, partial controllable of the fundamental variables are exactly the ones under the inquiry of strategic management research. That is to say, both the new industrial organisation based on game theory and strategic management deal with interactive decision situations in which players (firms) have some discretion over market variables. Therefore, in terms of explaining and predicting the logic of interdependent decision-making in competitive environment situations, new industrial organisation based on game theory seems to contribute much to strategy theory. More clearly, as Caves puts it,

> the problem of the manager who must anticipate a rival's next move is just the problem addressed by the agent in a game-theory model. What game-theory models predict is exactly what we want to teach future business managers about the consequences of competitive moves (Caves, 1994, p. 12).

Caves observes that game theory, in particular noncooperative game theory, in industrial organisation is proving easier to sell to business strategists and the business-administration classrooms than was the S-C-P paradigm because it caters to their interest in how firms make strategic moves given their rivals' responses.

New industrial organisation in form of game theory explicitly recognises firm heterogeneity. Heterogeneity is, and must be, a presupposition of the game theory since without it there would be no strategically logical interactive decision making possible. In other words, if all firms were homogeneous, there would be no need for strategic behaviour to influence rivals' expectation of its future behaviour.

Firms are assumed to be equipped with different *initial* endowments, and therefore, to face different *constraints and incentives*. Accordingly, they follow or select a *different set of strategic actions*. The sources of heterogeneous endowments can be their different cost structures, good or bad histories (reputations), timing (first mover advantages), R&D outcomes (innovations, patents), production and distribution capacities, degree of integration (horizontal and vertical), learning speed and processes, investments in physical capital and intangible assets, strategic control of information, contracting, economies of scale, privileged access to primary factors of scale and so on (Tirole, 1989;[13] Shapiro, 1989). In this respect, new industrial organisation also recognises both barriers to entry and mobility (modelling various entry deterrence and timing strategies), and barriers to imitation (modelling the dynamics of patent races, the licensing of intangible property, research joint ventures, investments in brand loyalties, etc.).

It is worth highlighting that game theory has not been fully exploited yet; it is certainly in a developmental stage. Therefore, it can be expected that it might well model any explanation of firm differentials and mechanism of their sustainability. In other words, as it takes the mould imposed by a particular theory, rather than imposing a predefined mould, various dimensions of strategic behaviour might well be modelled by using the tools of game theory.

## Hard Core Assumptions: Multiple-exit Situational Determinism

As we have already introduced, Industrial Organisation as a whole is a territorial expansion of neoclassical theory of market organisation rather than a new paradigm or research programme. In other words, Industrial Organisation extends the territory of neoclassical paradigm or research programme to cover imperfectly organised markets besides perfectly organised ones. In this respect, as a neoclassical sect, Industrial Organisation shares the hard core of the neoclassical research programme, introduced in the previous chapter. Yet, it has its own subdivisional hard core as a paradigm case of the research programme.

Arguably, the best way to identify and assess the hard core of Industrial Organisation as a paradigm case of neoclassical research programme is to take as a departure point the hard core of the other sect, perfect competition theory. The following assumptions, let us recall, constitute the hard core of perfect competition theory: (1) profit maximisation, (2) perfect knowledge, (3) independence of decisions, and (4) perfect market (Latsis, 1976, p. 23; 1972, p. 209). These are the necessary conditions for markets to achieve Pareto-optimal resource allocation. Industrial Organisation can, as we have discussed above, describe what things would be like if the world of business is imperfectly competitive. Therefore, the question is what conditions make it imperfectly competitive to render suboptimal resource allocation? Compared with the conditions of perfect competition, the conditions of imperfect competition can be stated as follows:

1. Constrained Maximisation vs. Global Maximisation Behaviour: In the theories of Industrial Organisation firms are still assumed to maximise profits. Nevertheless, they are not assumed to *maximise universally* but to *maximise under certain constraints*. Constraints stem from initial endowments that firms possess (e.g. cost structures, reputation, privileged access to primary factors of production, past performance, first mover advantages, capabilities of generating scale economies, etc.), market conditions in which they work (rivals' possible behaviours, demand and supply conditions, etc.), and legal bindings. Given the constraints, firms are not expected to make global choices. In this vein, the stress shifts implicitly to the importance of the firm's *historic* circumstances in determining its current set of opportunities. In this context, thus, maximisation means primarily the 'historical' rational maximisation under certain conditions. Clearly, this is a significant diversion from the ahistoric models of neoclassical perfect competition, according to which the set of alternatives are universally open to firms.[14]
2. Decision Making with Imperfect Knowledge vs. with Perfect Knowledge: In a perfectly competitive market, market price provides all the knowledge that is needed for making decisions, and that is known to everyone objectively. However, in imperfectly competitive markets there is not a unified price for every product but there are numerous products (differentiated) and associated prices; furthermore, firms are not price-takers but have some control over price. Therefore, market price does not reflect fully and correctly all relevant information in making decisions. In that case, firms need some other kind of knowledge than market price to make decisions. This knowledge could be about behaviour of the firm's rivals, behaviour of buyers, future conditions of product and factor markets, production process possibilities, etc. That kind of knowledge is neither comprehensively, readily nor objectively available. Decision makers form some *expectations* subjectively of what is most likely to occur, and make decisions accordingly. In other words, they have to make decisions with some sort of unknowability about behaviour of rivals, of conditions of supply and demand, of the firm and of its rivals' capacity (e.g. in generating scale economies, productivity, differentiation) etc., as it

is impossible to comprehensively and correctly predict them. Therefore, uncertainty predominates to a significant extent in imperfectly competitive markets. As Hey observes, 'take away the uncertainty ... from oligopoly, and one takes away the whole subject: uncertainty *is* the very essence of the problem' (emphasis in origin) (Hey, 1979, p. 33).[15]

3. Interdependent Decision Making vs. Atomistic Behaviour: Perfect competition theory assumes that the number of sellers in each market is so large that any one individual firm has only a negligible effect on market price. However, in imperfectly competitive (oligopolistic or concentrated) markets there is assumed to be a small number of firms, so that sellers are conscious of their interdependence.[16] That is, 'what makes oligopoly theory different from competitive market theory is the recognition by firms that outcomes of their decisions are affected by the behaviour of other firms' (Joskow, 1975, p. 271). Therefore, decisions are taken under some assumptions about probable reactions of those firms which the firm thinks will be influenced in some way by its actions. And relatedly, since the number of sellers in an imperfectly competitive market is small, it may permit them collectively to control market prices.
4. Imperfect Competition vs. Perfect Competition: The concept of imperfect competition arose naturally with analogous to that of perfect competition. Perfect competition is attained if a market is made up of firms with identical (cost) conditions, and if the number of firms is sufficiently large for firms' demand curves to be completely elastic; the result is perfect competition. In contrast, if a market is made up of firms with differing initial conditions, and of a small number of large enough firms in their industries so that they can exert a significant influence on market prices and the quantity of a product supplied, thereby affecting (distorting) in some significant sense the resource allocation pattern which follows, then the result is imperfect competition.

Within Industrial Organisation paradigm of imperfectly competitive markets none of the *auxiliary* assumptions of perfect competition notion, namely, homogeneous commodity, large number of sellers, and free entry to, exit from a given market and mobility of production factors, holds. The intensity and dimensionality of competition in imperfectly competitive markets depends on the spread in the capacities of firms to generate synergies, scale economies, rents, productivity, to build up some sort of barriers to entry, mobility, and imitation, to offer differentiated products, and so on, not on the mere number of firms in a market, offering *output* of the same good at the same unit price through free entry, exit and perfectly imitative competition (Demsetz, 1997).

Another important point regarding imperfect market assumption is that although the equilibrium idea is still held, a more sophisticated equilibrium assumption is made. Within in perfect competition theory markets a straightjacket equilibrium concept is assumed: profits are everywhere zero, or more generally, all opportunities have been exploited; and there exists only one equilibrium point, the Pareto optimal. The existence, optimality, and unbiasedness of perfectly competitive equilibrium depend only on the fact that consumers are maximising, and maximising universally. If they are maximising with what they individually know and control, unequal resource endowments, uncertainty, asymmetric information, adjustments, in a process, on the basis of new information, and interdependencies, then, it can be assumed, there exist more than one equilibrium point. In these markets large profits would be earned, firms' decisions to enter attractive markets could be slown down by some kind of barriers to competition, imitation might be gradual, sub-optimal firms might not go out of business promptly, etc. In these respects, as Hahn observes, 'economists are not agreed even what the appropriate notion of an equilibrium should be. But it becomes easy to show that plausible equilibria are no longer Pareto efficient ... when the no surplus condition is not satisfied' (1984b, p. 117).

Although perfect competition theory and the Industrial Organisation theories are within the same research programme, their subdisciplinary hard cores are so different that the former does not permit to investigation of strategic phenomena within its limits, whereas the latter provides a framework to explain and investigate the reasons for profit differentials between markets and firms within the markets, sluggishness of competitive equalisation of the differences, and strategic behaviour of firms.

The point needs elaboration. As we have discussed in the previous chapter, the distinctive character of neoclassical research programme can be stated, as Latsis argues, 'situational determinism'. Situational determinism as a research programme simply assumes a systematic relationship between market situations (structures) and outcomes. Under the conditions characterising perfectly competitive economic situation (certainty, atomistic competition, free entry and exit, etc.) the firm's course of action is reduced to a predetermined single choice, which Latsis calls the 'single-exit' situation. By 'single-exit' situation he means that once the objective function and constraints are specified, as in the paradigm case of perfect competition theory, a unique solution emerges directly. But,

Industrial Organisation modifies to a significant extent situational determinants, introducing uncertainty, interdependence of decision making, entry and exit conditions, and so on, into explanations. Under the modified conditions the firm's 'choice is *not* narrowly delimited by situational considerations' (emphasis in origin) (Latsis, 1976, p. 16) which Latsis calls the 'multiple-exit' situations: 'in oligopolistic market situations the awkwardness of a single-exit model is most apparent. In such situations, ... we are confronted with genuine multiple-exit decision-situations' (Latsis, 1976, p. 31). In other words, the single exit approach to theories of imperfectly competitive markets, such as monopolistic competition and oligopoly, is inadequate since the motivation and learning processes of the decision-maker need to be far more thoroughly specified.

Note that it is not, indeed, economic agents (for instance, their decision making capacity, their logic of choice, etc.) who change, but rather situations under which they make decisions. As we have mentioned above, under multiple-exit situations firms do not face objective conditions. They then form subjective expectations about rivals'-existing and potentials - possible responses (e.g. defensive and aggressive responses), about demand conditions (e.g. expecting growth or decline in demand), about what the firm and its rivals capable of doing (e.g. in generating scale economies, productivity, differentiation), etc. Moreover, they revise their decisions if they receive new information, they learn over time, etc. These are crucial factors in determining choices, and cannot be specified *ex ante*. In fact, it is only in these market situations that the firm has any role to play.

In this respect, under multiple-exit situations an area of discretion is introduced. For example, in these situations firms which do not maximise profits do not necessarily go out of business. In other words, 'sub-optimal behaviour is still viable' (Latsis, 1976, p. 31). Therefore, firm differentials in profitability are now recognised as viable competitive (equilibrium) outcomes. Or, from a more active sense, instead of the machine-like reactions of firms to prices, the firms are assumed to engage in interactive competitive situations, in which it will be necessary for them to take into consideration the decisions of rival firms (current as well as potential) from the point of view that other firms' decisions can be influenced by their own. Thus, as Hahn asserts, 'their choices will now be among strategies' (1984b, p. 117).

The idea of strategic behaviour of advantage seeking seems to solve also a deep problem with perfect competition theory. The problem originates in the fact that perfect competition theory postulates both rational self-seeking agents (economic agents act in their self-interest) and price takers (individual or firms act as if prices were given) at the same time. If the hypothesis of rational self-seeking holds, as Hahn asks, 'will not individuals or groups of individuals seek to find ways to exert market power [for example, in the form of price-making]?' (1984b, p. 116). The answer given by theorists of perfect competition is that 'there is no market power for individuals to exploit' (Hahn, 1984b, p. 116) due to perfect imitation abilities of economic agent (i.e., everyone in the economy, other than a given agent, can do as well when that agents trades as when he does not - Hahn, 1984b, p. 116) in a large economy. In this case, the conflict seems to be solved by postulating self-seeking agents with no opportunity of doing so, that is, self-interest seeking agents competing in a market environment that all opportunities have already been exploited, and, as a result, agents continue to exist doing exactly the same thing as they have been hitherto doing and/or to achieve the uncontroversial goal, i.e. Pareto-optimality. Otherwise they go out of business. But this event, a deeper problem emerges: not only the underlying logic of competition, which is that differences between firms create competition, but also the motive force for business behaviour, which is the self-seeking behaviour for advantages, is assumed away. In this respect, competition connotes no longer self-seeking behaviour for superior gains, rather, it means improving economic efficiency, where 'efficiency' is defined in terms of equilibrium welfare economics, which is a social rather than self-interest goal.

However, within Industrial Organisation theory of imperfect competition firms are assumed to seek for market power in their favour (for example, changing market structure, affecting market prices, involving R&D to innovate, etc.), whether efficiently or not, as a path to high profits. In consequence, they are not expected to allocate resources in a machine-like manner, to react to prices, but commit resources to long lasting investments such as product differentiation, scale economies, brand building, etc., to obtain and sustain advantages over rivals. In this respect, the conceptualisation of the market as an imperfectly competitive organisation (as a deviation from the Pareto-efficient ideal) captures the very essence of capitalist reality, which is the self-seeking behaviour for advantages.

It should be emphasised that in these markets firms are assumed not to behave with an eye on immediate, but rather long term gains. For instance, firms attempt to create conditions of imperfect competition, by building up some sort of barriers to competition (entry, mobility and imitation) - both individually and collectively - in order to sustain supernormal profits. Note that the kinds of barriers assumed are not *innocent*, i.e. barriers irrespective of the behaviour of incumbent firms, but rather *strategic*, i.e. barriers deliberately created by firms in a market or strategic group to make entry and mobility unattractive or to make imitation difficult.[17] Clearly, the creation of conditions of imperfect competition is a manifestation that firms follow a strategy (Barney, 1985). In game theoretical sense, since firms in imperfectly competitive markets are *behaviourally* interdependent, they act *strategically* to influence the behaviour of its rivals significantly by affecting its rivals' expectations of its future behaviour (Schelling, 1960). Or, from the efficiency approach viewpoint, firms have to *work to compete* via serving customers better, establishing reputation and brand loyalty, improving organisation, generating scale economies, seeking for legal protection in forms of patents, copyrights and trademarks against free imitation, and so on. Firms' effort of '*working to compete*' implies that they compete to seek for long term competitive advantages (Demsetz, 1973, 1997).

## Conclusions

Industrial Organisation is a territorial expansion of neoclassical theory of market competition, which approaches the market phenomena from the perspective of how the market is organised, and the impact of the way that it is organised on the economics of the market with regard to its social-welfare implications. Industrial Organisation extends the 'structure-oriented' neoclassical analyses to cover imperfectly organised markets (oligopolistic or concentrated markets) besides perfectly organised markets (atomistic markets). The paradigms in Industrial Organisation, namely, the S-C-P, efficiency, and game theoretical, though still neoclassical in character, relax the stringency of the assumptions of perfect competition, thus creating a strategic possibility not open to the firm in the perfectly competitive markets. In imperfectly organised markets the firm is assumed to compete for profit advantages, and when gained, to strive to sustain them. In other words, in imperfectly competitive situations firms are assumed to compete purposefully to acquire and/or maintain market power or superior efficiency capabilities, as a path to high profits. This requires that they behave strategically by making long-lasting commitments such as investments in brand building, quality improvements, scale economies, product development, etc. Thus, strategic phenomena are the direct domain category for Industrial Organisation research.

In this respect, Industrial Organisation provides a highly versatile groundwork for the investigation of strategic phenomena at market level. Indeed, Industrial Organisation has already played a highly significant role in the development of Strategy theory. Positioning and resource-based approaches, the two main approaches in the field of strategic management, build directly or indirectly upon the intellectual foundations of Industrial Organisation, namely, the S-C-P paradigm and game theoretical approach, and the efficiency paradigm respectively. In consequence, the intergroup debate between the approaches of strategic management reflects, in essence, the debate between the approaches of Industrial Organisation, regarding the sources of profit differentials (market structure or firm specific resources and capabilities) and the mechanism of sustaining them (barriers to entry and mobility or barriers to imitation).

## Notes

1. This field of economics is traditionally known as industrial organisation, but, especially in Europe, the term industrial economics is often applied in its stead (F.M. Scherer and D. Ross, 1990, *Industrial Market Structure and Economic Performance*, Third Edition, Boston: Houghton Mifflin Company). In this study we prefer the traditional line of naming.
2. The roots of that kind of endeavours goes back to the rising trend in the 1920s and 1930s of classifying markets, primarily according to the number of producers, and to derive equilibrium patterns of conduct of firms for each category. Most notable examples in that trend were Chamberlain's *Theory of Monopolistic Competition*, [Chamberlin, E.D., 1962 (first published in 1933), *Theory of Monopolistic Competition*, Cambridge, M.A.: Harvard University Press.] and Robinson's *The Economics of Imperfect Competition* [Robinson, J., 1969 (first published in 1933), *The Economics of Imperfect Competition*, London: Macmillan.]. As Mason later wrote, the influence of Edward H. Chamberlin [and Joan Robinson] had been profound: 'Chamberlin's [and Robinson's] theoretical insights were developed by his Harvard Colleagues in the messier areas of industry statistics, studies of particular firms, and antitrust policy.' They introduced the concepts of 'monopolistic competition' and 'imperfect competition', arguing that the determination of most market prices was the result of both competitive as well as monopolistic forces. Both models, now commonly referred to as the model of 'monopolistic competition, looked at the importance of differentiated products and the existence of advertising to competition and firm's behaviour. Historically, the development of this model must be seen as significant, as intermediate models of competition between perfect competition and monopoly now dominate much theoretical study of the firm in economics. The development of a model of monopolistic competition involved an examination of the theoretical relationship between industrial structures on the one hand, and prices and profits on the other, and it was just this type of relationship that pioneers of the field attempted to test empirically.
3. Like perfect competition, monopoly is also an extreme form of market structure. Monopoly theory is not going to be examined in this study since it does not seem relevant for 'competitive' strategy purposes.
4. The term of imperfect competition can be applied to cover all forms of market competition which exist between perfect competition and monopoly. The position of any particular market can be located along this spectrum by looking at the structure of that market in terms of the number of firms, ease of entry, and so on.

5. The diagram is taken from Reekie, but it is developed in some respects. For the original presentation see, W.D. Reekie, 1989, *Industrial Economics: A Critical Introduction to Corporate Enterprise in Europe and America*, Hants: Edward Elgar.
6. A large set of structural variables (growth, concentration, capital intensity, advertising intensity, etc.) have performed differently in different studies. Looking back almost three decades later, the theoretical arguments that are used to include or exclude a particular structural aspect from a list of explanatory variables are often *ad hoc* and imprecise, made without any clear reference to an underlying general model. See Jaquemin, A. (1987) *The New Industrial Organisation: Market Forces and Strategic Behaviour*, Oxford: Clarendon Press; Davies, S. and Lyons, B. (1992) (1989 first edition), Introduction, in S. Davies, B. Lyons with H. Dixon and P. Geroski (eds) *Economics of Industrial Organisation*, London: Longman.
7. See for example, J.M., Vernon (1972) *Market Structure and Industrial Performance: A Review of Statistical Findings*, Boston: Allyn and Bacon; F.M. Bass (1974) Profit and A/S Ratio, *Journal of Advertising Research*, Vol. 14, No. 6, pp. 9-19; W.E. Cox, Jr. (1977) Product portfolio Strategy, Market Structure, and Performance, in H.B. Thorelli, *Strategy + Structure = Performance. The Strategic Planning Imperative*, Bloomington: Indiana University Press, pp. 83-102.
8. See for example, Scherer and Ross (1990); Pickering (1974); Salop (1979); Ferguson and Ferguson (1994); Waterson (1984); McGee (1988); Schmalensee (1989); Sawyer (1981).
9. Chicago School is sometimes named as 'Chicago tradition,' 'efficiency paradigm' or 'efficiency-based theory.'
10. See Norman, G. and La Manna, M. (1992) *The New Industrial Economics*, Aldershot: Edward Elgar.
11. Besides game theoretical approach, contestable market theory (Baumol, W., Panzar, J., and Willing, R. (1982) *Contestable Markets and the Theory of Industry Structure*, New York: Harcout Brace Jovanovich) is also a part of the new industrial organisation current. Contestability theory describes situations where there are no sunk costs. As Shapiro argues (1989), 'this translates into a complete absence of strategic behaviour, since any action that is costlessly reversible has no commitment or strategic value.' (p. 127). The applications of contestable market theory has also been very limited. In the literature concerning the relationship between economics and strategic management, there is no significant reference to the theory; we also do not attempt to examine the theory since we believe that as a market theory, it does not offer a foundational service for the theory of Strategy, due to its strong assumption of free of exit barriers, which is a denial of long-lasting strategic commitments. For a critique of the theory of contestable markets, see Shepherd, W. (1984) '"Contestability" vs. Competition', *The American Economic Review*, Vol. 74, No. 4, pp. 572-587.
12. A game is said to be cooperative when players can make binding agreements; it is called non-cooperative when they cannot. For more information and applications, see F. Forges and J-F. Thisse (1992) Game Theory and Industrial Economics: An Introduction, in G. Norman and M. La Manna (eds.) *The New Industrial Economics. Recent Developments in Industrial Organisation*, Oligopoly and Game Theory, Hants: Edward Elgar, pp. 12-46.
13. See, in particular, Chapter 10.
14. It should also be pointed out that profit maximisation is not the only goal of the firm assumed in Industrial Organisation. As Sawyer argues, '[theories of oligopoly, in this context 'managerial' theories of the firm, put forward by Scitovsky, Baumol, Williamson, and Marris] share the common theme that the controllers of the firm pursue non-profit objectives [such as sales maximisation, market share or growth, and

individual objectives like status and salary] generally subject to achieving a certain level of performance in a profit-linked variable. ... [They] rely on the existence of barriers to entry into the industries in which their firms operate, so that potential supernormal profits are available to the firm. For if the firm could at most only earn normal profits, then it would have to maximise profits in order to survive. All the theories ... assume that the controllers of the firm are maximisers, but differ in terms of which variables the controllers are thought to seek to maximise.' (Sawyer, M.C., 1979, *Theories of the Firm*, London: Weidenfeld and Nicolson, pp. 89-90.) For the managerial theories of the firm, see T. Scitovsky (1943) A Note on Profit Maximisation, *Review of Economic Studies*, Vol. 11, No. 1, pp. 57-60; W.J. Boumol (1959) *Business Behaviour, Value, and Growth*, London: Macmillan; O.E. Williamson (1963) A Model of Rational Managerial Behaviour, in R.M. Cyert and J.G. March, *A Behavioural Theory of the Firm*, Englewood Cliffs, N.J.: Prentice-Hall, pp. 237-252; R. Marris (1963) A Model of the Managerial Enterprise, *Quarterly Journal of Economics*, Vol. 77, pp. 185-209.

15. For the importance of uncertainty in oligopolistic markets see in particular, Chapters 17 and 20.
16. Note that, as Latsis observes, 'the distinctive characteristic of oligopolistic models is not numerical fewness as such, but 'fewness' in the idiosyncratic sense that decisions are interdependent. ... In this idiosyncratic conception of 'fewness' it is important that industries with quite a large number of firms may nevertheless qualify for treatment in terms of an oligopolistic model ...' (p. 31). Latsis, S.J. (1976) A Research Programme in Economics, in S.J. Latsis (ed.) *Method and Appraisal in Economics*, Cambridge: Cambridge University Press, pp. 1-41.
17. For the categorisation of the barriers as innocent and strategic, see Salop, S. (1979) Strategic Entry Deterrence, *American Economic Review*, Vol. 69, pp. 335-338.

# Process-Oriented' Theories of the Market: Austrian and Evolutionary Schools of Economics

As we have demonstrated, the focus of neoclassical perfect competition and industrial organisation theories has been on 'market structure.' Elaboration within Industrial Organisation, while extending the theory to new market situations (imperfect factor markets and imperfect product markets), retains the basic framework and decision-making process postulated for perfect competition. Within the neoclassical construct the basic argument was that the particular market structure of the economy will influence the pattern of resource allocation.

In so doing, the neoclassical research has shed much light on how markets *look*, but it has not shown exactly how markets *work*. The Austrian and evolutionary schools of thought approach the market phenomena from the perspective of how the market functions, not on how it is organised. Thereby they shift the focus from 'market structure' to 'market process'. The intellectual effort is then put on understanding the driving forces of market change and competitive process. Then, the 'process-oriented' theories suggest investigations into market and competition as an *evolving* and *historic process*, rather than into making comparisons between markets within a particular economy at a specific point in time, which would only give a limited picture of market forces at work. In other words, they suggest approaching market or market competition as a process rather than a state.

In what follows, we examine the Austrian and the evolutionary theories respectively from the standpoint of their foundational offerings to strategic management approach to explaining the differential and competitive economics of market participants, namely, firms.

# Chapter 5

# Austrian School of Economics

## Introduction

The Austrian School of economics originated in Vienna in the 1870s with the writing of Carl Menger, *Principles of Economics* (1871), and the ideas were first propagated and extended by his near-contemporaries, Frederich von Wieser and Eugen von Bohm-Bawerk. The school has continually produced highly prominent figures thereafter, such as Ludwing von Mises, Joseph Schumpeter,[1] Fredrich Hayek, Ludwing Lachmann, Israel Kirzner, and recently Gerald O'Driscoll and Mario Rizzo.

It should be pointed out here that the phrase of Austrian School now has 'little geographical connotation' (Barry, 1991, p. 69). Today the term 'Austrian' represents a school of thought, whose common concern is with competition as a dynamic and ongoing *process* of change. The ideas associated with the school have largely gained prominence, and been extended and refined in England and the United States via, primarily, Hayek and Mises who helped spawn the 'British' and most notably 'American' generation of Austrian economists.

The Austrian School of thought was developed in parallel with neoclassical school. As we mentioned before, Menger was also one of founders of the neoclassical school. Therefore they share some common principles. The Austrian School, however, diverged from the neoclassical during the 20th century. More specifically, until the mid-1970s the Austrian ideas of economics, which were thought to be significant such as the subjectivist value theory and the theory of capital 'had been incorporated into the mainstream of economic thought and its *distinctive* characteristics had been confined to the more arcane texts in the history of the discipline...' (emphasis in original) (Barry, 1991, p. 69). In order to turn down the claim of the originality of the Austrian ideas, Milton Friedman once declared boldly that 'there is no Austrian economics - only good economics, and bad economics'[2]. As Dolan pointed out, Friedman did not mean 'Austrian economics as bad economics but rather to declare that truly valuable and original contributions of Austrian-school economists ... could be smoothly incorporated into the mainstream of economic theory' (1976, p. 4).

Nevertheless, after the mid-1970s, with the coincidence of the Nobel Prize in Economics in 1974 to Hayek, who was then accepted as the leader of the Austrian School, not only has the interest in the Austrian economics become a remarkable phenomenon, but the status of Austrian economics as a distinctive paradigm or research programme has been forcefully argued. The distinctive features of the school and its implications for strategic management field seems to lie in its view of competition as a discovery process and relating issues such as entrepreneurship, learning, etc.

## Problem Area: Competition as a Discovery Process

The question of what constitutes a legitimate problem for economic analysis receives careful attention in the Austrian School of economics. For example, one of the earliest founding fathers of the school, Menger, believes that the problem of social sciences is 'how can it be that institutions which serve the common welfare and are extremely significant for its development came into being without a *common will* directed toward establishing them?' (emphasis in original) (1963, p. 146). Menger argues that many social institutions are the results of human action but not of human design. He pointed out that actions do have unintended consequences, and made it very clear that economics is the science that is able to explain how these unintended consequences emerge in the market place.

As intellectual descendants of Menger, most Austrian economists have continued to concern themselves with the question of the existence of a spontaneously generated market order as the central question of economics. For example, for Hayek, whose writings are well-known for his emphasis on spontaneous order of market coordination, economics (indeed, the social sciences generally) as a discipline is 'to explain the unintended or undesigned results of the actions of many men' (1955, p. 25). In clearer terms, the task that he assigned to economic theory was 'to explain how an overall order of economic activity was achieved which utilised a large amount of knowledge which was not concentrated in any one mind but existed only as the separate knowledge of thousands or of millions of different individuals' (Hayek, 1967b, p. 91). The emergent basis of market order is premised upon the free decisions of many disconnected individuals, based upon knowledge. To him, although individual actions are governed by purposeful actions based on knowledge, market order is the unintended outcome of interactions (decentralised decision making), not the product of a single will (centralised decision making).

In fact the problem of spontaneous order is not unique to the Austrian School of economics at all. Much of nineteenth century economics and neoclassical economics revolved around the mystery of market order as a spontaneous phenomena. In particular, the problem can be traced back to Adam Smith and his invisible-hand explanation of coordination problem. Nevertheless, the striking point in the Austrian enunciation of the task of economic activity is a radical reorientation in the focus of economic thought of the coordination problem from the Smithian 'division of labour' to the 'division of knowledge', arguing that the former implies the latter (i.e., division of labour implies specialised knowledge). In other words, in the hands of Austrians, in particular Hayek, the problem of economics as a social science becomes 'the problem of *the division of knowledge*' (1949, p. 50). Within the construct of economy of knowledge, the determination of the optimal allocation of resources given all the relevant information, as Hayek holds, 'is emphatically not the economic problem which society faces' (1948, p. 77). What is important, then, is not much how markets coordinate specialised labour or allocate resources, but *how markets generate, disseminate, and respond to information*.

Kirzner assigns another task to economics alongside the investigation of spontaneous order: 'Besides ... the tracing out of the unintended consequences of action ... we have the requirement that it makes the world around us intelligible in terms of human action' (1976, p. 41). In other words, although market coordination is the unintended consequence of human actions, the market phenomena is conceivable only in terms of the interacting decisions of market participants such as consumers, entrepreneur-producers, and resource owners (Kirzner, 1973). Mises (1966) argues human actions can, in some way, only be conceivable through the cause and effect between the means chosen and the ends desired. Specifically, the idea of intended human actions establishes a basis for the investigation of the motives of participants involving in market making activities. For our purpose, the most important market participant is the entrepreneur-producer, who is at the centre of the Austrian analysis of market phenomena. As Kirzner maintains: 'a useful understanding of the market process requires a notion of competition that is analytically inseparable from the exercise of entrepreneurship' (1973, p. 9).

Investigations into unintended market order and into intended human actions together lead to a highly unique conceptualisation of market competition from that of the neoclassical. Austrian economists conceptualise the market as a 'discovery process' that mobilises dispersed knowledge among market participants. To elaborate the point, first of all, Austrians view market coordination as a 'process' rather than a state. For them, 'the passage of time is essential to give the concept of equilibrium any meaning' (Hayek, 1949, pp. 36-37). Hayek argues that introducing time dimension into the equilibrium analysis is the only way to approach the real world investigations of causal processes. Austrians view time as historical or irreversible. This is fundamentally different from the neoclassical perfect competition conception of spatialised time, in which, as in the geometry of lines, 'each point is identical to all others, except for its positions' (O'Driscoll and Rizzo, 1985, p. 54). These two different conceptions of time bring us to the centre of tension between equilibrium viewed as a composite of homogeneous time points (a certain market state) and equilibrium viewed as a composite of heterogeneous time extension (market process). As O'Driscoll and Rizzo observe, in the former 'the mere elapse of time does not produce or cause anything...' (1985, p. 55) to change. In the former, however, 'change ... is the *true* effect of time' (emphasis in origin) (O'Driscoll, et al., 1985, p. 57). The passage of time produce change, or 'causal efficacy' in terms of O'Driscoll and Rizzo referring to Capenk (1961), in bringing out source of novelty. For Hayek, if there were no change, there would be no economic problem: 'all economic problems are created by unforeseen changes...' (1949, p. 101).

As we have pointed out, in the neoclassical general equilibrium construct, there is a causal inertness. Since the passage of time does not produce any real change, time does not cause anything. All change is compressed into a single instant. The outcome of this 'causal inertness', as O'Driscoll and Rizzo put it, is 'its consequent determinism' (1985, p. 56). In other words, all choices have already been determined once and for all. In Hayek's terms, 'as long as things continue as before, or at least as they were expected to, there arise no new problems requiring a decision, no need to form a new plan' (1949, p. 82). In this static equilibrium construct, for example, 'once a plant has been built, the rest is all more or less mechanical, determined by the character of the plant, and leaving little to be changed in adapting to the ever changing circumstances of the moment' (Hayek, 1949, p. 82).

Secondly, the dynamic force behind the market process is assumed to be entrepreneurial discoveries. The assumed continuous change (disequilibrium) implies that there are yet, and will always be, unexploited market opportunities for mutually advantageous exchange. To put it differently, continuous change implies a never-ending process of 'competition as a discovery procedure' of marketable opportunities, as Hayek (1978) proposes to consider it.

The view of the market as a discovery process is diametrically opposite to that of the market as perfect competition view in which all profit opportunities have already been known and exploited, so that economy is in a Paretian-efficient state of rest. For Austrians, as Kirzner argues,

> [the] world *is* a grossly inefficient world. What is inefficient about the world is surely that, at each instant, enormous scope for improvements exists... At each instant, because the market is in a state of disequilibrium, genuine allocative inefficiencies remain yet to be removed simply because entrepreneurs have not yet noticed the profit opportunities represented by these in efficiencies. At each instant available technological improvements ... remain to be exploited; they remain untapped because entrepreneurs have not yet noticed the profit opportunities embedded in these possibilities (Kirzner, 1978, pp. 73-74).

In the Austrian construct, economy is an open-system, that is, open to grow. The dynamic force of economic growth is the increase in entrepreneurial knowledge of new marketable opportunities. In this world of yet uncovered profit opportunities, the task of competition is drastically different from that of perfect competition. As Hayek maintains, perfect competition is 'a *state* of affairs ... [that] leaves no room whatever for the *activity* called competition, which is presumed to have already done its task' (emphasis in origin) (1978, p. 182); however, 'the chief task [of market competition] is [to encourage prospectors] to discover yet unknown opportunities of a society in which in the past competition has not been active' (1978, p. 188). In the course of this entrepreneurial discovery process, Kirzner argues, 'new products may be introduced, new qualities of existing products may be developed, new methods of production may be ventured, new forms of industrial organisation, financing, marketing, or tackling risk may be developed' (1985, p. 30).

And thirdly, the causal efficacy of time on the basis of changes (discoveries) enters the Austrian equilibrium framework in the form of changes in the data of market participants previously held and of necessitating the acquisition of new knowledge by them and changes in their plans. To the Austrian economists, the importance of market economies as social institutions in the world of discoveries is to enable participants to communicate their discoveries to others and to learn of discoveries that other people have made, and thus helping individuals to coordinate their plans *towards* a mutually consistent state of plans via making continuous modifications of their plans and adaptations to ever-changing circumstances.

In the Austrian paradigm, although the price system still plays a significant role, its role is different from that of the neoclassical perfect competition paradigm. In the neoclassical paradigm the role of price mechanism, as we remember, was 'strictly confined to clearing markets [equalising supply to demand] and enabling a separation between agents in such a way that there was no need for them to act strategically [to outperform each other]' (Bohm, 1989, p. 207). Within the Austrian construct, however, price system enables entrepreneurs to make discoveries about individual wants at particular times and places, about advantages of hitherto unnoticed divergences between different parts in a present market (cross-sectional arbitrage opportunities), about advantages of yet unnoticed divergences between today's market and tomorrow's market (cross-time arbitrage opportunities), about erroneously overlooked opportunities, etc. Discovering and marketing all these opportunities requires a 'mechanism for communicating information', as Hayek calls it. This mechanism for communicating information is the price system.

Yet, in the Austrian paradigm it is recognised that 'current prices are only a very small section of the problem of knowledge' (Hayek, 1949, p. 51). In a world of discoveries, we go beyond information indicated by price system and 'find scope for the unpredictable, the creative, the imaginative expression of the human mind' (Kirzner, 1985, p. 58). The view of competition as a discovery process thus indicates that the market economy is an open system in that it is open to 'grow' into new possibilities not implied by price parameters.

The conceptualisation of the market as a discovery process, or, investigations into intended and unintended human actions, as we shall see, has important implications for strategic management. To start with, arguably the most important implication is that in the Austrian School, as in the theory of strategic management, it is assumed that the motive for competition is to search for marketable profit opportunities (intended human actions). Implicit in the concept of intended human action is the idea of seeking to replace a state of relative dissatisfaction with one of relative satisfaction. It implies a dynamic struggle for betterness, or, competitive advantage in a market place. In other words, new possibilities (discoveries) are searched for by entrepreneurs for their self-interest of seizing profit opportunities. As we remember, 'perhaps the primary limitation of the neoclassical theory of [perfect] competition is that it fails to provide a motive for the search for new products and methods (i.e., innovation)' (Jacobson, 1992, p. 785). However, in a market economy, profit seeking behaviour of entrepreneurs and competition are inseparable. Without a motive for earning economic profits, there seems to be no reason to become involved in competitive behaviour to search for new opportunities.

As to the unintended consequences of human actions, it is assumed that men act purposefully by using means (organisations called firms) to achieve ends (earning superior profits), yet the resultant performance of their actions are not always what they intend. In other words, firms act purposefully (rationally) to place themselves in situations that are the most preferred of those equally available alternatives of which they are aware, nevertheless they may end up with 'more' or 'less' preferred positions than that they pursue. By the presupposition of purposeful (rational) human actions, firms are meant to not *consciously* place themselves in less or undesirable positions. By contrast, they at any time pursue exploiting any known opportunity for achieving the most desirable position possible. So, why they may end up with undesirable situations. This is because their plans and expectations are continually imperfectly fulfilled because of learning, disappointments and surprises. There is nothing in purposeful action which by itself guarantees that man is free of fallibility and surprises that disturb his/her plans, perceives every available opportunity correctly and instantaneously, or gets what he/she intends (Kirzner, 1978). Without such considerations of learning, committing errors, and surprises, there seems to be no basis for an explanation of why firms sometimes fail in earning economic profits in the process of competition.

In the Austrian equilibrium construct, as Hayek deduces, '*wherever* the use of competition can be rationally justified, it is on the ground that we do *not* know in advance the facts that determine the actions of competitors' (emphasis in original) (1968, p. 179). But, an economic agent has limited ability of foresight, and 'may learn of new facts that make him change his plans...' (Hayek, 1949, p. 52). Implicit in the Hayekian presentation of learning is the indispensable element of disappointing or defeating some particular expectations and intentions. In his terms, 'if we do not know the facts we hope to discover by means of competition, we can never ascertain how effective it has been in discovering those facts that might be discovered' (Hayek, 1978, p. 180). Opportunities or errors, once discovered, cause the equilibrium position to alter in a previously unforeseen way due to distinctive learning schemata of different individuals. Therefore, market equilibrium is considered being a process characterised by profits and losses as the judgements made by economic agents turn out to be correct or incorrect. The importance of this point will be appreciated when we compare it with the perfect competition view of the economic agent as 'a quasi-omniscient individual' (Hayek, 1949, pp.

45-46), who does not need to learn, and is free of disappointments and surprises. In other words, in the perfect competition construct, economic agents have perfect foresight of future states, and they get what they want. In so assuming, no room is left for explaining why there are successful and unsuccessful firms competing side by side in a market. This is a denial of the domain subject of Strategy theory.

In short, an investigation into firm differentials constitutes a legitimate and significant part of the Austrian paradigm for investigations into intended human actions and unintended consequences of human actions. Yet, more specifically, does it offer an explanation for the sources of success or failure of firms, and for the mechanism of sustaining success?

## The Sources and Mechanism of Persistent Firm Differentials

The Austrian School explicitly recognises firm differences as an economic problem which is central to strategy theory: 'In fact, it need hardly be said, no ... two producers are ever exactly alike ... These differences are part of the facts which create our economic problem ...' (Hayek, 1949, p. 98). Firm differences are repercussions of either changing demand conditions or different resources and capabilities that economic agents possess:

> In conditions where we can never have many people offering the same homogenous product or service, because of the ever changing character of our needs and our knowledge, or of the infinite variety of human skills and capacities, the ideal state cannot be one requiring an identical character of large numbers of such products and services (Hayek, 1949, p. 104).

At the heart of all sources of superior profits lies the superior knowledge possessed by individuals. As we see above, for the Austrians, and in particular for Hayek, the economic problem is 'a problem of the utilisation of knowledge which is not given to anyone in its totality' (1949, p. 78). In this world of knowledge there are two kind of knowledge: scientific knowledge, which is 'the knowledge of general rules' (Hayek, 1949, p. 80), and the knowledge of the particular circumstances of time and place. For Hayek, it is the second kind of knowledge that is important for economic problems. And, from the sources of competitive advantage, obviously, it is this unique knowledge, not the knowledge of general rules, that leads to competitive differences. This is explicit in Hayek's analysis *Of The Use of Knowledge in Society*: 'It is with respect to this [the knowledge of the particular circumstances and place] that practically every individual has some advantage over all others because he possesses unique information of which beneficial use might be made ...' (Hayek, 1949, p. 80). This category of knowledge is not, and cannot be, readily at the command of everybody, and, in particular, in the form of statistical aggregates (scientific knowledge). This knowledge is localised, subjective and dispersed among millions of market participants.

In other words, as Rizzo (1978) observes, the existence of supernormal profits or entrepreneurial profits is postulated to be the outcome of some kind of special superior knowledge. Obviously, this world of superior knowledge is radically different from the neoclassical perfect competition world in which 'there is really no superior information: all agents have the same perfect knowledge of probability distributions' (Rizzo, 1978, p. 12). This knowledge could be the knowledge, as Hayek mentions in different contexts, of cost-reducing techniques, improving (differentiating), better management, rising opportunities from change, new ways of doing things better than they have been done before, and in short, of new possibilities in a wide sense. For Kirzner (1973) the superior knowledge of particular circumstances and place means specifically the superior knowledge of some kind of profit opportunities for arbitrage (cross-sectional and cross-time arbitrage opportunities).

The sources of competitive advantage are, in the Hayekian sense, another expression of the sources of competitive advantage put forward within the positioning view, namely cost leadership and differentiation, and within the resource-based view, namely superior resources and capabilities. Nevertheless, for the Austrians, the ultimate source of advantage is embedded in individuals' skills and capabilities in discovering such profit opportunities as low cost production processes or product differentiation. They view, as Armentano observes,

> this process [of discovering attractive opportunities to potential buyers] as *inherently* competitive since the key ingredient that makes the process function - entrepreneurship - can *never* be monopolized; hence the freedom to enter the market is absolute since no obstacles to entry can ever exist in a free market (emphasis in original) (Armentano, 1978, p. 100).

In fact, entrepreneurial discoveries bring new dimensions into competition, rather than limit it. Profit opportunities are dependent on the ability of entrepreneurs to perceive them. Entrepreneurial ability is based upon knowledge, often the most tacit and implicit knowledge, and therefore it is immune to immediate observation and imitation. In other words, in the Austrian construct, invisible assets or unobservable factors are the sources of superior success as well as the reason for their persistency.

Nevertheless, in the construct the explanation of persistency of profit opportunities does not seem very straightforward. For the Austrians, market process is assumed to have a strong *tendency* towards equilibrium, and in the process of equilibrating tendency superior profits are, thus, viewed to most likely be a *temporary* phenomenon. Is this practically thought of being so? In what follows, we argue that it is not that simple, and that there is ample room for assuming, within the Austrian paradigm, the persistency of superior profits in spite of competitive pressure.

Then, despite the attempts of economic agents to eliminate them, the persistence of profit differentials demands explanation. Persistent profits may be the case, as Hayek argues, 'in a market where adaptation is slow compared with the rate of change...' (1949, p. 103). In other words, as Littlechild argues, referring to Kenneth Boulding's analogy of the dog chasing the cat, that 'equilibrium for the dog where the cat is, but the dog might never catch the cat!' (1982, p. 95). That is, when the dog chases the cat, the cat does not stand still. As market participants chasing one equilibrium (i.e., fulfilling their individual plans), other forces might be disequilibrating (i.e., making adjustments in their plans, discovering new possibilities, entering to and leaving from markets, etc.). Therefore, running towards an equilibrium is running towards a moving target.

Note that, for Austrians, 'the concept of equilibrium is used to characterise not the *state* of the economy but the direction of *changes* in the state' (emphasis in original) (Littlechild, 1982, p. 95). As such, it is reminiscent of the conception of competition prevalent within the strategic management paradigm. There competition is also not a state but a direction of change. Competition between firms pressurises or forces firms towards the state of earning normal profits by nullifying differences in performance between them, via entry, exit and imitation. But the equilibration of differentials might never be attained because successful firms also seek for new ways of competing better, and thus creating ceaselessly new disequilibriums between themselves and imitators. There is, therefore, a continuous process of market equilibrium and disequilibrium or coordination and discoordination of the plans of market participants.

More importantly, from an empirical point of view, as Utton observes, the time period involved in the adaptation (equilibrating) process of erosion of profit differentials may be expected to vary from industry to industry or the stage of development reached (growth or maturity), but it cannot be inferred from the Austrian theory as to whether an above-average profitable position will be 'eroded within five years or fifty' (Utton, 1986, p. 1).[3] Needless to say, from this empirical point of view, there is not a significant difference between the Austrian and strategy theory. In strategy theory, persistence of profit opportunities are also always open to competitive pressure or forces to erode them, but it is assumed that the process of erosion can be slowed down by strategic actions of firms for a long enough time. This long enough time could be, in Utton's terms, five years or fifty.

## Hard Core Assumptions: Situational Indeterminism

In his *Mises and Lakatos: A Reformulation of Austrian Methodology* essay, Rizzo reconstructs the Austrian methodological framework along lines delineated by Lakatos's methodology of scientific research programmes (Rizzo, 1982). In what follows we take the reconstruction as given and assess whether the hard core of the Austrian economics facilitates the integration of the two bodies of knowledge, i.e. the knowledge produced within the Austrian and strategic management research programmes.

For Rizzo, the fundamental presupposition of Austrian economics is that man engages in purposeful behaviour.[4] This constitutes the basis of the Austrian enquiry of economic discipline in explaining, as we have argued, behaviour in terms of purposeful human action, and to what extent purposeful human actions can interact to produce unexpected outcomes. Rizzo suggests four hard core assumptions derivable from the presupposition, by pursuing the strand of thought in Austrian methodology to reconstruct the Austrian use of purpose with the rationality hypothesis often employed by economists:

1. Individuals Perceive a Decision-making Environment: All purposeful human actions are oriented towards the future, and the future cannot be objectively known. The future state can only be imagined or projected. In other words, human actions or plans are assumed to be based on subjectively perceived or known future states. Thus, the context in which actions take place to achieve ends varies from one economic agent to another.
2. Perceptions Take Place in a World of Uncertainty: For the Austrians, action in a world of complete certainty is logically impossible. If everything is certain, there would be merely automatic or reflexlike behaviour similar to the involuntary responses of cells and nerves to stimuli. This is not the same as purposeful human action. As Rizzo maintains, 'part of what we mean by human action is its lack of deterministic nature and consequent imperfect predictability' (1982, p. 57). Hence,

purposeful human action logically entails the existence of uncertainty.

3. Individuals' Perceptions Are Not Always Correct: Within the neoclassical formulation rationality is viewed as a purely formal relationship between means and ends, and independent of the accuracy of the individuals' information. Taking the objective circumstances as given, rationality is considered to be just a maximising exercise, which is always optimal. However, Rizzo argues, a decision is not independent of the accuracy of the individual's information. A decision can be optimal or rational relative to perceived data. If a situation is incorrectly perceived, and a decision is made accordingly, such a decision could be inefficient or ineffective but never irrational in the sense of instrumental rationality, i.e. means-ends compatibility, since means-ends compatibility still obtains given the knowledge of the situation.

   However, for the Austrians, there is no objective reality independent of interpretation of economic agents. If perceptions were always objective or correct, there would be no importance of uncertainty, perceptions, learning, competitive strategy, etc., but an automatic response to objective reality, and individuals and economy as a whole end up with equilibrium state.

4. Action is Coordinating: The tendency toward coordination follows directly from the action postulate itself. Actions are motivated by profit opportunities. Profit opportunities appear in the process of discoordination. But, the purposeful pursuit of profit sets also in motion a tendency toward elimination of this discoordination. For the Austrians, the tendency toward coordination is not the same as the full coordination assumed by neoclassists. The assumption of tendency toward coordination does not make any claim about the frequency with which coordination comes about. And, full coordiantion is viewed as unattainable. The emphasis is on the process of coordination.

As we have been arguing, the aim of Austrian economists is not to explain market situations (structures), but market *process*. The driving forces of market process are assumed to be purposeful human actions. Given the hard core assumptions, it is assumed implicitly that there is an element of significant indeterminacy in human action and thereby in the outcomes of these actions. In contrast to the neoclassical 'situational determinism' according to which we can, at least probablistically, predict what action (single-exit situation) or set of alternative actions (multiple-exit situations) will be taken in any given situation, in the Austrian construct, as Buchanan observes, 'there is no way, even conceptually, to predict what action will be taken in any particular circumstance' (1982, p. 14).

Purposeful entrepreneurial actions seeking marketable opportunities are as much consequences of the 'unpredictable, the creative, and the imaginative expression of the human mind' (Kirzner, 1985, p. 58). In other words, the entrepreneurial creative imagination of the future is not determined by the present situational facts but by the entrepreneur's subjective interpretation and creative imagination. Therefore, it is difficult to talk about a 'situational determinism' in the world of the creative actions (discoveries) of the entrepreneur. The world of entrepreneurial action is simply an open-ended system, brought into existence in an unfolding process. In other words, on the contrary to the neoclassical research programme that assumes market economy as a closed system in which economic agents' choices can be predicted, the Austrian research programme assumes market economy to be an open system in which economic agents make entrepreneurial choice that involves creative, imaginative or innovative thinking.

In fact, the bottom line in the distinction between situtional determinism and indeterminism is not about situational 'logic' in the sense that agents act appropriately to the logic of their situations, and, specifically, prefer a best alternative given their knowledge and means, but about 'situations' themselves in which economic agents make choices. Indeed, 'situational logic' in the above sense is, as Langlois (1982) argues, common to the neoclassical as well as the Austrian research programme. But, as Vaughn maintains, '[neoclassical] predictive, positive economics applies to those situations where humans respond passively to shifts in constraints ... [however, Austrian] subjectivism applies to situations where humans actively seek to alter their constraints' (1982, p. 21). In other word, the world of business is, for Austrians, the world of possibilities (discoveries), which is in a state of continuous becoming, rather than being.

In this respect, needless to say, the idea of entrepreneurial choice goes beyond that of the multiple-choice situations variant of situational logic since it still assumes a predictable set of choices. Nevertheless, explanations of entrepreneurial choice situation and multiple-exit situations seems to be not mutually exclusive but complementary. What seems to differentiate them is the assumed *degree* of uncertainty. In the entrepreneurial choice situations of discoveries and innovations the degree of uncertainty is extremely high, and thus past experience and present observation are not very helpful, whereas in the multiple-choice situations of interdependent decision making in established and stable markets, uncertainty is relatively low, and the set of choices available to decision makers is thus much predictable.

In this respect, both sets of situational assumptions seem to shed light on different aspects of strategic behaviour, namely, interactive and innovative. Yet, in order to eliminate a misunderstanding, it should be emphasised that in the Austrian research programme competition is indeed viewed as an interdependent relationship. Competition involves actions to gain advantage over rivals, or, as Hayek defines it, 'the action of endeavouring to gain what another endeavours to gain at the same time' (1949, p. 96). In this respect, it is worth mentioning that the concept of 'perfect' competition is unequivocally refused by Austrian economics. Perfect competition, as Hayek maintains, 'means indeed the absence of all competitive activities. ... Especially remarkable in this connection is the explicit and complete exclusion from the theory of perfect competition of all personal relationships existing between the parties' (1949, p. 96).

Nevertheless, this interdependent relationship is not assumed to be in the form of limiting competition (building some kind of barriers to competition) but promoting competition (adding new dimensions to competitive struggle via discoveries). In other words, in the Austrian paradigm, profit-seeking entrepreneurs compete continually to outperform and outdo one another by offering more attractive opportunities to potential buyers. As Singleton (1986) mentions in his analysis of the Austrian School with regard to antitrust considerations, entrepreneurs use a number of strategies, such as product differentiation, advertising, discovery of low cost production processes, and research and development, in their efforts to generate and respond to profit opportunities. All these strategies are assumed to be the essential part of competition, rather than deviations from it.

Finally, under the situations of uncertainty, entrepreneurs are assumed to follow some kind of rules.[5] Rule-following behaviour seems to be a direct resultant of the *knowledge problem* that is central to the Austrian research programme, in particular, after Hayek's seminal work *Economics and Knowledge*. The 'whole rationale of the phenomenon of rule-guided action' is, Hayek submits, to be found in our 'inescapable ignorance of most of the particular circumstances which determine the effects of our actions' (Hayek, 1976, p. 20). Thus, rule-following behaviour is assumed to be the product of ignorance, and of a process of evolution, and substitutes for the maximising behaviour of firms case-by-case calculation of static innumerable micro-variations. Rules are assumed to govern firms as well as markets (in fact all social agents and institutions working under uncertain conditions), as O'Driscoll and Rizzo argue that 'any model that explains social rules solely in terms of maximising behaviour fundamentally misconstrues the phenomena' (1985, p. 119). Stability and evolution of firm and market behaviour are due to the stability and evolution of rules, not the resultant of case-by-case marginal adjustments.

From the strategic management viewpoint, the idea of rule-following seems to shed light on the strategy-following behaviour of firms in the sense that the properties of rule-following behaviour of firms can easily be interpreted as the properties strategy-following behaviour. For example, one of the most important illuminations of rule-following behaviour is, arguably, the idea that rules enable us to manage organisations according to predetermined guides (strategic principles), saving us from having to assess each case separately. Or, rules 'limit our range of choice' (Hayek, 1967a, p. 90) by abbreviating 'the list of circumstances which we need to take into account in particular instances, and singling out certain classes of facts as alone determining the general kind of action which we should take' (Hayek, 1964, p. 11). This idea illuminates why firms do not and cannot chase each and every opportunity.

## Conclusions

Like neoclassics, Austrians attempt to explain the market-price system. But, for neoclassics market prices serve merely as parametric guidelines for the appropriate reconciliation of human preferences in the allocation of goods, whereas for Austrians they serve as indicators of opportunities for profit and loss, and thereby as a mechanism for plan coordination. More clearly, for Austrians the economic problem is to understand, in general, the mystery of spontaneous order which cannot be altered by human activity, and, in particular, the nature of the purposeful competitive activities by which men discover and market profit opportunities, and adjust their plans to ever changing circumstances of moment.

In so doing, the market is viewed as a process of discovery that mobilises dispersed knowledge among market participants. The dynamic force of this discovery process is viewed through entrepreneurial creative actions for generating and realising profit opportunities in a constantly changing market place. Market environment is assumed to be uncertain and subject to continuous change. Change and uncertainty bring about new profit opportunities, surprises, failures as well as successes, learning, etc. Markets are assumed to approach equilibrium, rather than at equilibrium.

Within the conceptualisation of the market as a discovery process sources of profit differentials between firms and the mechanism of their persistency over time are not only recognised but also viewed as legitimate and significant problems to be investigated. Firm profit differentials are assumed to be corollaries of differences in the idiosyncratic knowledge of the entrepreneur that each firm enjoys. Differences in knowledge lead to the reformulation of a product's function, the development of new manufacturing methods, distribution channels or new forms of organisation, or the discovery of dimensions of competition that competitors have hitherto overlooked. These are in fact strategies that entrepreneurs initiate to outperform their rivals. Entrepreneurial factor or superior knowledge is also assumed to be the source of sustainable competitive advantage because it is difficult to obtain or imitate due to its partly tacit character. Therefore, this invisible or difficult to observe asset is likely to generate supernormal and long lasting impact on firm performance.

## Notes

1. Though Schumpeter's work is too individual and too expansive to be confined within any one school. Nowadays he is generally associated with evolutionary school of economics, and we also examine his ideas there.
2. Friedman made this assertion when speaking informally at a conference. See, G. Dolan (1976) *The Foundations of Modern Austrian Economics*, (eds.), Kansas City, KS: Sheed & Ward, p. 4.
3. It should be pointed out that in both the neoclassical and non-neoclassical branches of economics, it is well established to make, implicitly or explicitly, the distinction between long-run and short-run, and then maintain that substantive firm differentials are only short-run occurrences. In the long-run it is assumed that disadvantageous firms are either selected out or pressured to reorganise or firm differentials are equalised. Therefore, implicit in economics considerations, for example the Austrian School, Chicago School, Schumpeterian version of evolutionary economics, transaction cost economics, etc. is the belief that the process of imitation, entry and exit will be relatively rapid. On the contrary of this pessimistic economic view of sustainability, theorists in the area of strategic management take an optimistic view regarding the length of the durability of competitive advantages, arguing that competitive advantages are 'strategic' since they are a matter of long-run.

   The essence of these divergent views originates in the fact that time dimension considered for the sustainability neither in strategic management nor in economics corresponds to an observable reality. Therefore, they cannot be subject to testability. For example, five, ten or twenty years may be considered to be long enough in strategy theory, but it may not be considered so in economics. This seems to be because the 'run' (length) of the decay of competitive advantage is not considered, in economics, in terms of the real time needed for entry, mobility or imitability to take place, but in terms of dependent variables (i.e. that is, the short-run is considered to be when production is variable but production capacity is fixed, however, in the long-run production capacity is considered to be, by extending the list of dependent variables, variable too - in the long-run all factors are considered to be variable). As Langlois and Robertson (Langlois, R.N. and Robertson, P. L. (1995) *Firms, Markets and Economic Change*, London: Routledge, p. 26) observe:

> the time that passes between the short run and the long run is ... 'operational time' rather than real time. The length of the run is defined entirely in terms of the variability of factors, not in terns of the external standard of a clock. The long run may come about in a week in some industries and a century in others.

As such divergent views between economics and strategic management regarding sustainability are not inconsistent but rather reflect their disciplinary orientations. Economics views, from a social welfare viewpoint, how markets are competitive or should be made more competitive as policy recommendation, whereas strategic management views, from a private enterprise viewpoint, how markets are or should be made inefficient enough to earn high profits over a long period of time. While economic theories highlight the dynamics of competition through which competitive advantages (innovations, rent-earning resources, profitable positions) are diffused and economic profits (competitive advantages) are driven down to explain the effective and efficient workings of free markets, strategy theory brings forth considerations of inimitability as a failure of market competition (product markets and factor markets), from its disciplinary viewpoint to explain behaviour of private enterprises. None the less, they might well indicate the same length of time but from a pessimistic or optimistic connotation, depending on the problem at hand or reflecting their disciplinary orientation.

4. Austrians argue that they have a distinctive methodology, which is called praxeology, the science of human action. Praxeology rests on the fundamental presuppositions of purposeful human action. According to this methodology, the postulates of the research programme are a priori true, and not subject to proof or disproof. For more details, see L. Mises (1963) (first published in 1949) *Human Action: A Treatise on Economics* (3rd revised ed.) Chicago; I.M. Kirzner (1976) On the Method of Austrian Economics, in E.G. Dolan (ed.) *The Foundations of Modern Austrian Economics*, Kansas: Sheed & Ward, pp. 40-51; J.B. Egger (1978) The Austrian Method, in L.M. Spadaro (ed.) *New Directions in Austrian Economics*, Kansas: Sheed Andrews and McMeel, pp. 19-39; M.J. Rizzo (1978) Praxeology and Econometrics: A Critique of Positivist Economics, in L.M. Spadaro (ed.) *New Directions in Austrian Economics*, Kansas: Sheed Andrews and McMeel, pp. 40-55; B.J. Caldwell (1984) Praxeology and Its Critics: An Appraisal, *History of Political Economy*, Vol. 16, No. 3, pp. 363-379.
5. For example, see F.A. Hayek (1976) and (1979), *Law Legislation and Liberty*; 1988, *The Fatal Conceit*; M.J. Rizzo (1985) Rules Versus Cost-Benefit Analysis in Common Law, *Cato Journal*, Vol. 4, pp. 865-884; G.P. O'Driscoll and M.J. Rizzo with contribution by R.W. Garrison (1985) *The Economics of Time and Ignorance*, Oxford: Basil Blackwell. See also for an excellent analytical work on rules in economics, and, in particular, the view of Hayek on rules, V.J. Vanberg (1994) *Rules & Choice in Economics*, London: Routledge.

Chapter 6

# Evolutionary School of Economics

## Introduction

In the 'structure-oriented' paradigms the nature of market economies is thought of from their fundamental, stable structural characteristics. In the 'process-oriented' paradigms structural characteristics are seen just as the manifestation of an underlying dynamic process. The basic nature of capitalist economic reality is then viewed from dynamic interactions between market participants and continuous change. Implicit though, this signifies a paradigm shift from mechanics to biology as metaphor of social economic existence.

Although there have been attempts by structure-oriented researchers, such as Alchian, to approach economic reality from an evolutionary standpoint, the aim was not to give a systematic account of economic interaction, diversity and change but rather to defend the neoclassical theory of the firm by replacing its strong motivational assumption (profit maximisation), which exposed the theory to severe attack, with a weaker assumption (positive realised profits) (Alchian, 1950). Therefore, that kinds of evolutionary approaches should be seen as the continuation of mechanistic world view since they still approach their phenomena of inquiry from a 'deterministic' (strong-form situational determinism, no matter whether it is physical or organistic) viewpoint, which does not seem to be much relevant for analysing social economic reality.

In contrast, modern evolutionary approaches view social economic entities (markets and firms) in forms of ever-increasing diversity, complexity and change. Although the effect of environmental pressure and chance events on the behaviour of economic agents is still acknowledged as important aspects of biological evolution, the central focus is on creativity, on entrepreneurial inherent tendency to create novelty, in the spontaneous emergence of increasing complexity and order. We then ask, what are the implications of the world view of evolution's creativity for explaining firm sustainable profit differentials as results of their strategy-following behaviour?

The seminal work of Nelson and Winter, *An Evolutionary Theory of Economic Change* (1982), has brought about the modern revival of evolutionary approach to economic phenomena as an alternative theory of economics to the mainstream neoclassical scheme of the mechanistic approach. Nelson and Winter's 'greatest intellectual debts are to Joseph Schumpeter and Herbet Simon' (Nelson and Winter, 1982, p. ix). From Simon they acquired the notions of bounded rationality and satisficing in order to build models of search and selection, and from Schumpeter they acquired the idea of economic development through the process of technological change and competition through innovative activities in order to build a workable framework for variation. They added the essential ingredient, i.e. routines as genes, to construct models and theories of evolution.

In what follows we also take the seminal work of Nelson and Winter as the basis of our examination since, as Langlois and Everett (1994) observe, 'present-day efforts in evolutionary economics almost all take their cues from Nelson and Winter'. Also, we give a special emphasis on Schumpeter's work since, as Nelson and Winter observe, 'it could reasonably be said that we are evolutionary theorists *for the sake* of being neo-Schumpeterians' (emphasis in original) (1982, p. 39). Simon's behavioural approach to economic phenomena is to be examined in the next part.

## Problem Area: Market as an Evolutionary Process of Search and Selection

It should be made clear at the outset that Nelson and Winter's evolutionary approach is not a theory of firm *per se*, but a theory of market. Individual firms are seen as instrumental for explaining what happens at industry level, as they clearly express:

> The emphasis is on the analysis of the larger systems [industries, sectors], not on the individual actors. And because the theoretical treatment of the latter is essentially instrumental to the investigation of other matters, that treatment is flexible and opportunistic in the traditional style (Nelson and Winter, 1982, p. 51).

Being in interested in developing a theory of industry behaviour, they diverge from behavioural theory,[1] which is to be examined in the next part. Nevertheless, more recently, Nelson has extended the evolutionary approach to the analysis of the firm arguing that economists must recognise firm differences explicitly.[2]

Nelson and Winter clearly state that their 'theory is a theory about market processes' (1982, p. 1). Specifically, the primary interest of Nelson and Winter lies in obtaining a realistic understanding of the process of technological change, or more generally, economic change, and of the Schumpeterian competition process through innovative activities. This was clearly stated on the very first page:

> In this volume we develop an evolutionary theory of the capabilities and behaviour of business firms operating in a market environment, and construct and analyse a number of models consistent with that theory. ... The specific models we build focus in turn on different aspects of economic change - the response of firms and the industry to changed market conditions, economic growth, and competition through innovation (Nelson and Winter, 1982, p. 3).

In essence, for them the primary economic problem is economic change. They argue that neoclassical orthodox theory deals in an *ad hoc* way with the effects of changes, in particular, with unexpected shocks, and treats radical changes such as significant technological advances quite mechanically. The result of this *ad hoc* treatment of change is that it is impossible to derive from neoclassical orthodox formalism an operative theory of firm and industry response to changed market conditions.

The evolutionary theory has emerged an alternative operative theory of firm and industry response to neoclassical formalism. In the evolutionary paradigm, choice set are not given and the consequences of any choice are unknown, and thereby there is no choice that is clearly best *ex ante*. Moreover, in stark contrast to the neoclassical assumption of given choice set, evolutionary theory assumes innovating or generating choice set. Given these assumptions, evolutionary theory presumes a diversity of firm behaviour in real situations due to interpreting and responding market signals differently, in particular, in the situations that the signals are relatively novel. In this alternative construct of market theory, there are two functions of competition assumed:

> One function of competition, in the structural sense of many firms, then would be to make possible that diversity. Another function of competition, in this more active sense, is to reward and enhance the choices that prove good in practice and to suppress the bad ones (Nelson and Winter, 1982, p. 276).

From an evolutionary selection viewpoint, the competitive system is assumed, over the long run, to promote firms that choose well on average and would eliminate, or force reform upon, firms that consistently make mistakes (the notion of the survival of the fittest). As such, in evolutionary paradigm, which is based on the assumption of market behaviour as promoting diversity and selection processes as well as that of firm behaviour as generating sets of choice and interpreting and responding market signals intentionally but with the possibility of making mistakes, seems to be a very suitable ground on which strategic research on firm diversity in performance can be treated. This is because within the evolutionary paradigm, as in the theory of strategic management, diversity of firms is assumed to be inevitable due to firms having different structures, different core capabilities (routines), and different responses (strategies) to changed market conditions. Therefore, some firms will prove profitable, some not, given the way markets evolve.

Note that the problem of economic change as the research focus of evolutionary theory is based on a background theory of firm diversity. More specifically, economic change is explained at the basis of the profit-oriented behaviour of firms that compete for opportunities and advantages. In terms of Nelson and Winter, '... much technical advance results from profit-oriented investment on the part of business firms. The profits from successful innovation are disequilibrium phenomena ... They stem largely from the lead over competitors that innovation affords' (1982, p. 28). As we have identified in Chapter 2, business strategy theory is in essence a theory of profits, or more specifically, a theory of firm profit differentials. Like the Austrian school, evolutionary school also provides a general theory of profit and profit differentials when dealing with the problem of economic change.[3]

Before entering into a more detailed examination of the sources of superior performance and of the mechanism that protect them from competitive equilibration in evolutionary theory, it seems better to give a general idea of Schumpeter's and Nelson and Winter's view of economic change and relate it to strategic thinking.

### *Schumpeterian Dynamism or Creative Destruction*

For Schumpeter,[4] 'the essential point to grasp is that in dealing with capitalism we are dealing with an evolutionary process. ... Capitalism, then, is by nature a form or method of economic change and not only never is but never can be stationary' (1950, p. 82). In this evolutionary process of economic change 'the fundamental impulse that sets and keeps the capitalist engine in motion comes from the new consumer's goods, the new methods of production or transportation, the new markets, the new forms of organisation that capitalist enterprise creates' (Schumpeter, 1950, p. 83). These prime movers of dynamic process 'incessantly revolutionise the economic structure *from within*, incessantly destroying the old one, incessantly creating a new one' (emphasis in original) (Schumpeter, 1950, p. 83). Therefore, this innovative process is a 'process of Creative Destruction', and 'is the essential fact about capitalism'[5] (Schumpeter, 1950, p. 83).

In the Schumpeterian construct, firms, thus, constantly compete for better production methods. In fact, in Schumpeter's view, the firms' struggle for better production method is not only through innovative activities, but also through imitative activities. As Schumpeter argues, 'the carrying out of new combinations is difficult. ... However, if one or a few have advanced with success, many of the difficulties disappear. Other can then follow these pioneers ...' (1934, p. 128). That is, firms also strive to imitate the more profitable methods which are currently employed by pioneer firms. Therefore, the evolutionary history of an industry is assumed to be moulded by outcomes of the pattern of technological process of innovation and imitation.

Placing the evolutionary process of innovation and imitation at its central analytical core, Schumpeter, thus, explains the dynamic evolution of the economic system. For him, while the occurrence of an innovation disrupts the existing structure (de-structure) of the industry, imitation processes bring about a new structure (re-structure). To put it in a more formal way, while the process of innovation incessantly upsets the equilibrating tendency towards a static order of an industry structure, the imitation process functions as an equilibrating force that pushes the industry towards a static equilibrium (behaviour in and out of circular flow). This process of de-structuring and re-structuring is assumed to be progressive, in contrast to the neoclassical static economising view, in the sense that it increases the technological efficiency of the industry as a whole in the long run.

The Schumpeterian construct of the dynamic connection between innovations/imitations as processes of market evolution seems to supply an ample ground for strategic theorising on the nature of strategic competition between firms. On the one hand, firms compete to innovate since innovations give rise to market power which enables innovative firms to earn monopoly profits or what is called entrepreneurial profits (first mover advantages). It is this prospect of gaining entrepreneurial profits that gives motivations for innovative activities, for example, investing in R & D. Nevertheless, they are not immune to imitation, although they do their best to pick the fruits of innovations as long as they can by erecting barriers to imitation or barriers to entry into the market. While innovation creates an opportunity for above-average profits, imitation works to reduce profit differentials. But this process never ends; innovation and imitation continually take place.

Another important aspect of this construct is that firms and industries are viewed as being interconnected, and growth, stagnation, and decline of firms and industries appear to be a fundamental feature of industrial evolution from within. Firms are assumed to play a central role in the dynamic evolution of economic system. It is firms that introduce new production functions into the economic system through new ideas. Industries as a whole emerge, grow, stabilise, and eventually decline as outcomes of historical progress of the pattern of technology through new combinations and emulations by firms. Thus, from a strategic theory point of view, this explains why some firms and industries rise and fall, why some firms and industries are more profitable than others. It thus explains the indeterminate behaviour of firms and industries arising from genuine uncertainty, where new possibilities are continually created.

By the view of the dynamic evolution of economic system, Schumpeter is also able to explain how industries or industrial structures come into existence and evolve. As Schumpeter holds, 'there is ... an obvious connection between innovation and the rise of new industries, although, of course, innovation may also rejuvenate old ones' (1950, p. 95). That is, innovations call for new industries, or more generally, new production functions. New production functions are introduced into economic system through new firms or new ideas. This view of industry formation helps strategy theorists explain not only the sources of competitive advantage but also the first mover advantages. Neoclassical formalism neglects disequilibrating forces and process, so it fails to explain disequilibrium behaviour of industries and firms and how industries come into existence and how equilibrium comes about unless making *ad hoc* assumptions. As a result of neglecting disequilibrium, a constellation of significant notions to economics, such as time, learning, error, innovations or discoveries, change, adaptation, etc., are all also left out of research concern.

In short, the 'creative destruction' view of market economy is drastically different from the neoclassical perfect competition view of the market as a signalling device for the allocation of scarce resources that serve to guarantee a state of equilibrium. The focus of economic analysis shifts from economising on existing resources (static efficiency) to generating new possibilities (new markets, new way of doing things, etc. and dynamic efficiency), from known or given resources to unknown or not given potentialities, from optimal utilisation of known resources to under-utilisation of the indefinite fruits of uncertain potentials, from marginal calculation to uncertain innovability and imitability, from determinism to discretion, from competing on given opportunities to struggling for generating new profit opportunities, and so on and so forth. In shifting the focus of economic analysis so, the market view of creative destruction supplies a very fertile ground for strategic theorising.

### *Nelson and Winter's Evolutionary Economic Change*

As we have pointed out above, Nelson and Winter have based their evolutionary theory of economic change on the Schumpeterian conception just introduced. The main difference between the Schumpeterian treatment and theirs seems to be their desire to develop a sound theory of institutions and institutional change. In the Schumpeterian (as well as the Austrian) construct, the institutional aspect has largely been neglected. The emphasis was mainly on individuals (entrepreneurs), although he recognised the institutional character of economic change. In other words, the position of Schumpeter regarding the prime movers of capitalist economic system seems to loom. In his early work, *The Theory of Economic Development* (1934), he sees entrepreneurs as prime movers, but in his later work, *Capitalism, Socialism and Democracy* (1950), he takes an institutional view and argues that the social function of entrepreneurs is being steadily undermined, as 'economic progress tends to become depersonalised and automatized. Bureau and committee work tends to replace individual action' (Schumpeter, 1950, p. 133). To him, this process of eliminating entrepreneurs has been at work through the growth of large corporations in which management and administration are bureaucratised, and scientific and technological progress is routinized. Nevertheless, he failed to build a workable framework in which the institutional economic evolution can be explained. It is this gap that Nelson and Winter mainly attempt to fill in.

Nelson and Winter conceptualise the firm as a 'routine-guided' organism by which they manage to explain the regular and predictable behavioural patterns of firms from an institutional point of view:

> In our evolutionary theory, ... routines play the role that genes play in biological evolutionary theory. They are persistent feature of the organism and determine its possible behaviour (though *actual* behaviour is determined also by the environment); they are heritable in the sense that tomorrow's organisms generated from today's ... (Nelson and Winter, 1982, p. 14).

For them, entrepreneurs and managers come and go, products and processes change, innovations break out and end, but the set of routines continues through replication and transmission. Routines developed in their evolutionary economics are 'a key repository of knowledge in the firm: the firm "know how" to do something because it commands the appropriate routines' (Winter, 1995, p. 152). That is, routines as a repository of knowledge are assumed to be the memory of an organisation, and thus 'organisational command of a routine is not reducible to the level of individual skills, because the context of each individual performance includes the performances of other members' (Winter, 1995, p. 152). Therefore the basis of team performance is the learned patterns of interpersonal coordination. But, for the same reason 'command of the routine does not reduce to the resource "team-embodied skills" because there is more the context of individual performance than just the performance of other team members' (Winter, 1995, p. 153). These other contextual features are, for example, the information flows from the environment that trigger particular performances or the equipment and facilities that establish the physical setting.

This conceptualisation of organisational knowledge involves, therefore, a unity of knowing and doing, and the shared practices of the group, and not simply of individuals. Moreover, this knowledge is 'tacit' in nature and cannot be reduced simply to 'information', which is assumed in neoclassical theory, since it is partly embodied in habits and routines, and so it cannot be reduced to, or transmitted in, a codified form. An important corollary of this conceptualisation of knowledge is that since the appropriate details of knowledge are liked to highly specific contexts, the knowledge is not available as such in the marketplace. This conceptualisation of knowledge is of importance from strategic management point of view, since it constitutes the basis for the argument of the sources of firm differentials (different organisations of knowledge) and of the mechanism of the persistence of the differentials (none codifiable, tacit, and consequently not-easily-imitated knowledge). As we have already demonstrated, this is exactly the same argument developed by strategy theorists such as Dierickx and Cool (1989), who work within the resource-based approach.

Following Schumpeter, they maintain that, in the pursuit of profits, firms engage incessantly in 'search' for new routines (better ways of doing things) that , if adopted, would likely increase the level of profits they earn. Nelson and Winter interpret search to cover the activities of innovation and imitation. And in turn, they interpret the search behaviour itself as a routine behaviour of firms.

More clearly, in their view, there are three analytically-separable kinds of routines:

1. standard operating routines, which govern short-run behaviour of the firm in determining inputs and outputs given its prevailing stock of plant, equipment, and other factors of production that are augmented only in the long run,
2. routines that determine the investment behaviour of the firm in determining the firm's capital stock (factor of production), and
3. search routines which operate to modify over time various aspects of their operating characteristics with the help of market analysis departments, operations research shops, and R & D laboratories.

Not all the three categories of routines have the same effect on firm behaviour. There is assumed to be a hierarchical relationship between routines, which 'define lower order organisational skills and how these are coordinated, and higher order decision procedures for choosing what is to be done at lower levels' (Nelson, 1994, pp. 234-235). Arguably, this is analogous to the three categories of firm behaviour in strategic management literature, as operational, tactical and strategic, as well as the assumed hierarchical relations between them. Recognition of a hierarchy from upper-level routines directing lower-level routines is of importance since it helps in analysing real-world firm behaviour from a managerial hierarchy point of view. The importance of hierarchy becomes more obvious when we consider firms as production functions assumed in neoclassical theory. As we examine in the next part, there is assumed to be no upper-level hierarchy defining firm policies and invoking lower-levels to accomplish them, but a hierarchy - less world in which all organisational problems are reduced to price and quality determination which are subject to mechanical marginal calculation.

Therefore, out of the three categories, search routines, like strategic behaviours, play the central role in the continuous evolution of firms and markets by entailing firm interaction with market in a competitive manner. Innovative activities create new routines (disequilibrating process), on the one hand, while, on the other hand, existing successful routines are replicated and imitated by firms (equilibrating process) in order to grow or survive. The evolution of industry structure is, therefore, the evolution of the organisation routines (knowledge of innovation and imitation). Routines in general play the role of genes in the evolutionary theory (stabilising forces). However, search routines stochastically generate mutations (variations, disruptions or differentials). Firms as well as markets learn and adapt. Knowledge disseminates from firms to the market as other firms imitate the better routines. Note that systemwide learning over time is not assumed to be the product of design, but spontaneous, as is assumed in the Austrian School. Firms and markets are considered to be historical entities displaying the futures of the path they evolve (path dependency). Time therefore plays an essential role in the process of change, as in the evolutionary biology.

In the interaction between firms and the market, the selection mechanism also works on the basis of firms ability to generate or emulate routines (to produce profits). Over time firms that are equipped with routines that are most adaptive to market and environmental change survive and grow while others are eliminated (the survival of the fittest). That is, 'the market determines which firms are profitable and which are unprofitable, and tends to winnow out the latter' (Nelson and Winter, 1982, p. 4).

### Firm Differentials and Mechanism of Persistent Differentials in the Evolutionary Theory

As we have seen, at the heart of the evolutionary construct lies 'search-and-selection' explanation. Firms intentionally *search* for different forms of behaviour and functional rules (routines). This is the element which is called 'mutation' in the evolutionary conception, which explains why there would exist, in a given time, considerable diversity across firms in productivity levels and profitability. Accordingly, firm diversity is seen as an essential aspect of the process that creates economic change or progress (diversity-driven dynamic). And, markets *select* more efficient rules and routines and eliminate less efficient ones. This is the other element which is called 'natural selection' in the evolutionary jargon, which explains why the relatively more efficient rules and routines will persist and grow in the population of firms. Therefore, the search-and-selection framework should also be taken as the basis for the explanation of firm performance differentials and their persistency in the evolutionary theory.

In other words, innovative search behaviour of firms, taken together with selection effects in the market, determines the profitability of firms. As implied by the conception of innovative search (routines), firm differentials are viewed, at least partially, as discretionary. As Nelson clearly puts it,

> ... discretionary firm differences within an industry exist and do matter significantly ... by the term 'discretionary' I do mean to imply a certain looseness of constraints, both in the short and long run, that gives room so that firms that differ in certain important respects can be viable in the same economic environment (Nelson, 1991, p. 62).

This is an explicit recognition of both the generation and function of firm diversity. Nelson argues that firm differences are at the heart of management, in particular, strategy inquiry, yet, he maintains, neoclassical theory often ignores intra-industry firm differences, or denies that they are significant for economic analysis. Then he argues that the differences between firms observed in the real world of business must also be recognised by economic theory.

Furthermore, Nelson goes on to argue that by the term 'discretion', he also does 'mean that to some extent these differences are the result of different strategies that are used to guide decision making at various levels in firms' (1991, p. 434). In the evolutionary context, strategies of firms are largely seen as 'search' behaviours or routines to explore new potentially better ways of doing things. This view of strategy is very compatible with the one developed within the resource-based view in the field of strategic management, which highlights such search routines as resources and capabilities as the basis of firm differentials.

From a decision making point of view, in the theory different firms are assumed to have different sets of rules or routines for making choices due to their different abilities to deliberate, interpret, implement and path dependencies. These differences in the processes of deliberating, interpreting, implementing, and histories are then seen as a central part of the explanation of why firms make different choices. Note that the nature of decision making assumed as such is, therefore, strategic in character in that decisions aim at creating competitive differences.

The kind of competition is also not simply seen as environmental pressure to keep prices in line with minimal feasible costs, and to keep firms operating at low costs through marginal calculation, but, like the Austrian School of economics, as exploring profit opportunities. Schumpeter makes the point as follows:

> In capitalist reality as distinguished from its textbook picture, it is not that kind of competition which counts but the competition from new sources of supply, the new type of organisation ... [In short,] competition which commands a decisive cost or quality advantage and which strikes not at the margins of the profits and the outputs of existing firms but at their foundations and their very lives (Schumpeter, 1950, p. 84).

As Schumpeter implies the kind of competition which counts at the margin is trivial compared with the latter in terms of doing things in a totally new manner. The latter kind of competition is essentially strategic because it commands a decisive cost or quality advantage, strikes at firms very foundations and lives, changes the very structure of markets (not merely adapts reactionary to changing markets or is managed by invisible hand operations), and creates profit opportunities that are not signalled solely by prices.

Competition in this respect, is a matter of winning or losing. For not all firms would be equally successful in generating new combinations (new products, new methods of production, etc.) or in coping with market changes (imitation). That is, those firms that are good at initiating new sources of competition or imitating good routines of rivals will tend to win, and those that are not tend to lose.

An important aspect of that kind of competition is that winning or losing competitive advantage is not just a matter of random selection or luck. But, as Nelson argues, 'winning is partly a matter of having a good strategy' (Nelson, 1986, p. 466). In the evolutionary construct, there seem to be two good strategies for winning: innovation strategy (discovering or generating new possibilities of competition) and imitation strategy (adopting currently successful way of competition). While innovation strategy gives first mover advantages due to being first in the field, imitation strategy gives the follower advantages due to following successful innovation. Innovation strategy is highly risky, costly and time consuming but very profitable, whereas, imitation strategy is less risky, costly and time consuming but also less profitable.

If we trace the sources of these competitive advantages in the evolutionary theory, we end up with such concepts as firm capabilities, skills, routines, histories, etc. Nevertheless, it is not difficult, as we argued above, to compose them under one title, that is, routines. Firms that have better routines, such as production technologies, the mechanisms for allocating the attention of management and the operations research staff, R & D policies, investment-project screening rules and so on, will tend to prosper and grow relative to those firms whose routines are less-suited to the current situation. Placing routines at the centre of competitive advantages means that sources of competitive advantage are internal to firms, as is presumed within the resource-based approach of strategic management. That is, in the evolutionary theory and the resource-based approach, firm ability to compete for advantages is heavily constrained by the level and nature of their routines or competencies.

But it should also be remembered that overall performance of individual firms is assumed to be the result of market environment (market selection) as well as of firms' ability (search routines), as Nelson and Winter maintain:

> We have already referred to ... the idea that is central in our scheme - the idea of economic 'natural selection'. Market environments provide a definition of

> success for business firms, and that definition is very closely related to their ability to survive and grow. Patterns of differential survival and growth in a population of firms can produce change in economic aggregates characterising that population, even if the corresponding characteristics of individual firms are constant (Nelson and Winter, 1982, p. 9).

In other words, whether firms' abilities prove profitable depends also on what other firms do and the way markets evolve. The level of firm profitability is, therefore, 'context dependent' (depends on the environmental conditions in which they operate). And the environment conditions may change (grow or decline). Firms may adapt well or badly to the changing markets, and thereby determine their level of profitability. In fact, in the evolutionary construct there is assumed to be a two-way interaction: while market structure is determined by firm new routines (knowledge), new routines (knowledge) also flows from market structure to firm. Therefore, market structure, besides firms' dynamic capabilities, also has a strong bearing on the level of profitability.

This view (firm routines as well as market structure as determinants of firm success) sheds light on the debate between the positioning approach and the resource-based approach on the sources of firm profitability (success). As we remember, the positioning approach proposes an externally based perspective, i.e. industry structure, of the sources, whereas the resource-based approach takes an internally-oriented view, i.e. resources and capabilities, of the sources. Consistent with both externally based and internally oriented, as Levinthal points out, the evolutionary theory 'encourages, if not forces, one to bridge these analyses of organisational level processes with an examination of population level of market forces' (1994, p. 168).

In other words, from the evolutionary theory viewpoint, the existence of profitability differentials reflects both industry-specific characteristics and firm-specific characteristics interdependently. But now the question is, for the strategic value of the existence of profitability differentials, 'Do profitability differentials persist or disappear within the general flux of evolutionary change?' The answer seems to be to some extent problematic. As we have argued above, on the one hand, innovations bring about above-average profitability opportunities, while the other, imitation ensures that successful techniques (routines) will gradually diffuse between firms once possibilities for above-average profits are recognised by other competitors, thereby levelling profit differentials. Therefore, within this dialectical approach to competition (the conflict between innovation process and imitation process), profitability differentials seem to be temporary.

Yet despite the general presumption of temporality, there is also a place for the persistency of profitability differentials in a strategic sense within the evolutionary theory. First of all, it is assumed in the evolutionary theory that firms are motivated for profit opportunities, and would never invest in R & D unless they could control the market long enough to insure a profitable return. Therefore, firms must enjoy protected market positions in order to innovate. This assumption constitutes the basis of strategic behaviour of firms towards innovative activities.

Second, the speed of the process with which the activities of innovating firms will be imitated and market power, together with above-average profits, will wane, is not rapid. As Schumpeter argues, 'in practice competition does not act promptly and hence enterprises remain in possession of surpluses for a considerable time' (1934, p. 209). The speed with which emulation equalises differentials varies depending upon the obstacles which exist for such emulation. The ability to block imitation by competitors, (for instance, in the cases of limiting price competition among advantaged firms and discouraging new entry, inability of firms, originating in path-dependency constraints, to emulate new routines, property rights, uncertainty in the real sources of success, the time span involved in the emulation, the locality of learning, the opaqueness of the environment) reduces the speed of emulation, so that innovative firms may enjoy above-average profits over some considerable period of time. The considerable period of time is, from an empirical point of view, statistically unspecified 'long time', as we have pointed out above, and it may indicate five years or fifty years. Over this long time profits are assumed not to converge on a common rate of return, making possible for some firms to earn above normal rates of return. Needless to say, this is drastically different from neoclassical instant equilibrating process.

Finally, there are assumed to be two categories of firms earning persistently above normal profits in the theory. One category is considered to be monopolies. For example, Schumpeter says, some railways have, if not a perpetual, yet an assured monopoly for a long time. For them, as for the Austrians, entrenched monopoly positions would never develop except with the help of government intervention because of the competitive erosion or 'perennial gale of creative destruction' (Schumpeter, 1950, p. 84). This category is not relevant much for competitive strategy studies due to its non-competitive nature. But, the second category, the category of leading firms, constitutes a direct case for strategic theorising and research. Schumpeter defines the second category as follows:

> Then there are kinds of enterprises which by nature and programme are continually doing new things and are really nothing but forms for continual

new enterprises. Here the aims alter incessantly and the leading personalities also change, so that it is in the nature of the thing that people of considerable ability always appear in the leading positions (Schumpeter, 1934, pp. 208-209).

Nelson (1990), in one of his recent works, examines this second category. He takes a more institutional view, and discusses these leading edge companies with reference to the concept of dynamic firm capabilities, developed by Teece et al. within the resource-based approach. Nelson argues that 'simply producing a given set of products with a given set of processes well will not enable a firm to survive for long. To be successful for any length of time, a firm must innovate' (Nelson, 1994, p. 235). He argues that the capabilities required are capabilities to innovate and to take advantage of innovations. The capabilities involve incessantly renewal and upgrading in order to innovate continually. In short, if a firm is able to lead its competitors in continual innovation, it will earn persistently above normal rates of return. Note that the idea that innovating, discovering, upgrading, learning, etc., faster than competitors may give 'sustainable' advantage to leading firms was put forward within the Austrian conception of market as well.

This view of earning persistent superior profits via leading positions is shared by both schools of thought, positioning and resource-based, in the field of strategic management. It is more so for the resource-based approach, in which resources and capabilities, or in one word, competences, are also seen in a dynamic perspective, and involve continual regeneration and upgrading. In the positioning approach, market positions that are occupied by firms involve continuous reassessment and improvements in order to continue to provide competitive advantages.

In brief, the existence and persistence of firm differentials find an ample place in the evolutionary theory of market. In fact, they constitute an essential part of evolutionary construct. Therefore, they become a 'legitimate' object of interest within the theory.

## Hard Core Assumptions: A Middle Ground Position Between Situational Determinism and Situational Indeterminism

Dosi, in his editorial article to the first issue of the *Journal of Evolutionary Economics*, asks, 'is there an evolutionary approach?' In his view, in a loose sense certainly, there is such an approach to economic phenomena that can be called 'evolutionary'. The focus of this approach is on such phenomena as 'institutional and technological change, disequilibrium interactions, non-linear dynamics, less-than-perfectly rational behaviours, history dependence of economic processes, effects of extra-economic institutions on economic variables ...' (Dosi, 1991, p. 5).

Dosi argues that one can find that any of these issues are dealt with through rather standard methodology. Even in this loose sense, evolutionary approach shares some underlying beliefs on the heuristic power of equilibrium models, micro optimising assumptions, etc. Therefore, on these grounds, 'there is no clear discontinuity between "orthodox" and "evolutionary" economics, but rather some fuzzy continuum' (Dosi, 1991, p. 5). Nevertheless, he also proposes a stricter definition of an 'evolutionary approach'. Although he proposes this definition as a personal view, which, he cautions, might not necessarily be shared by other economists who call themselves 'evolutionary, it seems that the definition expresses the view of the mainstream in modern revival of the evolutionary approach. In his view, the evolutionary approach makes, in general (that is, in most empirically relevant cases), the following, jointly-held, propositions.

1. The world is 'full of opportunities': In a world of continuous change and progress opportunities are never exhausted; on the contrary, at any one time, only a very small share is exploited. This proposition constitutes the very basis of the idea of economic change since there would be no change and progress if there were not some opportunities for change and progress. Schumpeter is, arguably, the most famous figure in putting forward the idea of the world full of opportunities. For example, follows in *The Theory of Economic Development* he expresses forcefully and elegantly the idea as:

   > In any kind of economic situation whatever, the number of possible innovations is practically unlimited ... Even the richest economic system is not absolutely perfect and cannot be so. Improvements can always be made, and the striving after improvements is always limited by the given conditions and not by the perfection of what exists (Schumpeter, 1934, p. 197).

   In other words, as Dosi argues, the extent to which opportunities are exploited is not constrained by 'nature', but, rather by economic agents' limitations on their own competences. Therefore, the challenge is to unleash constraints, and invent, discover and grab opportunities. Dosi goes as far as reversing the famous saying by Friedman, that there are always a lot of free lunches, provided economic agents uncover and take advantage of them.

This proposition constitutes also the very basis of strategic theorising, since, if there were no opportunities to exploit in the world of business, there would be no need for a strategy to take advantage of them. In other words, strategic behaviour is by definition an opportunity-driven behaviour. The important corollaries of this proposition are, as Dosi points out, that dynamic increasing returns (also above normal returns) are not only possible but also very frequent, that change is partly endogenous to the normal working of economic system, that is, change is a subject matter of managerial discretion, and that the non-convexities are the general rule, that is, economic growth, in consequent new strategic possibilities, are the case in the real world of economics, not exceptions.

2. Economic agents (individuals and organisations) present much less than the assumed 'maximising' behaviour by marginalists: No doubt, one of the hallmarks of evolutionary economics has been the proposition of non-maximising modes of behaviour by agents. This lower methodological stance (less than maximising behaviour) stresses what Simon and others termed bounded rationality and 'rejects the notion of maximising behaviour as an explanation of why decision rules are what they are' (Nelson and Winter, 1982, p. 14). As Nelson and Winter observe that maximising suggests that 'there is a global, faultless, once-and-for-all optimisation over a given choice set comprising all objectively available alternatives' (1982, p. 31).

   Firms, in an ongoing evolutionary framework, 'satisfice rather than maximise: they find niches to protect themselves from competition' (Hodgson, 1993, p. 29). The assumption of global maximisation rules out the possibility of the incremental and imperfect adjustments in an evolutionary process. Nelson and Winter propose the basic premise of bounded rationality as an alternative explanation of why decision rules are what they are in the sense that firms are profit-motivated but not profit maximising organisations, that decision rules and procedures are not too complicated and cannot be characterised as 'optimal', i.e. they reflect the results of global calculation taking into account information and decision costs, that firms actually employ relatively simple devices to cope with their severe information-processing constraints, which often have a key influence on the actions taken, that they fail sometimes to process, relate, and interpret internal and external signals into a message relevant to available choices, that the range of things a firm can do at any time is always somewhat uncertain prior to the effort to exercise that capability, that firms operate at all times with a status quo policy (history-dependent routines), and so on.

3. Interactions amongst economic agents are typically disequilibrium ones: Equilibrium interactions are pre-determined, mechanistic interactions. They are not, and cannot be, considered as descriptions of real world typical cases. In the real world, firms learn, err, succeed, fail, grow, die, strive for opportunities, etc. All these are manifestations of disequilibrium behaviours. From the strategic theory point of view, this means not only that strategic interactions belong to the disequilibrium category of competitive process but also that strategic behaviours aiming at creating and sustaining competitive advantages are only possible when the economy is in disequilibrium. These disequilibrium behaviours are typical, not exceptions.
4. Institutional rules/learning/discovery/innovation, on the one hand, and ex-post selection in the market, on the other, are the driving mechanisms of both coordinating and discoordinating (change). This proposition of pushing toward opposite directions is necessary to explain both competitive pressure to remove differentials (equilibrating/imitating process) and competitive struggle for creating differentials (disequilibrating/innovating process). Only within the two-pushing-opposite directions of the market functioning framework do such concepts as strategic behaviour, competitive advantage, sustainability make sense since it supplies a sort of 'externality' by which market participants enter into strategic competition to obtain and sustain advantages against others, and when failed, to be pushed out of business.
5. History and institutions are an integral part of economic 'explanations': Evolutionary theory emphasises 'the importance of the emergence, change, and death of social institutions in time-space for any kind of economic behaviour' (Magnusson, 1994b, p. 2). Neoclassical economics is based on the assumption of universal (history-less and non-contingent) individual. In contrast, evolutionary theory proposes a history-contingent process of economic change. Institutions are considered to be the creations of historical time and context-specific conditions. From the strategic management point of view, strategies are also made in historical

> time and contingent upon context-specific conditions. There cannot be universal strategies. Therefore, economic as well as strategic analyses are inevitably historic and context-specific.

First of all, it should be pointed out that, given the hard core assumptions, the evolutionary theory can be located between the neoclassical research programme of 'situational determinism' and the Austrian research programme of 'situational indeterminism'. As we remember, the former presupposes that the set of possible responses (either responding in a single and predetermined manner, or, in different ways to changes in environment) is determined by the structural environment facing the individual firm; the latter puts forward the view of the agent where his/her 'action bears no significant influence of the environment...' (Hodgson, 1988, p. 11). Evolutionary theorists take a middle ground position between these two poles, as Hodgson very well summarises:

> There are actions which may be uncaused, but at the same time there are patterns of behaviour that may relate to the cultural or institutional environment within which the person acts. Action, in short, is partially determined, and partially indeterminate: partly predictable but partly unforeseeable ... Human actions can be both routinized and conservative, and display flights of imagination or eccentricity which are beyond rational anticipation and bring the greatest surprise (Hodgson, 1988, p. 12).

This middle ground position seems to offer a much more promising foundation to Strategy theory than both situational determinism and indeterminism could do, since the emphasis is now on both entrepreneurial actions, which are manifestations of atypical insights or free thinking as well as managerial discreational actions, which are to a significant extent moulded by external environment. In respect of this middle ground, evolutionary theory has something of consequence to offer about both predictability, which seems necessary for building a model of business strategy that can generate predictions, and surprises and disappointments that are necessary in explaining what has actually happened differently from what was predicted to happen *ex ante*.

In the evolutionary research programme, as in the neoclassical and Austrian, economic agents are viewed as purposive and as operating according to a set of decision rules, which are the best rules the actors know about. However, they have developed a non-deterministic evolutionary economics. In their approach, as in the Austrian, error and the correction of error are important facets in the dynamic process. This is obviously different from ever correct calculations of maximising firms under the assumption of perfect predictability. Moreover, economic agents are assumed to have discretion in the sense that they can use resources in ways which are not known (innovation), initiate new policies to change market structure, etc. (assuming an open-ended economic system). But maximising agents are assumed to use resources in ways are already known, and are thereby stripped of any innovative discretion (assuming a closed economic system).

In evolutionary theory maximising behaviour is substituted for routine-following behaviour, in terms of Nelson and Winter. Routines are at the centre of their theory in explaining the behaviour of firms and markets. In this respect, in the Nelson and Winter's construct the rule/routine-following behaviour is integrated into the analysis in an absolutely indispensable manner, not in *ad hoc* way.

The idea of routine-following behaviour supplies a very fertile ground for theorising on the long-run strategic behaviours (strategy-following behaviour) of firms in explaining firm performance differentials as well as the persistence of the differentials, as outcomes of the cumulative-history dependent course of continuous market change and firm responses to market change over time. The assumed path-dependent behaviour not only brings about asymmetries between firms but also persists over time due to the length of time needed by rivals to replicate and uncertainty about how it developed. As has been discussed, maximising assumption is only able to explain short-run, case-by-case, marginal adjustment behaviour of firms. However, the assumption of routine-following behaviour enables us to explain the pattern of behaviour over a long period of time. In this respect, it certainly demonstrates a strategic property.

In fact, routines, in particular search routines, in Nelson and Winter's construct are analogous to strategies. The idea of routines as strategies is explicitly recognised by them, and is a significant ingredient, besides the Shupeterian idea of creative destruction and the Simonian bounded rationality, in their analysis:

> A line of work centred in the Harvard Business School has explored a concept of business strategy in its relation to the organisation of the firm ... We have considerable sympathy for these lines of analysis. In some of our models, the higher-order decision rules or policies with which we endow our firms may metaphorically be interpreted as their strategies. In these models firms have different strategies, and a central analytic concern is the viability or profitability of firms with different strategies (Nelson and Winter, 1982, p. 37).

They explicitly express their sympathy for Chandler's historical analysis of the organisation of the firm in relation to the concept of business strategy, and for his proposition that there is a dynamic interaction between a firm's strategy and for its appropriate organisational structure. They agree with Chandler that different firms adapt different strategies because of, in part, their subjective interpretation of opportunities and constraints, and, in part, because different firms are good at different things. In turn, the capabilities of a firm in doing different things are embedded in its organisational structure, so that it is better adapted to certain strategies than to others. Thus, strategies available to a firm at any time are constrained by organisation. However, a significant change in a firm's strategy is also likely to involve a significant change in its organisational structure.

In clearer terms routines function like strategies, in the sense that every firm has different routines and accordingly responds to its environment differently: a firm's routine not only largely determines its behaviour but also its ability to cope with environmental change; routines not only constrain the set of choice for an individual firm but also induce inertia because they are difficult for the firm to change once established; there is a hierarchy between routines and the higher-order routines determine the lower-order routines, routines help rationalisation of choices, and so on.

## Conclusions

Evolutionary theory attempts to explain economic change or, more concretely, dynamic growth of the potential aggregate supply. It holds that the driving forces of economic growth are firm unique skills (routines). Growth is likely to involve a substantial component of replication or partial replication of the routines underlying initial success. Some firms may have unique routines to be sources of revolutionary changes (innovations), while others may have an ability to adapt rapidly to whatever innovations might occur. Therefore, economic change is characteristically long term and cumulative. Like the Austrians, in dealing with the problem of economic change, evolutionary economists promotes the view of competition as a dynamic process involving uncertainty, struggle, and disequilibrium.

In the evolutionary construct, the central idea that each firm possesses a unique set of routines (skills, or a characteristic way of doing business) also accounts for profit differentials between firms. In other words, it is a firm's path-dependent, unique capabilities that are assumed to differentiate it from other firms, and enable it to enjoy supernormal profits via unique profit-seeking strategies. Therefore, firms need to engage in a struggle to develop those capabilities that will allow them to successfully compete in the changing environment. The notion of routines also provides a rationale for the relative rigidity that is necessary for the sustainability of superior performance since routines cannot be easily developed or imitated. The more existing routines of a firm underlying its success is assumed to involve tacit skills or otherwise resist codification, the more sustainable the advantages they generate. The concept of routine is also reminiscent to that of strategy. The theory holds that the behaviour and performance of firms can be understood in terms of a hierarchy of practised organisational routines, which define lower-order organisational skills and how these are coordinated, and higher-order decision procedures for choosing what is to be done at lower levels.

## Notes

1. See, Nelson and Winter (1982) p. 36.
2. See R.R. Nelson (1991) Why Do Firms Differ, and How Does It Matter?, *Strategic Management Journal*, Vol. 12, pp. 61-74.
3. It should also be pointed out that, with the research focus of economic change, evolutionary economists come closer to classics than neoclassics in being concerned with exploring patterns of long-run economic change of technological advance and capital formation. As is known, much of Smith's seminal work *The Wealth of Nations* is about what today would be called technical change and economic growth. For him log-run economic change means economic progress. This line of thought has been carried out further within the evolutionary theory of economic change. See Nelson and Winter (1982) pp. 43-45 for antecedents of their theory.
4. Although Schumpeter is often associated with the new resurgence of evolutionary theorising since the 1980s, he very occasionally employed the biological analogy in economics, and wherever employed, it is employed for clarity, not an analytical tool. Moreover, he explicitly rejected its usage, 'no appeal to biology would be of the slightest use' (Schumpeter, J.A., 1954, *History of Economic Analysis*, New York: Oxford University Press, p. 789). But frequently he uses the term 'evolution' in a developmental sense, though not in a process of evolutionary selection sense. However, his theorising is quite consistent with evolutionary approaches to economics since, in his view, firms strive for survival and growth. They innovate to grow and imitate to survive. When they fail to innovate or imitate, they are forced out of business.
5. By the concept of creative destruction, Schumpeter tries to capture the conflict between short-run consequences of disorder (adjustment cost) and long-run consequences of economic advance (increase in technological efficiency).

# PART III:
# FIRM THEORIES

In the previous part we have examined different conceptualisations of the market in economics from the viewpoint of whether they shed light on strategic phenomena at market level, so that strategy researchers may rely on them for their inquiry. In this part we carry on our examination of economics from the same viewpoint, but, this time, examine theories of the firm. The literature on the economics-strategic management relationship refers to five theories of the firm in the field of economics: neoclassical theory of the firm, transaction cost economics, agency theory, the theory of the growth of the firm, and behavioural theory of the firm.

Like theories of the market, theories of the firm in economics can also be categorised into 'structure-oriented' and 'process-oriented' theories of the firm. The structure-oriented theories, namely neoclassical theory of the firm and new institutional economics (transaction cost economics and agency theory), emphasis the formal or structural, rather than process, side of the nature of the firm. New institutional economics has distanced itself from neoclassical economics but it is still neoclassically-inclined in the sense that it not only deals with structural issues but also utilises neoclassical heuristics such as equilibrium, marginal analysis, and so on. The process-oriented theories, namely, the theory of the growth of the firm and behavioural theory of the firm break up their bonds with traditional neoclassical approach, focusing on processual issues and employing a distinctive set of heuristics, such as satisficing, rule following, and so on.

# 'Structure-Oriented' Theories of the Firm: Neoclassical Theory of the Firm and New Institutional Economics

In what follows, we examine the neoclassical theory of the firm and new institutional economics (transaction cost theory and agency theory) respectively. Neoclassical theory of the firm focuses on the reactive behaviour of the firm to market signals, and ignores the organisation and internal workings of the firm. In other words, neoclassical theory of the firm takes the existence of the firm for granted. Transaction cost economics attempts to account for the reason for the existence of the firm. Neoclassical theory also ignores all incentive problems within the firm. Agency theory initiates to rectify this.

It can be said that while neoclassical theory of the firm is an extension of the market theory of perfect competition, new institutional economics is reminiscent to imperfect market theories of industrial organisation[1]. Transaction cost theory of the firm extends the idea of imperfection to cover the firm as well. In other words, it proposes a more general framework of imperfection, that is, the concept of 'organisational failure', which implies that all organisations (market as well as firm) fail to work perfectly. Agency theory assumes a more efficient market, like game theory, but it does not rule out the possibility of sustainable firm differentials in the efficiently working markets.

## Note

1. See Williamson, O.E. (1985) *The Economic Institutions of Capitalism: Firms, Markets, Relational Contracting*, London: Macmillan, pp. 22-24.

## Chapter 7

# Neoclassical Theory of the Firm

### Introduction

As we have already identified, the primary concern of neoclassical theory has been with market in terms of allocative behaviour. In order to explain market behaviour, it developed models of the individual decision making units within the economy. Consumers and firms are the two types of such units, apart from the government sector. In other words, the theory of the firm has been developed for the theoretical explanation of the central problem of neoclassical economics, namely, resource allocation.

Neoclassical theory of the firm has been developed over the last one hundred years or so within the hands of many economists. During this long period of time, although it has been continuously criticised from many respects, it has been able to stand up and dominate the field. As we will see, all subsequent theories of the firm take their departure from it.

### Problem Area: Conceptualising the Firm as a Production Function

As we have just implied, the neoclassical 'theory of the firm' was constructed for the instrumental purpose of facilitating the theoretical explanation of the central problem of neoclassical economic analysis: the way in which prices and the allocation of resources among different uses are determined. As such, the theory of the firm is considered to be a part of the theory of allocation at market level and price mechanism, or more generally, apart of the wider theory of value.

In other words, the firm in neoclassical theory is viewed as a part of the operation and functioning of market price system. The role of the firm is not envisaged in the sense of decision making, but 'in the area of analysing the consequences for prices and output levels of particular courses of action in the market place' (Jones, 1976, p. 140). Consequently, as Jones rightly highlights, 'the level of aggregation at which the theory can most usefully be employed is not the level of the firm at all; it is the level of the market'

(1976, p. 140). In this respect, the firm is conceptualised as a market category, not a distinctive institution.[1]

The idea of the firm as a market category is, arguably, an extension of the Walrasian general equilibrium theory. The Walrasian equilibrium theory does not include a theory of production. Although the idea of the firm as a production function appears there, in the construct there is no special and specific mention of the firm as a significant institution within market economy. This seems to be because the Walrasian auctionering type of exchange (i.e. buying and selling inputs and outputs in spot market) takes place whether there are firms or not, however they may be owned, organised and managed, and no matter how they operate. As O'Brien maintains, markets ... could safely be analysed without firms' (1984, p. 38).

Yet firms exist and must fit somewhere in the construct. The place envisaged is, then, the intermediate position between resource suppliers and good demanders, that is, the role of production function converting inputs into outputs. That is, firms are thought of as intermediate agents between resource owners (resources are sold or hired *to* firms) and consumers (goods are bought *from* firms), and of 'black boxes' in between. Then the black boxes turn into 'production functions', converting inputs into outputs (Archibald, 1971). Under perfect market conditions firms are assumed as perfectly working production functions, since the production function includes all the technically efficient methods of production,[2] and in consequence, taken as homogeneous. Given the supply and demand curves, the equilibrium levels of price and output can easily be identified. Accordingly there remains no need to study them in terms of the reason for their existence, the determinants of their boundaries, and their various differences in profitability, management style, internal structure, decision making process, market position, resource and capabilities, strategic behaviours, etc.

This Walrasian-extension conceptualisation of the firm as a production function came to dominate economics during the 1930s, at the expense of the Marshallian more complex treatment of the firm. Marshall attempted to integrate a theory of exchange with one of production by exploring the nature of production and the determinants of supply.[3] Although he insisted upon the widespread application of perfect competition, he recognised, as O'Brien observes, that 'the allocation takes place within a continuously evolving framework of possibilities, leading to new techniques, new processes, new products - the overriding force behind all the changes - new profit opportunities' (1984, p. 26). Viewing the firm from this perspective not only provides an explanation for the reason for the firm to come into existence - to exploit profit opportunities - but also for the heterogeneity among them. For example, as O'Brien implies, the Marshallian idea of the 'representative firm' was employed, apart from its usage as a device to indicate the way in which price and output might respond to an increase in demand, in relation to the analysis of entry:

> Entrepreneurs outside an industry, who were considering entry into that industry, would look at the profitability of what they judged to be a representative firm, in order to decide whether entry was likely to be advantageous. The 'representative firm' was then, in essence, an informational device (O'Brien, 1984, p. 33).

This informational device sends signals for firms to enter (to come into existence) new markets for their profit advantages. Unfortunately, these and some other Marshallian insights, such as the vital role of management and the necessity of entrepreneurial energy for establishing and running the firm, which seem to be highly relevant for strategy theory, have been lost in the dominant neoclassical paradigm.[4]

## Can Persistent Firm Differentials Be Investigated Within the Conceptualisation of the Firm as a Production Function?

Since neoclassical theory of the firm is concerned with the allocation of resources, the question should then be that in what areas of strategic management can the economic principles be utilised to evaluate resource allocation? As we remember, neoclassical economics in general, and the theory of the firm in particular, has been conceived as one of the science of rational choice in a world in which resources are limited in relation to human wants. This led it to develop models of decision making units, namely, firms and consumers. It is assumed that the theory, in fact any economic theory, must solve three economic problems (Samuelson, 1980, p. 16): *what* goods to produce (scope problem) and in what quantities (scale problem), *how* to produce them (organisation problem), and *for whom* particular goods are produced (in which markets to compete).[5] The questions are strategic in nature since they relates to long term performance of the firm. Nonetheless, the answers given within the neoclassical frame of reference do not seem to shed light on strategic thinking and research at all. The conceptualisation of the firm in technological terms, namely as a production function, does not leave any room for strategic decisions and actions on the side of the firm. As Spulber observes,

> the firm's technology is taken for given, and so the choice of *what* to produce is simply a choice of output ratios from the production possibilities set, and the choice of *how* to produce is simply a choice from a set of available production processes (expressed as ratios of factors of production). Moreover, the choice of *for whom* to produce is not made by the neoclassical firm because the firm sells all of its output at the market clearing price by adding its output to the total supply pool (Spulber, 1993, p. 541).

That is, the choice problem is reduced to mere calculation of maximum or minimum points. Thus, in the theory, the problem and its solution are already given. Obviously, none of strategic choice problems of real firms can thus find a home within this special construct.

To put it in other way, within the conceptualisation of the firm in technological terms there are assumed to be only two strategic variables, namely output and price, that the firm can use. Nevertheless, the firm in a static but highly competitive environment (perfect competition) is assumed to be price taker rather than price maker, and to sell as many goods as it could under the prevailing market price. Thus the decisions of price and output are made automatically. In this respect, it is perhaps incorrect to refer to them as decisions at all. As Jones maintains, 'in perfect competition the firm has virtually no decisions to take. The perfectly competitive equilibrium is dictated by external conditions, and price and output follow automatically' (1976, p.25).

Under perfect competition conditions, such as the absence of uncertainty, of significant change in technology and production processes, of yet unxploited market opportunities, of transaction costs, and of limitations of decision makers in rationality, skills, etc., the function of the firm is almost nothing to do but calculating 'optimal point' of production quantities given market price for the product produced, which could be easily substituted with a computer. This straightforward technical exercise has no organisational implications such as, hierarchies, internal politics, culture, learning, improvements and so on. Such strategic actions as generating and exploiting opportunities (e.g. product differentiation or cost reducing processes), organising inquiry, communication and control, entrepreneurial motives, etc., are all condemned as wastes of competition or monopolistic misapplication (O'Brien, 1984; Loasby, 1981).

In the construct, firms are assumed to be homogeneous, passive and undifferentiated production functions. Accordingly there remains no need and room to study them in terms of their various differences in profitability, management style, internal structure, decision making process, market position, resource and capabilities, internal workings, strategic developments, and managerial problems, etc. If any difference occurs, highly competitive market (perfect competition) forces come immediately into force and nullify differences.

More specifically, firms in neoclassical theory are assumed to be homogeneous in every sense except in terms of the character of the markets they serve. As Nelson argues, economists working in the neoclassical paradigm recognise that computer firms differ from textile firms. Nevertheless, 'the differences aren't discretionary, but rather reflect differences in the contexts in which firms operate ... [so that] firms are forced to be different' (1991, pp. 61-62). However, from a strategy theory point of view, differences must be the result of some strategic discretionary behaviour of the firm.

Needless to repeat, firms in perfectly competitive markets do not have some kind of competitive advantages over each other since they have perfect imitation ability (i.e., firms are perfect substitutes for each other). As we have pointed out above, in perfectly competitive environments firms are price takers so that they do not involve in competition by offering a lower price. Instead, they involve in competition by offering output. But, the output offered is also assumed to be non-differentiated, thereby posing no strategic threat to the established firms; it is simply an imitative response to given market prices. As Demsetz highlights, in perfectly competitive markets:

> firms compete by offering *output*, especially by offering output through entry. The firm competes by entering a market and adding its output to that of incumbents, but all firms in a given market produce the same good and sell it at the same unit price. ... Competition ... is best described just so - *as imitative output competition* (emphasis in original) (Demsetz, 1997, pp. 137-138).

Clearly, the idea of 'imitative output competition' does not add any dimension to strategic conceptualisation of the firm engaging in a variety of activities in order to seek and sustain competitive advantages. Therefore, although the neoclassical theory of the firm may be useful for investigating how a firm's production choices respond to exogenous change in the market,[6] for our purpose, the type of problem has no use in investigating strategic phenomena with reference to it.

## Hard Core Assumptions: Single-exit Situational Determinism

As we have already argued, the theory of the firm in the neoclassical paradigm or research programme is merely as an extension of the theory of perfect competition. Therefore, the initial conditions assumed to be necessary for markets to work perfectly, apply also to the firm to operate (perfectly) as a production function. In this vein, Latsis mentions the same set of hard core assumptions for both the market as well as the firm theory (1972, p. 209). Yet, it seems reasonable to argue that the theory of the firm has its own subdisciplinary assumptions besides those of perfect competition. That is, since it is assumed that the firm is operating within a perfectly competitive market, both the firm and the environment specific features must be taken as initial conditions in order to understand the firm behaviour.

In this respect, the hard core assumptions are:

1. the sole objective of the firm's activities is to maximise profits,
2. demand and supply conditions, and the production function are all constant and known with certainty,
3. the firm is a price-taker in that it has no control over the price (atomistic decision making and no collusive behaviour), and
4. the firm operates in perfectly competitive product as well as factor markets.

Note that the firm in neoclassical theory can be examined with regard to the decision-making processes of resource allocation in a variety of market structures. Yet, what is known as the theory of the firm in neoclassical theory is the theory of the firm operating in perfectly competitive markets. Therefore, the assumptions of perfect market apply also to the firm. Yet the theory of the firm is also based on the following peculiar assumptions:[7]

1. The existence of a production function for each firm: The firm as an economic agent purchases factor inputs, and transforms them by some production mechanisms into some output(s). The relationship expressing the quantity of the output(s) as a function of the quantity of the inputs is termed the production function. The production function represents the technology of the firm, which imposes the present limits of the firm's technical production possibilities. The production possibilities reflect the best possible operations of the firm, given the state of technology. The firm cannot be maximising its profits (revenues minus costs) if it is not operating on the production function. The problem then becomes one of selecting the rate of output which maximises the difference between costs and revenues.
2. The Law of Diminishing Returns: Given a state of technologically feasible possibility, as the quantity of one factor of production is

increased, and the other relevant factors are kept fixed at a certain level, total product will continue to rise up to a point where the increase in total product per extra factor diminishes. In other words, the underlying technology is typically assumed to be subject first to increasing returns to scale, which imply a declining average cost curve, and then to decreasing returns to scale, which drive average cost up. The initial fall is assumed to reflect economies of scale which continue until output is raised to an optimum plant size; thereafter diseconomies of scale are assumed to set in. Economists working in neoclassical paradigm look to the causes of the rise of the long-run cost curve such as the limitations of management (upward sloping cost curve) or of the market (downward sloping demand curve). That is, the long-run average cost curve of a firm is assumed to be U-shaped and the optimum size of the firm is indicated as the lowest point of the average cost curve for its given product.

3. Factor substitution: The inputs into the production process are divided into categories which can be continuously substituted for one another.

The description of the firm in technological terms together with that of the environment within which it is assumed to operate, strengthens the idea of single-exit situational determinism. Under the single exit situation, as Blaug argues,

> there is no internal decision-making machinery, no information search, no rules for dealing with ignorance and uncertainty, and no entrepreneurship of any kind whatsoever: the problem of choice among alternative lines of action is so far reduced to its simplest elements that the assumption of profit maximising automatically singles out the best course of action (Blaug, 1992, p. 155).

As has been highlighted, from the Machlupian point of view, the role of the firm envisaged in neoclassical theory is, in essence, to adjust output and prices of imaginary (homogeneous) products to very simple specific changes in data (wage rates, interest rates, import duties, excise, etc.). In so conceptualising, the role of the firm in allocating resources is highly ambiguous since, as is understood by many neoclassical theorists, its function is to 'respond' market signals (changes) almost 'automatically'. In Blaug's terms, the 'theory turns the decision maker into a cipher' (Blaug, 1992, p. 156).

Given the perfect competition conditions in which the firm is assumed to operate and the knowledge of the state of technology, there seems to be no need to 'manage' resource allocation with discretion. In this regard, as we discuss in the next chapter, it is not the visible-managerial hand that coordinates firm activities, but the invisible hand of the market functioning. As Kay argues, 'the firm can be regarded as a "black box" with no discretion over resource allocation questions; the perfect competition rules must be obeyed, or the firm leaves the field' (1982, p. 2). Therefore, 'working out allocations of resources which are in the core becomes a matter of mere calculation' (Ricketts, 1994, p. 5).

In the theory problems as well as solutions are already given. That is, the theory of the firm is *a priori* in the sense that its behaviour can be deduced from assumptions that describe the environment and the technological possibilities that it faces. Such a priori theoretical construct could be useful for *model* predictions though, it is not useful for explaining and predicting real world phenomena such as strategic behaviour of business firms.

## Conclusions

The theory of the firm is simply an extension of the theory of perfect competition. Thus, the study of firms *qua* firms has been a neglected facet of neoclassical economic theory. The firm is conceptualised in technological terms. Given the specifications of perfectly competitive market and the state of technological knowledge, firms are assumed to choose only quantities of commodities from a predetermined set of possibilities. All the firms comprising of a market offer the same commodity (no differentiated product), and sell it at the same unit price (no competitive pricing activity). They all also deploy homogeneous resources using universally available production functions and, select that combination of resources and products which maximises profits. In this respect, in the neoclassical construct the firm is not treated in terms of the determinants of its success and failure, but of its function in converting inputs into outputs in an 'optimal' way, and thus in assisting to explain how price system works perfectly.

Although the theory may be useful for investigating how a firm's production choices respond to exogenous change in the market, for our purpose, the type of problem and the initial conditions assumed for modelling does not allow to investigate strategic phenomena within its construct. Firms in the construct are taken to be identical except in terms of the product market they serve. Yet, differences originating between firms as the result of the market they serve are in terms of the technology they employ rather than in terms of discretionary (competitive) profit differentials.

To avoid committing the fallacy of misplaced correctedness, it should be pointed out that the theory is not false but the conditions required to apply it are ones that make redundant any investigation into the sustainable firm differentials in profitability on the basis of the firm's strategy-following behaviour. In other words, our analysis has shown, not so much whether the theory is true or false, but it is no use for employing it in an alien environment in which strategic phenomena is prevalent.

## Notes

1. It must be emphasised that this procedure, i.e. the instrumental function of the firm, is not wrong at all from a model-building point of view. It is perfectly defensible for the (problem dependency) purpose of analysis of market level allocation. In fact, this position has been defended explicitly and strongly by contemporous neoclassical theorists. For example, Machlup, when faced with severe criticism about the unrealistic conceptualisation of the firm in the theory he responded: 'The model of the firm in that theory is not ... designed to serve to explain and predict the behaviour of real firms; instead, it is designed to explain and predict changes in observed prices ... as effects of particular changes in conditions ...' (Machlup, F., 1967, Theories of the Firm: Marginalist, Behavioural, Managerial, *The American Economic Review*, Vol. 57, No. 1, pp. 1-33, p. 9.) For him, the firm is a necessary 'theoretical construct' in explaining and predicting the causal connection between changes in prices (quoted, paid, received) and particular conditions (wage rates, interest rates, import duties, excise taxes, etc.). In this respect, he warns that the firm as a theoretical construct or heuristic fiction should not be confused with the firm as an empirical concept or a real organisation, dealing with internal workings, structuring, etc. of the firm.

   Accepting the idea of the firm as a heuristic fiction designed to explain some certain phenomena (problem dependency), notwithstanding, we examine, for the purpose of the present study, the conceptualisation of the firm in the neoclassical construct from, not whether it is realistic or unrealistic, but, whether this heuristic fiction enables strategy researchers to explain and predict the firm's strategic behaviour of seeking and securing competitive advantages, point of view. Apparently, this requires an assessment of the theory not much in its own terms but in strategic management's terms. That is, the study involves in analysing, and then judging, from a pragmatic viewpoint, the usefulness of the theory in terms of whether or not it sheds light on strategic phenomena given its intellectual foundations, not from a methodological viewpoint in terms of whether or not it represents reality. Accordingly, we continue to analyse its intellectual foundations, and, then, make an informed judgement for its usefulness for strategic theorising and research.

2. Note that 'the production function represents the technology of a firm of an industry, or of the economy as a whole.' A. Koutsoyiannis (1979) (first ed. 1975) *Modern Microeconomics*, London: Macmillan, p. 67.
3. See Marshall, *Principles, and Industry and Trade*.
4. In this study, we restrict ourselves to the examination of the dominant theory of the firm in neoclassical construct and its relevance for strategic thinking and research. For the examination of the Marshallian view of firm, see D.P. O'Brien (1984) The Evolution of the Theory of the Firm, in F.H. Stephen (ed) *Firms, Organisation and Labour: Approaches to the Economics of Work Organisation*, London: MacMillan, pp. 25-62; B. Loasby (1971) Hypothesis and Paradigm in the Theory of the Firm, *The Economic Journal*, Vol. 81, pp. 863-885; C. Knudsen (1996) The Competence Perspective: A Historical View, in N.J. Foss and C. Knudsen (eds.) *Towards a Competence Theory of the Firm*, London: Routledge, pp. 13-37. See also E. Penrose (1959) *The Theory of the Growth of the Firm*, Oxford: Oxford University Press. Penrose's The Theory of the Growth of the Firm is a Marshallian-oriented theory of the firm, rather than that of Walrasian. It differs from the dominant paradigm in some significant aspects such as firm as a bundle of resources rather than production function, a managerial organisation rather than one managed by invisible hand of market, etc.
5. See Spulber for how the problems relate to strategic management (D.F. Spulber, 1993, Economic Analysis and Management Strategy: A Survey, *Journal of Economics & Management Strategy*, Vol. 1, No. 3, pp. 535-574).
6. For example, it makes such predictions: 'an increase in demand leads to a rise in both output and product prices'; 'a lump sum tax on business profits will have no effect on output'; a rise in money wages causes a fall in employment; and so on.
7. In his analysis, taking the Lakatosian research programme as a heuristic device, Fulton identifies the below mentioned set of assumptions, but from a different perspective. To Fulton, the application of the idea of the research programme as an analytical tool in economics has been fault. In his view, hard core assumptions exemplified by Lakatos when introducing the ideal of research programmes, are highly technical. In this vein, he argues that the hard core assumptions identified for neoclassical research programme by Latsis and Remenyi are, indeed, 'presuppositions', i.e. statements that are made prior to outlining the hard core. Then given the presuppositions, he identifies the three features for each firm. For more details, see G. Fulton, 1984, Research Programmes in Economics, *History of Political Economy*, Vol. 16, No. 2, pp. 187-205.

Chapter 8

# New Institutional Economics: Transaction Cost Theory and Agency Theory

## Introduction

In the neoclassical analysis of the firm, the firm is taken as a technological production function for transforming inputs into output, rather than an organisation within which the inputs are organised and coordinated. The institutional economics emerged out of a critique of the neoclassical economics for the failure to explain the existence of capitalist institutions, in particular corporations. The old institutionalism appeared in the USA during the early years of the twentieth century and was based around the work of T. Veblen (1948) and J.R. Commons (1951). The 'new' is used to distinguish the post-Coase (1937) developments from the older institutionalist school. Williamson suggests that the work of Commons does provide a link between the two institutional approaches since it was him who first suggested that the ultimate unit of economic analysis should be the transaction (1975, p. 3).

The new institutional economics embraces property right theory, transaction cost theory, and agency theory. As Thompson argues, 'all the current strands in 'New Institutional' economics share an important ancestor in Coase's (1937) contractual view of the firm. They differ primarily in emphasis, and should be seen as complementary rather than rivalrous' (Thompson, 1988, p. 65). The focus of the new institutional economics is on the forms that organisations, especially capitalist firms, take.

In parallel to studies on the relationship between economics and strategic management from a 'legitimist' viewpoint (i.e. attempting to find the kind of economics on which strategy theory could be drawn), in this study we will also not examine property right theory.[1] In fact, most of the ideas of property right theory in accounting for strategic phenomena are similar, if not the same, as those of transaction cost and agency theory[2]. In what follows, transaction cost and agency theory are examined for their potential service to strategy theory, given their problem area and hard core assumptions.

## Problem Area: Conceptualising the Firm as a Governance Structure (Transaction Cost Economics) or as a Nexus of Contracts (Agency Theory)

It seems useful to examine the problem areas of the theories separately in order to avoid possible misunderstandings that may stem from a combined explanation since they 'have significant features in common and each could probably be expressed in terms of the other' (Rowlinson, 1997, p. 45). First, the problem area of transaction cost economics, then, of agency theory will be examined.

## Transaction Cost Economics

Transaction cost economics emerged largely out of a critique of neoclassical treatment of the firm as a market category, i.e. governed by market price mechanism. The whole theory of perfect competition has taken the existence of the firm for granted. In consequence, in the neoclassical construct, market price mechanism was seen as the sole coordination of resource allocation, that is, no other mode of coordination of resource allocation was recognised.

In his direction-setting article, *The Nature of the Firm*, published in 1937 Coase observed that there is a contradiction in the theory of market price mechanism which proposes that, on the one hand, resource allocation in market economies takes place through the price mechanism, and, on the other, such allocation depends on the entrepreneur-coordinator. Apparently, the proposition is laden with a contradiction for the invisible hand of market mechanism is not the same as the visible hand of entrepreneur-coordinator. In other words, Coase maintained that spontaneous coordination through price mechanism is by nature different from planned coordination through authority. Thus he drew attention to the organisation of the firm as a distinct and alternative coordination structure or governance structure, in terms of Williamson (1979), of resource allocation to market coordination. Thus, in recognising firms as distinct and alternative governance structure of resource allocation, Coase added another coordinator to the mono-coordinator world of neoclassics.[3] Coase provided a rationale for why there should be firms in a market economy: because it is sometimes costly to use the price system to coordinate economic activities.

As we have already seen, the Walrasian model assumes that the cost of transacting is zero. For example, under the conditions of perfect information of exchanged products, there is no need for organising marketing activities (e.g. advertising) since imperfect information is a precondition for marketing activities. All information needed for exchange is codified in and revealed through market prices. Thus, the economic universe is assumed to be free of transacting costs or they are assumed to be insignificant.

Coase (1937) argued that the firm cannot be comprehended through a model that assumes away transaction and information costs. For him transaction and information costs are not 'details' to be neglected, but the reason for the very existence of the firm because if it is prohibitively expensive to coordinate resource allocation through price mechanism, then resource allocation is coordinated through hierarchies such as firms in order to economise on transaction and information costs. In terms of Williamson, 'if transaction costs are negligible, the organisation of economic activity is irrelevant, since any advantages one mode of organisation appears to hold over another will simply be eliminated by costless contracting' (1979, p. 233).

To put in other words, why do firms exist?, ask theorists of transaction cost economics. In clearer terms, if market price mechanism controls all resource allocation activities and solve all allocation problems, why are firms needed? In the transaction cost paradigm this is because the price mechanism *fails* to control and solve all resource allocation problems; firms then come into existence to carry out the job as an alternative authoritative resource allocators.

In the Coasian presentation market failure was taken as exception, so that hierarchical governance structure of firms seemed to be exceptions to non-hierarchical market price governance structure. Arrow (1970) attempted to demonstrate that transaction and information costs is a general category of market failure attached to any market and to any mode of resource allocation (market, firm or state).

Furthermore, taking this general category of organisational failure as basis, Williamson argued that transactions are not homogeneous, so that identifying the critical dimensions with respect to which transactions differ is crucial. He proceeded to identify the critical dimensions that gave rise to the high (low) costs of transacting. He asserted that it is the co-existence of such human attributes as bounded rationality and opportunism with such environmental factors as uncertainty, small numbers exchange relationships (oligopoly situation) and asset specificity (transaction-specific assets) that give rise to significant transaction costs.[4] Organisational failures lead into such transaction problems as information asymmetries, incomplete contracting, bilateral dependencies, the limits of third-party enforcement, and so forth. These transaction problems carry costs, and these costs are the '*comparative costs of planning, adapting, and monitoring task completion under alternative governance structures*' (emphasis in origin) (Williamson, 1985, p. 2). In other words, the costs of negotiating, monitoring, and enforcing a contingent claims contract to ensure against the possibility of transactional problems are called transaction cost.

Displaying the complications and working out the organisational ramifications of these behavioural and environmental factors and their consequent transactional problems describes much of what transaction cost economics has been up to now. More specifically, within this organisational failure framework, transaction cost economics aims to explain the *nature*, *existence* and *boundaries* of the firm.

According to transaction cost theory, what distinguishes non-market forms of organisation (such as the firm) from market organisation is the nature of their organisation. In the former, organisation is administrative, whereas in the latter, it is spontaneous. As Coase argues: 'a workman moves from department Y to department X, he does not go because of a change in relative prices, but because he is ordered to do so' (1937, p. 387). The mode of organisation in markets is the price system, whereas firms develop their own managerial hierarchies to coordinate resources. The difference can be viewed, in terms of Chandler (1977), in the market system resources are coordinated automatically by the 'invisible hand' of market prices, firms involves the use of the 'visible hand' of the conscious authority of management.

As such, firms are alternative governance structures to market organisation in the resource allocation process. The question then is 'why firms emerge?' Coase's path-breaking reply was that 'the main reason why it is profitable to establish a firm would seem to be that there is a cost of using the price mechanism' (1937, p. 390). This was a recognition of the fact that 'there are costs of making transactions in a market economy' (Coase, 1937, p. 390). In other words, the penetrating insight by Coase is to highlight the fact that markets do not operate costlessly, and he takes the costs of using or running markets as the reason to form contracts, as his basic explanation for the existence of firms.

By pointing out that every transaction involves cost, transaction cost theory diverges from the perfectly running institutionless neoclassical world in which transactions, such as communication-information difficulties, problems of search, negotiation, policing, appropriability and enforcement, are not a problem. Transaction cost economics emphases that unless the transaction activities are not taken as problematic and related costs are introduced into economic analysis, nonmarket organisations, in particular firms, have no purpose to exist; the very existence of the firm is to economise on transaction costs.

The third issue for transaction cost theorists is the demarcation of the boundaries between the firm and market. In terms of Coase, the question is 'Why is not all production carried on by one big firm?' (1937, p. 387). More clearly, 'what determines which activities a firm chooses to coordinate 'internally' and which it leaves to be coordinated 'externally' by the market, that is, it procures from others. In now fashionable terms, the issue is that of 'make-or-buy'.

As we remember, the answer given by the neoclassical theory of the firm was that the natural boundaries of the firm are defined by technology, such as economies of scale and technological non-separabilities. In other words, as Coase cited earlier treatments by Kaldor (1934) and Robinson (1932), the determinant of the limit of the firm size proposed by neoclassics was because of 'diminishing returns to management' (1937, p. 395). However, Coase argues that markets and firms differ in transaction cost respects. Decisions to make or buy will be determined by transaction cost economising. In fact, Coase uses the same rationale as the neoclassics do, which is 'marginality'. A rising cost curve is, of course, vital to the marginality argument: the firm grows until its costs of organisation are equal to that of using the market. This means that there are costs of internalising transactions within the firm, and, the boundaries of the firm are set by the point at which organising a transaction internally is marginally more costly than buying in the necessary good or service. Internalising process will continue up to the point where the marginal cost of covering a further transaction by the firm is equal to the marginal cost of conducting the transaction by the market. The problem is properly regarded as part of the optimisation problem. This is why one big firm does not organise the whole economy.

## Agency Theory[5]

Transaction cost theory is concerned with the problem of under which conditions activities are coordinated under managerial hierarchies rather than the price mechanism (markets versus hierarchies dichotomy), 'without a clear spelling out of organisational considerations', as Spulber observes

(1993, p. 559). However, the replacement of price mechanism by managerial procedures within the firm naturally raises, as Spulber maintains, questions regarding the internal workings of the firm, in particular those regarding internal incentive structures: what will motivate subordinates in the firm to carry out the objectives of shareholders or management? In this respects, agency theory, arguably as a complementary theory to transaction cost theory,[6] addresses the design of incentives and control mechanisms to mitigate problems created by divergence interests between various groups (management-subordinates, shareholders-management, etc.).

The relationship between power and control (e.g. shareholders and managers) is labelled as an agency relationship, defined as 'a contract under which one or more persons (the principal(s)) engage another person (the agent) to perform some service on their behalf which involves delegating some decision-making authority to the agent' (Jensen and Meckling, 1976, p. 308). The agency problem emanates from the 'separation of ownership and control' observed in modern large business corporations as well as such organisations as large professional partnerships, financial mutuals, and nonprofits (Berle and Means, 1932). The problem of separation of ownership and control leads to conflicts of interests between employer (whose aim is the maximisation of his/her wealth) and employee (who is motivated by self-interest). Yet, agency theory can deal potentially with any kind of agency relationships involving the delegation of power and control such as employer-employee, lawyer-client, buyer-supplier, and doctor-patient (Eisenhardt, 1989). In the context of the firm theory, it concerns chiefly with the relationship between the owner of the firm and the manager of the firm who makes decisions which affect the value of the firm, on behalf of the owner.

As Eisenhardt observes, two aspects of the agency problem are cited in the formal literature: moral hazard and adverse selection.

> Moral hazard refers to lack of effort on the part of the agent. The argument here is that the agent may simply not put forth the agreed-upon effort. That is, the agent is shirking. ... Adverse selection refers to the misrepresentation of ability by the agent. The argument here is that the agent may claim to have certain skills or abilities when he or she is hired. Adverse selection arises because the principal cannot completely verify these skills or abilities either at the time of hiring or while the agent is working (Eisenhardt, 1989, p. 61).

Put it simply, the former refers to unobservable effort and the latter unobservable information. Note that the agency problem arises in situations of asymmetric information, where the principal has less information concerning the agent's actions than the agent does himself so that the agent has some scope to pursue his own interest that cannot be directly observed by the principal. In these situations, 'it is generally impossible for the principal or the agent at zero cost to ensure that the agent will make optimal decisions from the principal's viewpoint' (Jensen and Meckling, 1976, p. 308). Therefore, the principal (owner) needs to 'monitor' opportunistic behaviour of the manager, and the manager to 'bond' the owner, but which still leaves a 'residual loss'. In other words, agency relationship leads to costs of (1) monitoring expenditures made by the principal, (2) bonding expenditures made by the agent to reassure principals, and (3) residual loss due to unresolved conflicts of interests between the two parties.[7]

The conflicting interests of principals and agents in situations of asymmetric information in turn raises the question of how can a principal (a firm owner) delegate power to his/her agents (managers), and, at the same time, design an appropriate governance structure (control system) to align the agents' actions more closely to his/her interests (Jensen and Meckling, 1976; Eisenhardt, 1989). In terms of Eisenhardt, 'because the unit of analysis is the contract governing the relationship between the principal and the agent, the focus of the theory is on determining the most efficient contract governing the principal-agent relationship' (1989, p. 58). That is to say, the theory looks for contracts which minimise agency costs.

Agency cost economics theorists make suggestions for solving employment contract problems such as the development of efficient ways of monitoring the performance of individual managers (or management teams), providing incentive contracts which reward agents only on the basis of results, bonding (where the agent makes a promise to pay the principal a sum of money if inappropriate behaviour by the agent is detected) and mandatory retirement payments. Jensen and Meckling focus their analysis on the corporate form of organisation with diffused ownership, and stress the importance of minimising agency costs as an explanation for corporate financing decisions. These include incentive schemes for managers which reward them financially for maximising shareholder interests. Such schemes typically include plans whereby senior executives obtain shares, perhaps at a reduced price, thus aligning financial interests of executives with those of shareholders (Jensen and Meckling, 1976).

As it may have been clear so far, within the agency construct, the firm is conceptualised as a 'nexus of a set of contracting relationships among individuals' (Jensen and Meckling, 1976, p. 311). The view of the firm as a nexus of contract diverts attention to the internal workings of the firm in contrast to the neoclassical view of the firm which defines it as a black box:

> Defining the firm as a black box diverts attention away from what is going on within the firm. The nexus of contracts definition of organisations, on the other hand, focuses attention on the problems that the contracts are intended to solve, i.e., on how things get done within the organisation (Jensen, 1983, p. 331).

Since the firm is viewed as a nexus of implicit and explicit contracts between various groups, then contractual relations with banks and other creditors, suppliers, employees and customers are seen 'an essential aspect of the firm' (Hart, 1996, p. 205). Contracts specify the procedures of internal workings of the firm, or, the rule of the game within the firm, in terms of Jensen (1983, p. 326), including the performance evaluation system, the reward system, and the assignment of decision rights. The view of the firm as a nexus of contracts also,

> serves to make it clear that the ... *firm is not an individual* ... [but] is a legal fiction which serves as a focus for a complex process in which the conflicting objectives of individuals (some of which may 'represent' other organisations) are brought into equilibrium within a framework of contractual relations (emphasis in original) (Jensen and Meckling, 1976, p. 311).

In this respect, agency theory offers a complex view of the firm. Yet it still shares, as Chandler observes, the neoclassical view of 'the firm as a legal entity with a production set ... but gives it a managerial hierarchy' (1992, p. 488). Note that the view of the firm as a managerial hierarchy is common to both transaction cost and agency cost economics.

## Transaction Cost Economics and Agency Theory's Implications for Investigating into Persistent Firm Differentials

Clearly, the Coasian insight that the firm and market are alternative governance structures is invaluable for strategic management theory since it provides a rationale for the firm in its existence as a managerial structure. Given the idea of the firms as a managerial structure assumed in both the transaction cost and agency cost constructs, the firm is no longer considered to be an individual (uni-brain) maximising profits without facing any organisational problems (zero conflict, zero decision making costs, no information and incentive problems). On the contrary, management is called into action to contend, within a framework of contractual relations, with internal workings of the firm, more specifically, the internal organisational structure, incentive systems and control mechanisms, which cannot be taken as given, as is done in the neoclassical theory of the firm. All these require managerial effort of coordinating, adapting, and monitoring.

The recognition of managerial existence refers explicitly to the 'organisational' side of the firm: how does a group of individuals cooperate and achieve organisational objectives on grounds of self-interest? [8] Both theories assume the 'visible' hand of management, rather than the 'invisible' hand of price mechanism, in solving the organisational problem. In other words, they draw attention to the need for the managerial structures to coordinate and direct human capital to achieve organisational objectives, rather than simply presume that it is done by virtue of market mechanism. Yet, they do not rely managerial structures (authority) alone to solve the organisational problem. In both theories the emphasis is put on the significance of incentive structures (good management), in dealing with the organisational problem. Thus, the idea of hierarchical structures as well as incentive structures interrelates individual and organisational levels of analysis, that is, makes it possible to understand how employees work to achieve impersonal 'organisational' objectives on the basis of their personal 'self-interest' seeking behaviour. The organisational perspective provides a valuable framework for strategic management thinking since it explains why there is a need for management, and moreover, a good (strategic) management in governing internal affairs of the firm to achieve its long-term objectives.

Apart from this general framework, they offer some practical applications concerning strategic aspects of the firm. As Williamson argues, 'transaction cost economics deals with many of the key issues with which business strategy is or should be concerned' (1991, p. 90). He gives, *inter alia*, examples of make-or-buy decisions, corporate finance and corporate governance, and employment relation. For example, to demonstrate the relevance of the transaction cost approach to business strategy one of the best example in case is 'make or buy' decision. The 'make-or-buy' decision, as Buckley and Michie maintain, is fundamental to business strategy, since 'the overall composition of all decisions determine *the scope of the firm* (emphasis in original) (1996, p. 2). In other words, the decision about where to compete (in which direction the firm should grow by internalising markets or externalising businesses) is a major component of business strategy. The decision of 'make-or-buy' is essential to a wide variety of firms in involving vertical integration (adding a stage in the manufacturing process, either backward toward raw materials or forward toward the market), horizontal integration (doing more of the same), conglomerate diversification (controlling an unrelated business) and multinational firms (doing business in different nations).

Agency theory also deals with many of organisational issues, almost similar to transaction cost economics, such as, *inter alia*, corporate finance, corporate governance, and employment relations with which business strategy is or should be concerned. Agency theory can be applied to highlight specific internal and external agency relationships from a strategic viewpoint. For example, one of the main issue with which agency theory is concerned is corporate governance, which addresses the question of how the design of organisation structure helps the executive to formulate and implement plans for long-term high corporate performance. In this respect, Fama and Jensen[9] mention the board of directors as a monitoring device that stockholders within large corporations could use to monitor the opportunism of top executives, such as the adoption of a short-term, risk-aversive attitude in strategic investment decisions for the sake of stability and the protection of management's own control position, or the excessive pursuit of diversification as a strategy to increase the firm's size and the managers' associated prestige and status (Kosnik, 1987). The board works as a monitoring device to help control top executives' misuses of corporate funds by governing and assessing management's decisions and their impact on the long-term value of the firm (Breeley, and Myers, 1988). As Rumelt *et al.*, maintain, the corporate governance perspective supplies a valuable framework for strategic management thinking and research since 'by recognising the existence of "bad" management, identifying remedial instruments, and emphasising the importance of proper incentive arrangements, it takes a more normative stand than most other subfields of economics' (Rumelt, Schendel and Teece, 1991, p. 15).

Leaving aside the implications of the transaction cost economics and agency theory for strategic management theory, for our purpose the fundamental question is, 'Can the central research problem of strategy theory, i.e. the sources and mechanism of persistent firm differentials, be taken as a legitimate research subject within the incentive paradigm of transaction and agency cost approaches?'

To start with, the analysis hitherto must have made it clear that the focus of transaction cost economics is on the relation between the firm and market (firm versus market), not on the relation between individual firms (firms versus firms). In other words, the focus is on *comparative* advantage between alternative governance structures (markets and firms), not *competitive* advantage between the same governance structures (competition among firms). In one of his recent articles, Coase implies this point from the viewpoint of firm differences in organising activities:

> I did not investigate the factors that would make the costs of organising lower for some firms than for others. This was quite satisfactory if the main purpose was, as mine was, to explain why there are firms. But if one is to explain the institutional structure of production in the system as a whole it is necessary to uncover the reasons why the cost of organising particular activities differs *among firms* (emphasis added) (Coase, 1988, p. 47).

Agency theory, too, does not investigate the reasons why agency costs differ among firms, or more specifically, interrelate organisational incentive structures with strategic competitive behaviour of firms for advantage over each other. Yet, although Coase acknowledges that transaction cost economics has not treated firm differences in organising particular activities, he implies that this could be a complementary research agenda. The implication is that firm differences are recognised and that the reasons of cost differences among firms in organising particular activities or in dealing with agency problems, thereby leading into advantages in competition, can be taken up a complementary or legitimate research question.

Although such a complementary research initiation is still in its early stages of development, it supplies rich enough indications for the assessment.[10] To demonstrate this, it seems better to start from the explanation of the transaction cost approach to the economics of firm differentials since it has already been elaborated in this respect. Williamson asserts,

> That the profits differ in two firms in the same industry using the same technology selling to the same customers is not because the managers in the one are working harder than managers in the other. Instead, managers in the two firms are working equally hard but one is working smarter-better organisation form; better internal incentives and controls; better alignment of the contractual (interfirm and intrafirm) interfaces (Williamson, 1991, p. 78).

Firm differences are not interpreted in terms of managerial utility (the managerial capacity is more utilised in one firm than in another in terms of reducing waste, bureaucracy, slack, and so on). Rather the position taken is that the sources of firm differentials stem from different governance structures. Needless to say that that line of reasoning holds for the agency theory explanation of firm differential, i.e. some firms are better than others in structuring incentive structures to reduce agency costs. Agency theory offers an even a more suitable theoretical framework within which incentive structures can be connected with strategic competition and performance.

To elaborate, that hierarchical structures vary in the way they manage transactions and/or agency problems in their internal procedures and control systems influences the process of goal formation and business performance. In clearer terms, the argument put forward by both theories is that governance structures or incentive structures play a significant role in the determination of firm (strategic) goals, behaviour and performance. In consequence, differences in performance are thus explained with different governance or incentive structures followed by firms.

The firm as a governance structure or a nexus of contracts does not ensure an automatic efficiency advantage in managing transactions over market or in solving agency problems. To be able to do so, internal workings of the firm, more specifically, the internal organisational structure, reward systems and control mechanisms need to be put in and managed (Williamson, 1990). Therefore, the idea of the firm as a governance structure or a nexus of contract, like strategy theory, suggests that internal structure, incentives and control systems of the firm are all variables subject to managerial endeavour, and thereby firms vary in their performance outcomes according to these variables.

Governance or incentive structures are required to economise on costs of negotiating, monitoring, and enforcing contingent contracts to ensure against the possibility of transactional/agency problems originating in the firm or market. Firms are assumed to economise on transaction/agency costs by using the long term hierarchical employment relations based on contracts,[11] first, (1) in directing the work activities of the employee from day-to-day, thus overcoming the problem of dealing with spot market relations; and (2) in closely monitoring the employee's performance, thereby minimising the problem of opportunism; and, second, in creating an environment of trust between employees much more readily than a market can between trading parties, thus reducing opportunistic tendencies and in consequence the need to monitor their performance (Ouchi, 1980).[12]

In both constructs, it is recognised that complex institutions commonly serve a variety of objectives, including gaining market power, which is important from a strategic behaviour of the firm point of view, but it is proposed that the economic institutions of capitalism have the main purpose and effect of efficiency.[13] More clearly, the study of firm differentials from the incentive theories of the firm viewpoint is to assess the properties of various organisational modes (governance or incentive) by comparing their relative efficiency characteristics.

This view of the incentive theories suggests a different direction towards the inquiry into firm differentials. As we remember, focusing on the strategic purpose of the firm (gaining competitive advantage), the approaches in the field of strategic management, i.e. positioning and resource-based, direct attention to external market structure and internal firm resources and capabilities respectively for the inquiry of differentials. However, the incentive theories suggests another way of looking for differentials, that is, capacities of different governance or incentive structures in achieving efficiency. Although the incentive theories of the firm draw attention from the external market workings (neoclassical theory of the firm) to the internal firm workings to explain economics of the firm, they do not highlight, in explaining firm differentials, idiosyncratic and mainly informal (intangible) resources and capabilities that firms possess, as is argued by the theorists of the resource-based approach in the field of strategic management, but *formal* institutional arrangements, i.e. governance or incentive structures.[14] The idea of formal institutional arrangements as the source of firm differentials seems to be a challenging proposal to the ideas of market position of or idiosyncratic resources and capabilities of the firm, and may lead into new avenues illuminating strategic phenomena.[15]

As to the question of the persistency of firm differentials, the theories does not supply a straightforward answer. When transaction cost theorists explain the process through which an efficient institution such as the firm replaces an inefficient one such as the market, or vice versa, they employ, in general, 'evolutionary' arguments to explain the replacement process. For example, Williamson (1975, 1985, 1991) takes this evolutionary view of efficiency-based market selection in explaining the persistency of firm differentials. He maintains that in the competitive market selection process the winners and losers are determined by efficiency. For him, if strategy is concerned with long term superiority, economising is the best strategy because only those firms that economise will survive in the long run. Moreover, he argues that superiority based on sources other than efficiency, such as first mover advantages, strategic ploys, resource dependency, historical accident, luck, and so on, will not persist due to competitive market operations such as new entry, imitation, etc. Put differently, he invites us to see and appreciate the difference between persistency of good strategy (economising) and temporariness of bad strategy (market power gains or resource-dependency rents), given market selection. This explanation is an explicit acceptance of the persistency of firm differentials based on 'good strategy'.

Parallel to transaction cost theorists, agency theorists also theorise on survival of the fittest grounds. For example, Jensen argues, in discussing the manner in which they use tautologies to develop the theory, that in addition to the tautology that agency costs are minimised, 'the survival of the fittest tautology completes most of the major building blocks of the analytical framework for creating a theory of organisations' (1983, p. 331).[16] As in the transaction cost economics form of analysis, in the agency cost economics it is assumed that the form of economic organisation which minimises agency costs will be the form to survive or flourish.[17] Minimising agency costs is the best strategy in long term, to use Williamson's terms, and those organisations persist to survive that are able to achieve low cost control of agency problems.

The essence of these evolutionary arguments is the neoclassical variant of efficiency-based market selection, put forward by Alchian in 1950.[18] The view can simply be stated that competition in the face of pervasive scarcity dictates that the more efficient institutions will survive and inefficient ones perish. Nevertheless, the problem with that kind of reasoning is that it does not say anything about how the market mechanism selects, how long it takes to eliminate superiorities not based on economising transaction costs or minimising agency costs, etc. The process of the withering away of firm superiorities (based on other than efficiency) cannot be foreseen; that is to say, 'even with intense efficiency-based selection pressures it would take several years for the inefficient enterprises to get weeded out' (Carrol, 1993, p. 238).

In this respect, it can be argued that, given the organisational failure framework employed by the transaction cost approach, firm differences not based on efficiency, might persist long enough to enjoy competitive advantage due to market and firm failures. On the contrary to the transaction cost economics' reliance on organisational failure explanations, agency theory takes an efficient market view in explaining how market institutions (such as labour market, product market, banks) can play a part, alongside internal incentive structures, as a control on management.[19] Nevertheless, it can still be argued that market competition or market institutions may discipline but not necessarily eliminate swiftly those firms that earn high profits because of their market positions or idiosyncratic resources and capabilities, due to ubiquitous information asymmetry and bounded rationality.

Therefore, it can be asserted that firms that possess a superior market position or resource position may continue to be in a competitively advantageous position for a sufficiently long period of time. This argument can be made because

1. the assumed 'withering away' process does not correspond to an observed reality (it could be from five years to fifty years), and

2. such an assumption can be accommodated within the constructs without causing them significant damage, on the ground that markets and firms may continue to fail to equalise differentials for a significant period of time due to evolutionary sluggishness.

## Hard Core Assumptions: Multiple-exit Situations

As we pointed out previously, the neoclassical construct of the economic world is analogous to that of the physical world. In this physical world, the firm as a production function, like a frictionless machine, is assumed to work smoothly, i.e. free of transaction costs. Note that like a frictionless plane in physics, a costless transaction is a hypothetical construction. In this hypothetical construct there appears no need for 'managing' a frictionless or costless running machine. Employing this machine-like, technology-based concept of the firm, Willimason argues that when a good or service is transferred across a technologically separable interface, transfers may not occur smoothly. Thus he introduces frictions into the construct to explain the nature of the firm:

> In mechanical systems we look for frictions: Do the gears mesh, are the parts lubricated, is there needless slippage or other loss of energy? The economic counterpart of friction is transaction cost: Do the parties to the exchange operate harmoniously, or are there frequent misunderstandings and conflicts that lead to delays, breakdowns, and other malfunctions? Transaction cost analysis supplants the usual preoccupation with technology and steady-state production (or distribution) expenses with an examination of the *comparative costs of planning, adapting, and monitoring task completion under alternative governance structures* (emphasis in original) (Williamson, 1985, pp. 1-2).

In a similar chain of reasoning agency theorists argue that neoclassical theory of the firm is based on a hidden assumption that agents always execute the agreements they make with principals (a frictionless machine, free of agency costs, in terms of Williamson) (Pratt and Zeckhauser, 1985). Therefore, it ignores the ubiquitous agency costs that arise from having to ensure that agents do, in fact, fulfil the agreements. However, organisations need to be designed, they argue, to overcome agency problems (frictions), through some devices such as the alignment of objectives, monitoring and incentive.

As has been explained above, theorists working within both the transaction cost and agency cost constructs argue that organisations emerge chiefly to 'manage' the unavoidable costs, transactional or agency. Here, the question is, 'Why do frictions or transaction/agency costs occur?', or more precisely, 'Under which conditions do transaction/agency problems or costs appear and increase or decrease?'. According to Williamson, frictions or transaction costs emerge and differ (increase or decrease) in the economic system because of a set of *human factors* together with a set of *environmental factors*. According to agency theorists agency costs emerge because of human factors. The primary human (behavioural) factors, which are common to both theories, producing transactional/agency difficulties are:[20]

1. Bounded rationality: People are assumed to try to make rational decisions but their ability to do so is constrained by their cognitive and language limits on capacity to gather and process information to formulate and solve problems. For example, boundedly rational economic actors are not able to figure out and take full account of all future situations that might necessitate changes in the terms of a transaction or a principal-agent relation. Therefore, transactions or agency relations that require long-term relations cannot be specified, organised and agreed upon, taking all future contingencies into consideration and incorporated into contractual agreements. Bounded rationality gives rise to transactional/agency problems when decisions have to be taken with incomplete knowledge in the presence of uncertain and complex environmental situations and/or in face of inescapable moral hazard and adverse selection.[21]
2. Opportunism: Opportunistic behaviour is not only a self-interest motivational attribute, but also self-interest with 'guile'. In Williamson's terms, 'opportunism effectively extends the assumption of self-interest seeking to make allowances to self-interest seeking with guile' (1981, p. 1545). Opportunism is a deceitful kind of self-interest seeking behaviour. This kind of opportunism is different from that of the standard economic analysis assumption that 'men will reliably fulfil their promises' (Williamson, 1986, p. 152). Opportunistic behaviour may find excuses for the non-fulfilment of promises, disclose selective pieces of information, distort information, misrepresent intentions in the form of false or empty promises regarding future contract, etc. Needless to say, not all economic actors are assumed to have such an inclination towards opportunistic behaviour; and indeed the degree of opportunistic behaviour among them may vary.[22]

Both transaction cost and agency cost theorists argue that these two behavioural assumptions, individually or in combination, have profound implications for economic organisation. Given the former, all complex contracts are unavoidably incomplete, and given the latter, contract-as-promise unsupported by credible commitments is hopelessly naive. Williamson argues that together they require the following organisational imperative: 'organise transactions so as to economise on bounded rationality while simultaneously safeguarding against transactions the hazards of opportunism' (1990, p. 12). Almost the same dictum holds from an agency viewpoint: design contracts in a way that improves the flow of information, mitigates opportunistic behaviour and motivates agents to behave in accordance with a principal's interests.

The environmental factors causing transaction costs are:

1. Small numbers: This refers to small a number of participants in bargaining market circumstances, for example, oligopolistic situations. When the number of market participants is small, bilateral monopoly situations may arise which create uncertainty and, given opportunistic behaviour, can result in substantial transaction costs.[23]
2. Uncertainty: Transactions are considered to be conducted under conditions of uncertainty. Uncertainty relates to ambiguity as to transaction definition and performance. Uncertainty together with behavioural assumptions (bounded rationality and opportunism) and small number bargaining conditions may give rise to information impactedness, i.e. asymmetrical distribution of information among the exchanging parties (some participants are better informed than others who cannot acquire the same information without substantial costs). In the presence of information impactedness, the ability of participants to make detailed plans for the future is limited, and given the initial conditions, some participants may be in an advantageous position.[24] Under these circumstances the future of details of a transaction can be settled only when uncertainty is resolved by the passage of time. Given circumstances, then, the form of organisation required is adaptive.[25]

Williamson calls the combined effect of all these conditions 'atmosphere', which refers to the nature of the exchange process itself. He summarises the interactive effects of all these human and environmental factors as follows:

> ... associate bounded rationality with uncertainty/complexity on the one hand and opportunism with a small-numbers exchange relations on the other hand. Information impactedness is a derived condition, mainly due to uncertainty and opportunism, which in turn can give rise to a small-numbers result. That exchange takes place within a trading atmosphere ... that surrounds the human and environmental factors which appear in the organisational failures framework (Williamson, 1975, p. 39).

He argues that the atmosphere can influence the way people interact, by affecting the attitudes and behaviour of individuals. Note that the atmosphere describes virtually the same situations under which agency problems arise and influence business behaviour.[26] The atmosphere affects both production and transaction/agency costs, and the choice of modes of organising transactions or agency relations.[27] The atmosphere can thus be seen as a multiple-exit situation, in terms of Latsis, where the obvious course of action is not determined uniquely by objective conditions. Ostensibly, governance/incentive structures, by definition, involve some authority and conscious and discretional planning. But, note that further discretional decisions are now seen merely in terms of improving the efficiency of the firm rather than fulfilling grand, inspiring plans for competitive advantage, as is assumed by the industrial organisation approaches (the S-C-P, Chicago School, and game-theoretical approach).

Also, note that under the atmospheric situations not only uncertainty and imperfect information but also psychological and social psychological behaviours prevail and affect the way the firm behaves. The psychological, situational and cognitive assumptions seems to be consistent with or reinforce those of strategic management. Clearly, under the atmospheric conditions, as strategy theorists assume, strategic phenomena appear to be the case. The atmospheric conditions explain why markets and firms fail in operating smoothly. The assumptions individually and their atmospheric outcome together describe an environment in which exchange/agency relations besides production operations are problematic, and need to be managed, and managed efficiently. Under competitive conditions organisations will seek hierarchical and incentive structures that economise on transaction/agency costs since the choice of governance/incentive structures influences efficiency.

In both theories, the firm behaviour is a function of market circumstances, economising and strategic considerations, and the internal compliance process, the latter three being in turn affected by organisational form. Williamson suggests a typology of organisational forms based on the informational properties of different organisational configurations. In particular, he suggests two basic organisational forms or structures: the U-form (the unitary form or functionally organised single business firm in which each operating unit performs a specialised function, such as marketing, finance and manufacturing, in collaboration with all of the specialised units), and the M-form (multidivisional organisation which consists of a set of functionally self-contained operating business divisions). Within the former organisation at the top of the hierarchy is the chief executive officer (CEO) who is responsible for both strategic decisions and day-to-day operations of functions. However, the latter form is characterised by a separation of strategic decisions which is left to general office and the day-to-day operating decisions which are left to the divisional managers. In other words, within an M-form firm top management is assumed to be specialised in 'performing strategic planning (diversification, acquisition, divestiture, and related activities)' (Williamson, 1985, p. 284). Fama and Jensen suggest another typology of organisational form based on the nature and type of agency problems that organisations face (Fama and Jensen, 1983).[28] They also recognise the hierarchical distinction between strategic decisions and day-to-day operations.

The recognition of hierarchical relationship between organisational decisions endorses explicitly the 'strategic' side of management: how 'allocative control over strategic decision-making' and 'operational control over the production process' interact to achieve the 'long term' organisational objectives (such as maximising the value or performance of the firm). In other words, they provide a conceptual framework within which the interaction between 'strategic role of top management' and 'operational role of lower levels' can be dealt with. The theories presume that contractual structure, and therefore organisational form, shapes the allocative parameters within which operational decisions and mechanisms are formulated and implemented. Contractual structures also indicate some sort of relatively permanent establishments. But, contractual structure or the set of the rules of the decision making and human interaction is not wholly determined. It changes over time in response to the changing ways in which the decision making and human interaction takes place. Therefore, contractual structure or the form of organisations is assumed to be endogenous, and thus changeable, subject to the human factors.

Before proceeding, it seems useful to touch upon the Willamson's criticism of strategic thinking and research on the basis of their power considerations, and neglecting of efficiency considerations in their explanation of economic organisation. He argues that most firms lack market power that is routinely assumed by strategy literature. He distinguishes two kinds of power, the market power (positioning approach) and resource dependency (resource-based approach). With reference to the first, for him, economising is more fundamental than market power considerations because market power advantages are temporary. 'It is fatuous', for him, therefore, 'to ascribe strategic importance to temporary market advantages' (Williamson, 1991, p. 80). With reference to the second kind of power, resource dependency, he asserts that it does not also play a significant role in the transaction cost construct 'both because initial endowments are ordinarily taken as *given* and because the contracting process is examined in its entirety' (emphasis added) (Williamson, 1991, p. 80). He points out that taking endowments as given is, for the heuristic reason, in order to isolate particular problems to start somewhere. In this respect, net gain opportunities from resource dependency are, in theory, assumed away.

However, it is highly difficult to separate efficiency and power considerations altogether. As Malcomson (1984) forcefully argues in the context of (labour) power considerations, the existence of transaction costs themselves is precisely one of the sources that gives firms market power. Under perfect competition conditions of market-clearing equilibrium there would be no transaction costs, so that there would be no possibility of market power exercises. But, when anything that results in markets not clearing, more generally, when markets do not clear, because markets are either not perfectly competitive (the idiosyncratic exchange case) or do not function well (prices do not reflect all necessary information for exchange or planning), there will be substantial transaction costs, and 'the existence of transactions costs allows the existence of market power ...' (Malcomson, 1984, p. 125). This is so because, given substantial transaction costs under the atmospheric conditions, many efforts to economise, such as organisational form, internal incentives and controls, and inter- and intra-firm contractual interfaces, which Williamson discusses, might well result in market power (competitive advantage), even if that power is not exercised. In other words, economic efficiency without market power is a characteristic of equilibria of well-functioning perfectly competitive markets. However, under the atmospheric conditions, efficiency is not a characteristic of equilibria, but, on the contrary, of disequilibria, and thus a source of competitive advantage.

Secondly, Williamson argues that market power is not worth exploiting because of its temporary nature. To him, 'efficiency will always win out in the end'.[29] Firms should not, therefore, rely on short-run market power, which will be 'fatuous', from a strategic viewpoint. However, given that the atmospheric conditions cause markets either not to be perfectly competitive or not to function well, 'an essential feature of the world

Williamson is interested in ... is not one in which one can simply assume that economic efficiency will win out in the end' (Malcomson, 1984, p. 126). Competitive advantages are the outcomes of the atmospheric conditions and hence can be used and sustained only where these conditions exist. In this regard, it can be put forward a counterargument that advantages might well persist, given continuity of the atmospheric conditions. In fact, strategy theorists may develop the argument of the persistency of competitive advantages given the same set of conditions. Moreover, as we argued above, transaction cost theorists, *inter alia*, use such a language about the temporarity of competitive advantages (market power in their terms) that does not correspond to an observable reality; thereby the degree of verisimilitude cannot be assessed.

## Conclusions

Transaction cost theory attempts to provide a rationale for the existence of the firm, its boundaries and internal organisation. Agency theory tries to provide a deeper understanding of organisational aspect of the firm from the divergence of interest between economic actors (agency problem) viewpoint. In other words, the former focuses on the governance structures which administer transactions between parties, the latter is more concerned with the incentives that are used to structure the agency relationship. Both theories use contracting as a basis for analysing governance structures or incentive structures in contractual relationship. In explaining contract structure, and therefore organisational form, they rely on a similar set of hard core assumptions, especially behavioural assumptions (bounded rationality and opportunism), and take an evolutionary perspective. Therefore, their promises for strategy theory are on the same footing.

They conceptualise a problematic situation due to opportunistic inclinations of economic actors in face of observability and information problems. This provides a basis for the explanation why managerial hierarchical structures and incentive structures are called into action. Management must contend with internal workings of the firm, more specifically, the internal organisational structure, incentive systems and control mechanisms. Thus, they provide a valuable framework for strategic management thinking since it explains why there is a need for management, and moreover, a good (strategic) management in governing internal affairs of the firm to achieve its long-term objectives.

From the institutional perspective, firms as governance structures or nexus of contracts are considered to vary in the way they manage transactions (e.g. in the form of contracts between the principal and agent) and in their internal procedures, incentive regimes, and control systems. Thus they differ in their performance outcomes. At any time, each firm will therefore have differential advantages and/or disadvantages with respect to others. Firms' superior profit differentials may persist for a period of time because of the slow pace of market evolution. Yet, market competition is not a well-developed concept within the conceptual framework of the theories.

The explanation for the sources of firm differentials, i.e. differing governance or incentive structures among firms in managing transactions, suggests a different direction towards the inquiry into firm differentials from those of the dominant approaches in the field of strategic management. As we remember, they focus on external market structure (the positioning approach) and internal firm resources and capabilities (the resource-based approach) for the inquiry of differentials. However, the theories of the new institutional economics direct attention to *formal* organisational arrangements (governance or incentive structures). Note that even the resource-based approach, which highlights internal *informal* (intangible or unobservable) aspect of the firm, neglects the formal aspect of the firm in explaining firm differentials, let alone the positioning approach, which emphasises the external (market structure and firm position within the market) aspect of the firm. Arguably, the idea of formal organisational arrangements as the source of firm differentials seems to be a challenging proposal, and may lead into new avenues illuminating strategic phenomena.

## Notes

1. For property right theory see, A. A. Alchian (1965) Some Economics of Property Rights, *Il Politico*, Vol. 30, No. 4, pp. 816-829; H. Demsetz (1967) Toward a Theory of Property Rights, *American Economic Review*, Vol. 57, No. 2, pp. 347-359; H. Demsetz, (1983) The Structure of Ownership and the Theory of the Firm, *Journal of Law and Economics*, Vol. 26, No. 2, pp. 375-90; O. Hart (1995) *Firms, Contracts and Financial Structure*, Oxford: Clarendon Press.
2. For an explanation how the three theories are connected, see O.E. Williamson (1985) *The Economic Institutions of Capitalism*, New York: Free Press, pp. 23-29.
3. In a later study, *The Problem of Social Cost*, published in 1960, Coase went a step further and recognised another coordinator or governance structure, the law and the state, for the coordination of economic activities. He argued that the law and the state are also institutional devices for the allocation of resources, different to both markets and firms. Thus, he recognised a multi-institutional market economy. See, R.H. Coase (1960) The Problem of Social Cost, *The Journal of Law and Economics*, Vol. 3, pp. 1-44.

4. It should also be pointed out that an increasing emphasis has been put on asset specificity (specialisation of assets with respect to use or users) a key factor in explaining when markets will fail and be replaced by hierarchical organisations. Williamson argues that the existence of asset specificity is a prerequisite for the existence of transactional problems in contractual situations. For more details see Williamson (1985), pp. 31-32.
5. Jensen (1983) describes two approaches to the development of a theory of agency which he labels the 'principal-agent' and the 'positive theory of agency'. The former generally has a mathematical and non-empirical orientation, the latter has a non-mathematical and empirical focus. In this study we examine only the latter.
6. See Williamson (1985), pp. 23-32. For a more detail comparison between transaction cost economics and agency theory, see Williamson, O.E. (1988) Corporate Finance and Corporate Governance, *The Journal of Finance*, Vol. 43, pp. 567-591. In the latter source, in particular in the first section, Williamson observes that 'terminology aside, in what ways do agency theory and transaction-cost economics differ? ... My "objective" view is that these two perspectives are mainly complementary' (pp. 567-568). Then he goes on to identify commonalties and leading differences between the two theories of the firm. In fact, agency theory focuses on transactions as well, but in a specific form, in the form of contracts between the principal and agent.
7. See Jensen and Meckling (1976), especially pp. 308-310. Also, note that agency costs are seen predominantly from an *ex ante* incentive-alignment in point of view, while transaction costs are seen from an *ex post* governance structure point of view.
8. Note that the organisational problem (how a group of self-interest-seeking individuals bound by some common purpose to achieve the firm's objectives) is implied but not solved by the neoclassical theory of the firm. There, theorists have dealt with maximising behaviour but left out of concern the problem of self-seeking interest behaviour, which is the other part of rationality assumption.
9. Fama and Jensen (1983). Alongside the board, they suggest two more mechanism for the corporate agency problem: use of high levels of debt to commit management to payouts and hostile takeovers, which involves replacing old with new management teams.
10. For a research agenda on firm differences in organising activities, see O.E. Williamson (1991) Strategizing, Economizing, and Economic Organization, *Strategic Management Journal*, Vol. 12, pp. 75-94; and M. Aoki (1990) Knowledge: Its Acquisition, Sharing and/or Asymmetry, in M. Aoki, B. Gustafsson and O.E. Williamson (eds.) *The Firm as a Nexus of Treaties*, London: Sage Publications, pp. 26-52.
11. It should also be pointed out that in the theories the source of firm differentials is assumed to stem not only from *internal* contractual relations with employees, but also from establishing distinctive and long-term contractual relations with customers, shareholders, suppliers, creditors, etc. The distinctive set of contractual relationships can give a firm a unique advantage which its rivals (existing and potential) may lack, and find costly and time-consuming to develop.
12. Ouchi explicates this view in the context of transaction cost economics; but the view applies to agency theory even without involving modifications.
13. See Williamson (1985), pp. 26-30. Accepting that firms may gain competitive advantages for a variety of reasons via their strategising activities, Williamson argues that 'as between economising and strategising, economising is much the more fundamental' (1991: p. 75). This is because, to him, (i) strategising is relevant only to a small number of firms that possess market power, whereas economising is relevant to all firms, more generally, to all organisations; and (ii) strategising initiatives will rarely prevail if they are seriously flawed in economising respect. He forcefully asserts that

'economising is more fundamental than strategising - or, put differently, that *economy is the best strategy*' (emphasis in original) (1991, p. 76). He admits that 'economising and strategising are not mutually exclusive', (1991, p. 76) and, more often, strategising efforts can be used to promote economising outcomes, as in the case of pricing with reference to learning curve costs.

14. However, in the Porterian strategy construct, economising is, in a broad sense, one of the three generic strategies, that is, cost (economising), quality (differentiation), and focus (on a market niche). Even so, note that one important difference between the strategy and transaction cost concept of economising as a strategy is that while the former assumes economising as a way of gaining market power, the latter does not see it as a vehicle for anti-competitive behaviour (such as building up entry barriers). In fact, the 'competitive' dimension of economising as a strategy in the transaction cost construct is still poorly developed. In other words, it still deals with comparative advantage rather than competitive advantage. Nevertheless, the comparative advantage in the above sense is relevant for the study of firm differentials in performance. Whether comparative advantages lead into competitive advantages can be argued on the grounds that the conditions of transaction costs (organisational failures) are also the ones for competitive advantages, and competitive advantages can be gained as the outcome of comparative advantage (see the next section for this argument). As we recall, this rationale is employed in the Porter's argument of 'cost leadership' strategy.
15. It should be pointed out that there is a close similarity between the concept of asset specificity, one of the central elements of transaction cost explanation, and firm specific resources and capabilities, the central analytical concept in the resource-based approach. Both asset specificity and idiosyncratic resources and capabilities are chiefly intangible and expensive to develop in short time. Nevertheless, asset specificity in transaction cost economics is treated highly differently from idiosyncratic resources and capabilities in the resource-based approach. Asset specificity is assumed to exacerbate cooperation problems of effectively utilising organisational capital, in particular human capital (i.e. it is a source of transaction costs), rather than to enable the firm to seek and sustain competitive advantage.
16. Note that the formal side of the firm has been hitherto neglected in explaining strategic phenomena by strategy theorists, in particular by the resource-based theorists who focus on firm idiosyncrasies. Arguably, the formal and informal explanations complement each other in explaining strategic phenomena.
17. Alchian's evolutionary approach to economics is cited as the main authority.
18. See Jensen (1983), pp. 331-332.
19. As Barney and Ouchi maintain, 'while agency theory adopts these transaction-cost assumptions [bounded rationality and opportunism] about managers, the primary theoretical "engine" driving agency theory is not capital market failure but, rather, capital market efficiency' (p. 206). The implication of the efficient market view is not that 'firms cannot profitably do what they would like to do because of these market disciplines ... the efficient markets that surround a firm cannot be denied for long' (p. 212). (Barney, J.B. and Ouchi, W.G., 1986, Agency Theory: How Market Forces Affect the Management of a Firm, in J.B. Barney and W.G. Ouchi (eds.) *Organisational Economics*, London: Jossey-Bass Publishers, pp. 205-213.) In terms of Williamson, 'both agency theory and transaction cost economics invoke natural selection. Although agency theory assumes that natural selection processes are reliably efficacious ..., transaction cost economics is somewhat more cautious-subscribing, as it does, to weak-form rather than strong-form selection ...' (1988, p. 573).
20. As Barney and Ouchi observes, 'instead of assuming that managers are simple utility maximisers, most agency theorists adopt the assumption that managers are boundedly

rational and that they may act opportunistically. These are, of course, the same assumptions employed by transaction-cost theorists ... ' Barney and Ouchi (1986), p. 205.

21. As Williamson observes, economists of agency theory are 'reluctant to use the term bounded rationality, ... the term ... has nonetheless become the operative assumption'. Williamson (1988), pp. 569-570.
22. Again, as Williamson observes, agency theory 'refers to "moral hazard" and "agency costs" rather than opportunism. But the concerns are the same, whence these are merely terminological differences' (Williamson, 1988, p. 570).
23. It should also be pointed out that the assumption of asset specificity (specialisation of assets with respect to use or users) has been gaining significance.
24. Note that uncertainty or information impactedness in the above sense is implied by agency theory as well since agency problems arise when there is information asymmetry and uncertainty in face of moral hazard and adverse selection. As Eisenhardt argues, in agency theory, 'organisations are assumed to have uncertain futures. The future may bring prosperity, bankruptcy, or some intermediate outcome, and that future is only partly controlled by organisation members. ... Agency theory extends organisational thinking by pushing the ramifications of outcome uncertainty to their implications for creating risk. Uncertainty is viewed in terms of risk/reward trade-offs, not just in terms of inability to preplan. The implication is that outcome uncertainty coupled with differences in willingness to accept risk should influence contracts between principal and agent' (p. 65). To put it another way, as Reekie maintain, 'in risk-free situations, where the outcome of a relationship is directly observable and totally predictable ... no agency problems exist. When there is an indeterminate outcome and attitudes to risk differ between the two parties, however, then an agency problem does exist.' (Reekie, W.D., 1989, *Industrial Economics. A Critical Introduction to Corporate Enterprise in Europe and America*, Aldershot: Edward Elgar, p.175).
25. On the contrary to transaction cost concern with *ex post* governance design, agency theory is more concerned with *ex ante* incentive-alignment contracts.
26. The following statement by Eisenhardt describes a similar atmosphere: ' ... the theory identifies various contract alternatives, and ... indicates which contract is the most efficient under varying levels of outcome uncertainty, risk aversion [the risk attitudes of the principal and agent], information, and other variables [bounded rationality and opportunism] ...' Eisenhardt (1989), p. 60. To Eisenhardt, transaction cost economics and agency theory share bounded rationality and opportunism but each has unique independent variables. These are asset specificity and small numbers bargaining in the transaction cost theory; the risk attitudes of the principal and agent, outcome uncertainty, and information systems (p. 64).
27. Williamson (1985) argues that transactional difficulties and transaction costs increase when transactions are characterised by: (1) uncertainty, (2) infrequency (that is, transactions which are seldom undertaken), (3) asset specificity. 'Asset specificity has reference to the degree to which an asset can be redeployed to alternative uses and by alternative users without sacrifice of productive value' (Williamson, 1990, p. 12). Transactions require investments which are specific to the requirements of a particular exchange relationship. 'Specific' investment refers to investment which has very little or no value in alternative uses. Unspecified investments pose few hazards, but specified investments have important cost-bearing and hazardous consequences. Some theorists, in particular Alchian and Demsetz argue that asset specificity is the key to unlock a series of organisational puzzles, and even to explain the existence of the firm, without it there is no known reason for firms to exist (see, for example, A.A. Alchian and H.

Demsetz, 1972, Production, Information Costs, and Economic Organisation, *American Economic Review*, Vol. 62, pp. 777-795).

28. To them, firms can be organised as corporations, as limited partnerships, or as sole proprietorships.
29. Malcomson summarises his view so (Malcomson, 1984, p. 119).

# 'Process-Oriented' Theories of the Firm: The Theory of the Growth of the Firm and Behavioural Theory of the Firm

As we have seen, the neoclassical theory of the firm focused on resource allocation at market level. Transaction cost economics led an extension of the neoclassical research programme into problems of hierarchical or administrative resource allocation. Common to both theories seems to be over emphasising the structural features of market and firm respectively, and neglect important process issues. An alternative set of theories emerged to fill this gap, explaining economics of the firm through the passage of the time. These are, most notably, the Penrosian *Theory of the Growth of the Firm* (1959), and the Cyert, March and Simonian *Behavioural Theory of the Firm* (1963). These alternative theories broke up their bonds with traditional neoclassical approach, employing a distinctive set of analytical tools, that is, instead of using equilibrium, maximising, optimality, and marginal analysis, they introduced a distinct set of analytical tools, such as productive resources, bounded rationality, satisficing, rule following, etc.

The process-oriented theories of the firm have not gained much acceptance and coverage in the scientific community until recent decades. This neglect seemed to be because of the dominant position of neoclassical theorising and research. But the picture has been changing in favour of process-oriented theories (firm as well as market) in recent decades because of the growing unsatisfaction with explanatory power of structural theories (firm as well as market) in dealing with real world problems. These process theories of the firm have been integrated into evolutionary theory, developed by Nelson, Winter, Dosi, etc. From strategy studies point of view, the process theories of the firm (as well as market, in particular evolutionary theory) have been incorporated into strategy theorising and research, in particular, the resource-based approach, so extensively that it seems highly difficult to understand the resource-based approach to strategy, which is getting dominance in the field of strategic management in the recent decade, without the process theories of the firm (as well as market). In what follows, the Penrosian growth theory is first examined, then the behavioural theory will be examined.

# Chapter 9

# The Theory of the Growth of the Firm

## Introduction

It should be pointed out at the outset that, while developing a *Theory of the Growth of the Firm* (1959), Penrose did not seem to be aware of the Coase's article, *On the Nature of the Firm* (1937), or, at least, she did not make any reference to it. Therefore, the Penrosian growth theory was not developed as an alternative to transaction cost theory, but emerged out of a criticism of the neoclassical theory of the firm, in which there was no satisfactory explanation of the reasons for, and way of the growth of the firm. Nevertheless, her conception of the firm as an administrative organisation (1) constituting a bundle of heterogeneous resources for the purpose of producing goods and services for sale on the market, (2) directed and controlled by its managers who will be strongly motivated towards growth, and (3) whose boundaries are determined by its managerial capacity, supplies a distinctive view on the nature of the firm from that of transaction cost approach, although they are largely consistent with each other. To some extent this will be touched upon below.

In essence, Penrose was interested in building a theory of the *growth* of the firm, but in doing so, she also constituted a 'foundation' for a theory of the *firm* on which the growth aspect of the firm phenomenon could be based, and thereby examined. In this respect, the theory is versatile in many respects. But, as She did, we focus, mainly, on the analysis of the growth behaviour of the firm. Growth behaviour of the firm, in the Penrose' conception, is a matter of a historical process, and based on the cumulative effect of the firm's idiosyncratic (collective) knowledge and purposive investment decisions.

## Problem Area: Conceptualising the Firm as a Repository of Productive Resources

In her introductory chapter, Penrose clearly expresses the problem area of her inquiry:

> I am not asking what determines whether a particular firm can grow, but rather the very different question: assuming that some firms can grow, what principles will then govern their growth, and how fast and how long can they grow? Or alternatively, assuming that there are opportunities for expansion in an economy, what determines the kind of firm that will take advantage of them and to what extent? (Penrose, 1959, p. 7).

In so posing her questions for investigation, she does not subscribe to a model building approach for the examination, starting with stating necessary and sufficient conditions (which one cannot determine in advance, she argues) for successful growth, thus enabling us to make *determinate model predictions* on *a priori* grounds (fictitious time), rather, she follows an analytical way of dealing with the phenomenon, thereby offering a *basis* for predicting a firm's size and rate of growth at any particular future time (historical time).

In her inquiry into principles governing the growth of the firm, she looked at the dominant neoclassical paradigm for the answer. Given the conditions of equilibrium analysis, the underlying logic behind the neoclassical theory of the firm necessitates a position of 'optimum size' of the firm. In other words, of the two variables, prices and quantities, only the latter is under the discretion of the firm since the firm is assumed to be price-taker. Then, given 'equilibrium prices', the 'equilibrium of the firm' is, in essence, the 'equilibrium output' level that the firm could produce for a given product or a group of products. Therefore, the question of what limits the size of the firm in the neoclassical construct becomes the question of what limits the amount of output it will produce of the given product or products. The crucial question in turn becomes what prevents the indefinite expansion of output of the individual firm. Two explanations were basically offered in the construct: an upward-sloping supply curve (the firm's long-run average cost curve is assumed to be U-shaped, so that there is assumed to be an 'optimum' point of size of the firm, where the level of output corresponds to the lowest point of the U) due to technological or managerial diseconomies to scale under conditions of perfect competition, or a downward-sloping demand curve (falling revenue as additional quantities of the product are produced) under conditions of imperfect competition.

Penrose argued that, regarding the idea of technological diseconomies, given the possibility of expansion by multi-plant operation, the technological diseconomies of scale did not seem, on theoretical grounds, satisfactory. As to the idea of managerial diseconomies (management's greater difficulty of coordinating a large organisation), she argued, implicit in it was the treatment of management as a 'fixed factor'. In establishing causation between the nature of the 'fixity' and the nature of the managerial task of 'coordination' there have not been satisfactory identifications, on theoretical grounds. On empirical grounds, there was certainly evidence that managerial diseconomies did exist, however, large firms, even the very largest ones, appeared extremely successful and there was no evidence at all that they were managed inefficiently, and were unable effectively to compete with smaller firms. The second idea, downward-sloping demand curve was also rejected, on the theoretical grounds. She argued that implicit in the idea that the firm was limited by its original market, it nevertheless always had possibility to diversify into other product markets, when appropriate resources are available.

In other words, Penrose rejected the neoclassical explanations in two respects: management is not a fixed factor and the firm always has possibility to diversify into new markets. She observed that behind the notion of managerial fixity lay the neoclassical 'mono-brain' conception of the firm, thus, given the implicit indication that the capacity of any human being is finite, they assumed that the limited capacity of the individual would limit the size of firms. However, the firm is not 'single-minded', on the contrary, it is an administrative framework in which a managerial team and resources are bound together. Also, she found no reason why a firm should confine itself to its existing products only. However, given the fact that a firm is endowed with productive resources that can be used in many ways and can be increased by the acquisition of additional resources, she argued that, there are many reasons why a firm should search for opportunities of using its productive resources more effectively.

Thus, on these grounds, she released the size of the firm from these two constraints assumed by neoclassics. So, what does then determine the firm's growth and necessarily limit its rate of growth? The direction-setting answer to this question given by Penrose was based on an endogenous view of growth. She argued that there must be something *inherent* in the very nature of the firm that promotes its growth as well as necessarily limits its rate of growth.

Thus she turned her enlarger of inquiry onto the 'inside' of the firm. She observed that 'a firm is both an administrative organisation and a pool of productive resources' (Penrose, 1971a, p. 43). In planning expansion, the firm considers two categories of resources: inherited resources available in the firm and obtainable resources from market. In order to carry out the expansion program,

> all expansion must draw on some services of the firm's existing management and consequently the services available from such management set a fundamental limit to the amount of expansion that can be either planned or

> executed even if all other resources are obtainable in the market (Penrose, 1971a, p. 43).

In other words, particular emphasis was put on managerial services. She argued that a 'single-mind' alone cannot do everything by himself or herself, by contrast, the managerial task in large corporations that tend to grow must be performed by a managerial group. In other words, the workload that an existing managerial group can undertake is, at any point of time, limited, and managerial group takes time to establish. Therefore, managerial services required for the management of growth, at any one moment, determines the firm's growth and necessarily limits its rate of growth. Thus, the idea of managerial constraint was reached. The idea of managerial constraint in the above sense was Penrose's most innovative view in explaining the growth of the firm.

Note that Penrose still keeps the essence of the idea of managerial diseconomies, i.e. the firm's size is limited by the inability of the firm's management to handle the coordiantion problems, but she now sees it 'not a static phenomenon, related to scale, but a dynamic, transient problem which is more related to the rate of growth' (Slater, 1980, p. xii), not its absolute size. Also note that she assumes that the managerial constraint is the *determining* factor on the firm's growth, nevertheless, she also recognises a number of *affecting* factors, such as the market opportunities available to the firm to internalise.

The managerial constraint is coined by Marris as the 'Penrose effect' (Marris, 1964). The idea of the Penrose or managerial effect has been incorporated into a variety of micro- and macroeconomics, in particular in the field known as 'the Corporate Economy'. The idea was most used in the Marris' *The Economic Theory of Managerial Capitalism* (1964). Marris suggested a formal model of growth equilibrium in which management derives utility from growth. He argued that there are increasing costs of growth in terms of profits, therefore, more and more growth may depress the stock-market value of the company below the level that could potentially be gained. In this respect, growth will be limited by the fear of takeover. In the last two decades the Penrosian resource-based view of growth has also been substantially incorporated into evolutionary theory (Nelson and Winter, 1982), in particular in terms of the firm's specific resources and skills being developed as routines within the firm, which give impetus to innovate and expand.

Before proceeding to examine the theory from the strategic viewpoint, it should be briefly compared with transaction cost economics. The Penrosian growth theory is built on the assumption of firm heterogeneity in resources. As we remember, transaction cost theory assumes homogeneity of firms in this respect, but makes the assumption of the existence of transaction costs in using markets for theory building. The growth theory also recognises the existence of transaction costs, but they are not assumed to be decisive factors in internalising activities. Nevertheless, in spite of different departure points for theory building, they arrive at similar conclusions. Like transaction cost theory, the growth theory also recognises the essential differences between market organisation and firm organisation, as Penrose puts it: 'The essential difference between economic activity inside the firm and economic activity in the 'market' is that the former is carried on within an administrative organisation, while the latter is not (Penrose, 1959, p. 15).

Nevertheless, Penrose does not use the dichotomy (market versus hierarchy) reasoning of transaction cost theorists in explaining the boundary between administrative and market coordination. The dichotomy logic necessitates a state of equilibrium between market and firm. This is, in essence, a static approach. However, Penrose approaches the boundary problem of the firm from a dynamic viewpoint, and does not make any assumption of equilibrium. Given that growth is a matter of process, the firm may not reach an equilibrium state:

> The attainment of such a 'state of rest' is precluded by three significant obstacles: those arising from the familiar difficulties posed by the indivisibility of resources; those arising from the fact that the same resources can be used differently under different circumstances, and in particular, in a 'specialised' manner; and those arising because in the ordinary processes of operation and expansion new productive services are continually being created (Penrose, 1959, p. 68).

The boundaries of the firm are assumed to be determined not by comparative costs considerations of organising activities either by using market or administration, but, instead, by particularly unused managerial resources, which require time-consuming, and thereby costly efforts to imitate. In this respect, growth is, essentially, a source of competitive advantage since those firms that have unused productive resources are able to take advantage of opportunities in a growing market. The primary purpose of the firm, is not to economise on transaction costs, but 'to make use of productive resources for the purpose of supplying goods and services to the economy' (Penrose, 1959, p. 15) for 'a desire to increase total long-run profits' (Penrose, 1959, p. 29). Therefore, 'from the point of view of investment (make-or-buy) policy, *growth and profits become equivalent as the criteria for the selection of investment programmes*' (emphasis in original) (Penrose, 1959, p. 30).

## Heterogeneity in Firm Resource Endowments as the Source of Persistent Competitive Advantage

Penrose observed that the collection of human and other productive resource endowments that each firm has at any particular time are unequal and firm-specific, and it is these unequal firm specific endowments that determine the set of opportunities of which it can take advantage. In Penrose's words:

> It is the heterogeneity, and not the homogeneity, of the productive services available or potentially available from its resources that gives each firm its unique character. Not only can the personnel of the firm render heterogeneous variety of unique services, but also the material resources of the firm can be used in different ways, which means that they can provide different kinds of services (Penrose, 1959, p. 75).

This was the answer given by her to the research question that she set out at the outset, i.e. 'assuming that there are opportunities for expansion in an economy, what determines the kind of firm that will take advantage of them and to what extent?' (Penrose, 1959, p. 7). More clearly, she observed that it is the firm specific resource position that determines the kind of firm that will take advantage of market opportunities in a growing economy.

The research question and the answer given lies at the very centre of the resource-based view in the field of strategic management. In fact, in the development of the resource-based view, the growth theory played a central role and supplied a firm foundation to it, since common to both was the view that it is the firm's specific resources, not product market opportunities, that are sources and determinants of its persistent competitive advantage.[1] In both constructs 'growth [and competition] is [assumed to be] governed by a creative and dynamic interaction between a firm's productive resources and its market opportunities' (Penrose, 1971a, p. 43), but it was, in the final analysis, the resource position that is assumed to determine the competitive position of the firm and the direction of its growth. Thus, for them, the primary focus of analysis should not be product-market opportunities or positions of the firm, but the internal resources that enable the firm to take advantage of opportunities.

Available resources are assumed to limit competitive ability and expansion on the one hand, and productive resources (in particular unused ones including technological and entrepreneurial), which it is assumed to exist at all times within every firm, are 'a challenge to innovate, an incentive to expand, and a source of competitive advantage' (Penrose, 1971a, p. 44). Yet, she maintained that in many cases the ability of a firm to use these resources 'depends on increases in knowledge and improvements of technique' (Penrose, 1971b, p. 36). In other words, a firm achieves competitive advantage not because it has better resources, but rather because of its ability to make better use of its resources.

The view of unused resources as a challenge and incentive for innovation, expansion, and of the necessity to make better use of them for competitive advantage was also developed by Hamel and Prahalad, from the resource-based approach. In a more proactive manner, they argued that it is the resourcefulness of the firm, i.e. the way an organisation uses, supplements, and upgrades its resources as stretch and leverage, not existing resources, that provide competitive advantages (Hamel, and Prahalad, 1993). The view of unused and better use of resources as a challenge, incentive and source of competitive advantage provides not only a basis for the explanation of a sustainable growth but also that of a dynamic and continuous strategic struggle for competitive advantage, in contrast to that of the static and one-off first mover advantage explanations, as is the case in the structure-conduct-performance theory of industrial organisation.

As to the question of the persistency of firm differentials, the Penrosian growth theory also provides a profound and satisfactory explanation. It should be pointed out that the question was not directly addressed in a manner to indicate how competitive advantages can be sustained, but it has been touched upon at several occasions where the question of the sustained growth was discussed. In this respect, although it does not give a systematic explanation of the problem of persistency among firms, it recognises and illuminates it on many grounds.

To start with, as we said above, she argues that managerial resources are a bottleneck factor in the process of growth in that not only do they prevent the firm growing indefinitely but they also take time to develop. In other words, managerial resources cannot be developed at once. They can only be created and improved in the passage of time. Therefore, this time impediment may prevent equalising differentials for a long period of time.

That the reason behind the idea of managerial resources as a bottleneck factor is given by Penrose is that the development of managerial resources involve both socialisation processes as well as the difficulty of passing on substantive knowledge. To Penrose, managerial resources or, more specifically, managerial groups, are not just a collection of individuals, but one interacting as a team, accumulating experience by interacting, and establishing itself through the passage of time:

> Businessmen commonly refer to the managerial group as a "team" and the use of this word implies that management in some sense works as a unit. An

> administrative group is something more than a collection of individuals; it is a collection of individuals who have had experience in working together, for only in this way can "teamwork" be developed. Existing managerial personnel provide services that cannot be provided by personnel newly hired from outside the firm (Penrose, 1959, p. 45).

In other words, managerial resources are not based on individuals' skills, which can be bought in factor markets whenever needed, but 'organisation specific skills' developed within the firm as the outcome of long-term teamwork, trial, learning, and evolution. In this respect, managerial resources are more than human capital. Rather they are 'social capital', as Coleman (1988) describes, created through interpersonal relations, like 'organisational culture', as Barney (1986a) might call it. Therefore, they can not be easily replicated elsewhere.

The other reason given is the difficulty in transmitting experiential knowledge attached to individuals. This second reason seems to be complementary to the first one, but more on an individual basis. She distinguishes two categories of knowledge on the basis of their nature of transmittability: objective knowledge, which is independent of any particular individual or group of individuals and can be transmitted on equal terms in many formal ways such as books or blueprints, and experiential knowledge, which is 'the result of learning, but learning in the form of personal experience ... [and] itself can never be transmitted; it produces a change-frequently a subtle change-in individuals and cannot be separated from them' (Penrose, 1959, p. 53). This implies, if we simply need to replace 'person' by 'firm' that experiential knowledge is by its nature highly specific, tacit, and intangible. It cannot be transmitted or transferred from one firm to another without some kind of loss. In other words, experiential knowledge specific to a particular firm cannot be decoded and imitated by competitors.

Note that both notions, managerial resources and experiential knowledge, were captured by Nelson and Winter (1982) in the concept of firm routines in the sense of organisational learning, path dependencies, uncodifiability of knowledge embedded in routines, etc. Hence, to them, it is routines that determine the organisational capabilities, and thereby sustainable competitive advantage.

## Hard Core Assumptions: A Middle Ground Position Between Situational Determinism and Situational Indeterminism

Penrose did not specify in a systematic way the conditions under which the growth of the firm, as such, takes place. Nevertheless, scattered throughout her book are references, sometimes detailed, that she makes about them. These initial conditions that we identified as hard core assumptions of the theory are very similar to those of evolutionary theory. The hard core assumptions can be enumerated as follows:

1. Uncertainty: The environment in which the firm is supposed to grow is essentially uncertain. She clearly points out in several places that environment is not something 'out there' or an objective fact, but it is subjective in its offerings to how observers perceive it. In her terms:

   > The environment has been treated not as an objective 'fact' but rather as an 'image' in the entrepreneur's mind; the justification for this procedure is the assumption that it is not the environment 'as such', but rather the environment as the entrepreneur sees it, that is relevant for his actions (Penrose, 1959, p. 215).

   In fact, uncertainty as such is not a feature of external environment, but a quality of decision maker. In this respect, she argues that the effect of uncertainty on the behaviour of the firm must be in essence considered as 'subjective' uncertainty. She traces subjective uncertainty to two sources: temperament (for example, self-confidence) and awareness on the part of decision maker that he or she possesses insufficient information about factors expected to determine the future course of events. Both factors are interrelated in the sense that uncertainty stemming from the awareness that one has insufficient information gives rise also to a lack of confidence in the soundness of the judgements that lie behind any given plan of action. To eliminate lack of confidence in the completeness of planning, decision makers attempt to gather further information, yet no amount of obtainable information can completely eliminate 'uncertainty' because of 'the fact that the future can never be known with accuracy' (Penrose, 1959, p. 56). Therefore, growth plans must be based on expectations about the future which are held with varying degrees of confidence.
2. Bounded Rationality: Although Penrose does not use the concept of 'bounded rationality', the idea is there. The assumption of bounded

rationality very closely relates to that of uncertainty. Note that uncertainty, as she understands, refers to the decision makers' confidence in his expectations. The expectations of a firm, i.e. the way in which it interprets its environment, depends its resource position, more clearly, the personal qualities of its decision makers. In this respect, bounded rationality indicates the *psychological* dimension of the decision makers, which has been put forward by Simon introducing the notion of bounded rationality, and will be examined in the following chapter.[2]

Suffice to say here that, to Penrose, it is not 'objective facts' but 'expectations' that are immediate determinants of a firm's behaviour, although there may be a relation between them. The degree of the growth of the firm or of taking advantage of opportunities is assumed to be restricted to the extent to which the firm does not see opportunities for expansion, underestimates their future value, or is unwilling to act upon them. Given bounded rationality, hence, no firm ever perceives the complete range of opportunities and possible services available from unused resources, because the range of opportunities and services recognised is for the most part confined by the management's existing ideas as to the perceived state of the environment and possible combinations of resources.

To Penrose, the neoclassical assumption of 'complete rationality' means (1) that decision makers are supposed to 'know absolutely the consequences of their acts when they are performed, and to perform them in the light of the consequences' (Penrose, 1959, p. 55),[3] and (2) the knowledge is assumed to be 'objective', which is uniformly accessible to everybody.

As stated earlier, the knowledge is not assumed to be objective, but of an experiential kind that leads to growth initiations, and is thereby not accessible to everybody, and uncertainty is unavoidable even though it forces the firm to gather information, digest, and reach conclusions about the possibilities of actions which the firm has not confidence. Note that the neoclassical assumption indicates that predictions or expectations are always correct. However, in the growth theory decision makers are likely to fail in their efforts to predict the consequences of any actions taken, and, therefore expectations may not be correct.

3. Unused Productive Services: It is assumed that at all times there exists within every firm, pools of unused productive services. The unused services do not often exist in the visible form of idle man-

hours but rather in the concealed form of unused abilities. If there is not scope for the full use of the unused services in the firm, a pressure to expand will be exerted on the firm. The existence of the unused services in the firm is of significance for exploiting the 'external' opportunities for expansion as perceived by the firm. If they can be used profitably, they may provide a competitive advantage for the firm possessing them.

4. Heterogeneity of firms: All firms, like individuals, are different in terms of their resources and capabilities at any moment of time. Their resource and capability positions with respect to the external world provide the frame of reference from which external phenomena are approached and the point of origin of all plans for actions.
5. The Existence of the Opportunities for Expansion: There always exist market opportunities for expansion, and some firms will always see them and take advantage of them. Market opportunities may arise from growing demand for particular products, changes in technology, discoveries and inventions, etc. The environmental conditions are not given, rather they can be altered by the activities of firms. Therefore, opportunities are not independent of firms' activities.
6. Markets for Managerial Factors are Imperfect: Productive resources required for the management of growth are firm-specific. They cannot be instantaneously imported or purchased at full efficiency from factor markets. In other words, managerial resources are not in perfectly supply. Managerial resources required for growth must be developed within the firm, as has been explained above. Their development is time consuming as well as costly.

It should be, first of all, pointed out that, given the hard core assumptions, the growth theory, like evolutionary theory, can be located between neoclassical research programme of 'situational determinism' and Austrian research programme of 'situational indeterminism'. This middle ground position recognises both entrepreneurial creativity, and of the firms' state of unused productive services in a given time, as the determinants of the behaviour of the firm. Both shape together the scope, direction and rate of growth of the firm.

The above mentioned assumptions clearly describe an environment in which strategic behaviour of the firm is required. The growth in the above sense is itself a strategic activity, and thereby the management of growth essentially involves strategic management. In terms of Penrose, decisions for expansion are *enterprising* decisions in the sense of being in search of prospective profitability:

> The decision ... to investigate the prospective profitability of expansion is an enterprising decision, in the sense [of] ... committing resources to the investigation of whether there are further opportunities of which it is not yet aware. This is a decision which depends on the 'enterprise' of the firm and not on sober calculations ... (Penrose, 1959, p. 33).

She points out that assuming that firms are 'in search' of profits already implies some degree of enterprise since it is not an automatic task that no particular quality of enterprise is involved. Note that this is exactly opposite to the assumption of marginal calculation, which requires no particular quality of enterprise. She argues that, 'in any case, the decision to search for opportunities is an enterprising decision and require entrepreneurial intuition and imagination. Furthermore, she clearly argues that 'enterprise is by no means a homogeneous characteristic, and the 'quality' of enterprise, that is to say, the particular types of entrepreneurial service available to a firm, is of *strategic* importance in determining its growth' (emphasis added) (Penrose, 1959, p. 35).

In fact, the growth theory recognises strategic intent in consciously differentiating itself for competitive purposes. As Penrose puts it, 'growth is essentially an evolutionary process ... in the context of a purposive firm' (Penrose, 1995, p. xiii). In other words, 'successful expansion must, in the usual case, be preceded by planning on the part of the firm. Firms do not just grow automatically, but in response to human decisions' (Penrose, 1971b, p. 31). Without the idea of a purposive firm, at least to some extent, there would be no room for strategic behaviour of a firm to play a significant role in determining its competitive position and growth. This point was forcefully made by Penrose (1952) in her discussion with Alchian (1950), who, from a biological viewpoint, argued that firms that make profits are selected by the environment, and others are rejected, without seeing necessary whether firms consciously try to make profits or not. She argued that the biological variant of the growth approach leaves no room for human motivation and conscious decision, and that it should be rejected on that ground. Although sharing with the biological variant the same view that a predisposition to grow is inherent in the very nature of firms, she insisted that growth depends on human motivation as is the case of the businessman's search for profit. As we remember, firm discretion is one of the cornerstones in evolutionary theory put forward by Nelson and Winter (1982) as well.

## Conclusions

The Penrosian growth theory represents a non-neoclassical theory of the firm in contrast to neoclassically-inclined transaction cost theory, which is in essence an extension of neoclassical market theory to cover firm theory. The departure point for theorising in the growth construct is the assumption of firm heterogeneity in resources, which is taken as given in the transaction cost construct. The Penrosian growth theory offers a very versatile ground for strategy theorising and research since it offers very convincing explanations for both the sources and mechanism of persistent firm differentials in profitability. Its central assumptions about firm heterogeneity in resources, productive resources as a bottleneck factor due to their time consuming development processes, untradebility, and costly-to-imitate features, and growth as an investment policy being equivalent for a search for long term profits are all not only consistent with strategic management theorising, but also suggests a highly compelling research agenda into the persistent firm differentials in profitability.

In fact, the growth theory has already been extensively used in the field of strategic management either directly, or indirectly through evolutionary theory of which it constitutes a significant part. The environment under which growth is assumed to take place is also assumed to involve strategic behaviour on the part of individual firms. In this respect, decisions for growth are considered to be strategic (enterprising) decisions. In short, the growth theory, like evolutionary theory, suggests an alternative paradigm or research programme to the neoclassical theory of the firm, and its variant, transaction cost economics. And, it offers a much more basis for strategic theorising and research than its counterparts.

### Notes

1. See, for example, B. Wernerfelt (1984) A Resource-based View of the Firm, *Strategic Management Journal*, Vol. 5, pp. 171-180.
2. See H.A. Simon (1976) From Substantive to Procedural Rationality, in S.J. Latsis (ed) *Method and Appraisal in Economics*, Cambridge: Cambridge University Press, pp. 129-148.
3. She makes this quotation from F.H. Knight (1921) *Risk, Uncertainty and Profit*, Boston: Houghton Mifflin, p. 77.

## Chapter 10

# Behavioural Theory of the Firm

### Introduction

The behavioural theory of the firm also emerged out of a critique of the neoclassical theory of the firm in early 1960s in the work of, most notably, Simon (1959), and Cyert and March (1963) of American Carnegie School. They questioned whether firms could engage in the type of rationality, i.e. global maximising rationality, postulated in the neoclassical construct, and proposed an alternative set of behavioural concepts. Simon introduced the concepts of bounded rationality and satisficing in his explanation of organisational decision making processes. Cyert and March joined economic and behavioural approaches to understanding firm behaviour. Thus a new paradigm emerged in the field.

Behavioural assumptions have showed a wide influence on both economic and strategic management literature. But the influence of the theory as a whole has been negligible due to the lack of its predictive ability, and perhaps, of the dominance of neoclassical paradigm in economics discipline. Nevertheless, the behavioural theory, in particular its set of behavioural assumptions, has been integrated into evolutionary theory developed by Nelson and Winter (1982), thus has gained a new momentum recently. Behavioural assumptions have also played a significant role in the theoretical and empirical studies of the 'process' of strategy formation or strategic decision making.

### Problem Area: Conceptualising the Firm as a Coalition of Interacting Groups

As we remember, in the neoclassical construct, the firm is assumed to have a single decision criteria (profit maximising) and an ability to get all information that it needs to make decisions from the external market. In other words, the information encoded in prices received from the market is assumed to enable the firm to apply its decision criteria. The rest will be done by the market, that is, the competitive system then proceeds to allocate resources and produce output. Apparently, the emphasis in this construct is on external market. There is no room for analysis of the internal decision-making processes, nor are there any organisational problems. In the construct, all of the empirical content is assumed to be *a priori*, i.e. the firm behaviour can be deduced from the propositions that describe the external environment (Cyert and March, 1963, pp. 4-16).

The behavioural theorists attempted to give more empirical content to the theory of the firm by specifying some aspects of the firm's behaviour. They concentrated on making empirical analyses of decision processes of individual firms and on incorporating the results into models of the firm. Thus, they aimed to study how firms really do take decisions in practice, instead of hypothesising about how rational men respond (or should respond) to various situations.

Towards this end, they did not feel that a simple integration of an organisation-centred and market-centred theory of the firm would be adequate to explain the behaviour of the firm. Therefore, they started, instead, to build up an alternative theory of the firm. In constructing a new theory, they exposed their aims as follows:

> *Our conception of the task we face is that of constructing a theory that takes* (1) *the firm as its basic unit,* (2) *the prediction of firm behaviour with respect to such decisions as price, output, and resource allocation as its objective, and* (3) *an explicit emphasis on the actual process of organisational decision making as its basic research commitment* (emphasis in original) (Cyert and March, 1963, p. 19).

In other words, the unit of analysis is no longer market, but the firm. This shifts the focus from the market to inside the firm. Yet, it still continues to focus on predicting the price, output and resource allocation decisions of the firm, so, in this respect, it shares at least one similarity with the neoclassical theory of the firm, and remains an economic theory of the firm, not a purely behavioural theory (or a decision making model). Nevertheless, the emphasis is put on behavioural side of decision making processes, which is the distinctive aspect of the theory.

Cyert and March then discarded the neoclassical idea of the firm as a 'strange bloodless creature ... [engaging] apparently in the simultaneous purchase of inputs and sale of outputs at constant rates' (Boulding, 1950, p. 34), and developed instead a theory of the firm describing internal organisational behaviour and the behaviour of oligopolistic markets, in which the decision making process is 'adaptively' rational, with multiple objectives and continuing organisational learning in determination of prices, outputs and resource allocation.

Thus, the firm is no longer seen as a single production function but a complex 'organisation': 'Recognition of the separation of ownership and control in a modern corporation requires that the managers of such a firm be viewed collectively as an organisation' (Cyert and Kamien, 1972, p. 92). This complex organisation is no longer a 'uni-brain' in terms of Machup (1967, p. 10) (one major decision maker such as the entrepreneur), as is assumed in the neoclassical theory of the firm. Rather it consists of a 'coalition of conflicting interest groups' such as departments, managers, employees, shareholders, customers, suppliers, etc.[1] The members of the coalition are assumed to have different and conflicting goals such as production, sales, market share, inventory and profit. The formation and maintenance of the coalition is the result of a process of bargaining and compromise through which conflicting preferences and beliefs are resolved.

Therefore, the management of the firm itself becomes problematic since the conflicting interests of the coalition necessitates 'managing the coalition' (Stephen, 1984, pp. 8-10). The members of the coalition negotiate with each other continually. The dichotomy of the goals may be clarified in the process of decision-making within the firm, but it is not necessarily resolved, so that there may be only quasi-resolution of conflict. Thus, the firm is conceptualised as a coalition of partially cooperating and partially competing interests.

Secondly, the complex organisation is assumed to operate in situations of uncertainty. In the face of uncertainty, managerial behaviour is assumed to be characterised by bounded rationality to review, even imagine, all possible alternatives to obtain 'optimal' performance. In other words, managers are assumed to try to make rational decisions but their ability to do so is bounded by their cognitive limits on their capacity, relative to the complexities of the environment, to collect, assimilate and process information in decision-making situations under uncertain conditions.

Bounded rationality then necessitates formulating a noncomprehensive modelling of the world (taking limited account of all possibilities), and making a 'rational' decision within the limited set of possibilities. Therefore, managers do not follow a global maximisation rule, but rather the rule of 'satisficing', i.e. simply trying to attain an acceptable level of performance rather than an optimal performance. Given that the aspirations of the sub-units vary, there is a multiplicity of goals which take the form of aspiring to achieve satisfactory levels of performance in various aspects of the firm's work. If performance falls short of the satisfactory level, a search begins for alternative ways of achieving it, or the aspiration level is adjusted down to levels more likely to be achieved. They gave cost-plus pricing as a form of satisficing which has empirical support.

Also, in the face of uncertainty, firms operate according to a process described as problemistic search. That is, instead of devoting resources to wide-ranging searches and basing decisions on long-term strategies, firms operates on the basis of current information and are motivated to search by problems which need to be solved. When a satisfactory (not necessarily optimal) solution is found, search activity ceases. In the process firms learn, and thus adapt in the light of its past problems and error or of its experiences, more generally. They learn via individual learning, and in the process of learning and adapting, goals as well as search procedures may be modified.

Thus, behavioural theory suggests, on the contrary to much of modern decision theory, which has been concerned with the problems of decision making under risk and uncertainty but in fact 'the solutions involved have been largely procedures for finding certainty equivalents (e.g., expected value) or introducing rules for living with the uncertainties (e.g., game theory)' (Cyert and March, 1963, p.119), that firms avoid uncertainty by

1. making decisions when the need arises, on the basis of current information rather than on the basis of anticipation of long-run uncertain events, and
2. trying to arrange a 'negotiated environment', thus avoiding to anticipate future behaviour of other parts of their environment such as suppliers, customers, etc. In short, firms operate on the basis of problematic search rather than complete alertness.

One highly significant influence of the behavioural theory has been directing interest shown by economists into the internal organisation of the firm. Most significantly, Simon's ideas of bounded rationality, satisficing, rule following, etc., led to an alternative (neoclassical) way of approaching economics, from which more explicitly firm-oriented work such as Nelson and Winter's (1982) evolutionary theory proceeded:

> We accept and absorb into our analysis many of the ideas of the behavioural theorists. Our basic critique of orthodoxy [neoclassical theory] is connected with the bounded rationality problem. We base our modelling on the propositions that in the short and medium run the behaviour of firms can be explained in terms of relatively simple decision rules and procedures (Nelson and Winter, 1982, pp. 35-36).

The behavioural-oriented approaches focus attention on the process of decision-making in the firm in terms of variables that affect organisational goals, organisational expectations, and organisational choice, rather than show a preoccupation with the result of rational choice, which neglects the process by which choice is made.

## Behavioural Approach in Explaining Persistent Firm Differentials

The behavioural theory of the firm reflects a realistic description of internal and external environments of the firm, which seems to be compatible with that of strategic management. Both internal and external environments are assumed to be problematic. External environment is inherently uncertain and competitive, and internal environment is made up a coalition of conflicting interest groups. These problematic environments necessitate visible hand of management, unlike neoclassical environments in which all possibilities as well as future situations are known with certainty and in which all possible competitive activities have already ceased to take place at the equilibrium point, and there is zero conflict of interest among decision makers who run the firm.

That is, management of the firm, in itself a problem due to conflicting interest of managerial group, has to manage both the uncertain and competitive external environment and the internal coalition. For example, conflict between departments necessitates directing departments towards the achievement of some overall objectives, even though a consensus on the overall objectives is not attained, or uncertain competitive environment necessitates gathering and processing information about environmental forces in order to identify the firm position *vis-à-vis* them, even though the motivation for search is motivated by problems.

More specifically, the theory may contribute, or has contributed, to strategic management theory in explaining the processes involved in making strategic decisions. Implicit in any definition of the concept of strategy (strategy formulation, strategic planning or strategy formation) is some implications of decision making processes. Therefore, the theory seems to be most useful for strategy thinking and research in enabling investigation into the process of how strategic decisions are made. The significance of the contribution may be better seen when we take into consideration the fact that the dominant neoclassical theory assumes that the decision alternatives are known and that decision criteria is already available. This makes strategic decision making and the process involved uninteresting.

As to the sources of the firm performance, in the behavioural construct, strategy and performance are seen ultimately as a reflection of the actions, judgements, biases, experiences, negotiation, compromise, relative power and struggle, and so on, of the coalition members who run the firm. Top management team or dominant coalition of the firm set organisational goals and aspiration levels, make investment, pricing, employment and locational decisions, decide how they cope with complexity and uncertainty, and put them into effect in a processual, bargaining, and learning manner. Therefore, the performance is assumed to be an outcome of the decision making and implementation processes.

In this respect, to investigate 'why firms perform the way they do' and thereby explaining performance differentials between them, top management or dominant coalition must be, the theory suggests, seen as a decisive factor. In the face of environmental complexity and uncertainty as well as organisational human composition (relative power and struggle among the coalition members, biases, negotiation, trading, etc.,), it is assumed, no two top managements of two firms perceive and prefer the same array of options for the firms, and they certainly do not implement them identically. In other words, the theory assumes a causal association between top management behaviour and organisational outcomes.

Therefore, for our purpose of explaining firm performance differentials, the behavioural theory of the firm provides 'valuable [insights] as a backdrop for process research of how strategic outcomes are arrived at, as well as for content research under conditions which the nature of the process has a non-trivial effect on the outcomes' (Seth, and Thomas, 1994, p. 175). In other words, the behavioural approach might well contribute to understanding the dynamic of interactions among individuals and organisational sub-units as they endeavour to influence strategic decisions, and the resultant performance.

This means that within the behavioural construct, 'the impact of various strategic decision making processes on profit performance' can be taken a legitimate research question. This may illuminate the 'process' aspect of strategic phenomena. It may compensate for the neglect in most studies of strategic management of the decision processes leading to strategic choice along side strategy content. Nevertheless, although such a research question can be legitimately taken up within the behavioural frame of reference, the theory, as it is, fails to analyse the relationship between the observed decision making processes and firm performance differentials. But, the theory can be considered an open-ended framework, and furthered in this respect. Such an extension would fit well into the theory since the theory already emphasises that behavioural and political processes can critically affect any stage of a decision making system, and thereby outcomes.

As for the problem of sustainability, behavioural theorists contend, as Whittington observes, that 'it is to the very imperfections of organisational and market processes that managers owe their strategies and [sustainable] competitive advantage' (Wittington, 1993, pp. 22-23). Due to political bargaining and bounded rationality, 'the need for change will only be imperfectly recognised, and anyway change is suspected because it is likely to set off a period of internal civil war until a new 'dominant coalition' is established' (Whittington, 1993, p. 24). Markets are also assumed to be 'typically quite tolerant of underperformance. Firms often enjoy sufficient market power to be able to earn reasonable profits without maximum effort' (Whittington, 1993, p. 24). Shareholders generally have insufficient information or knowledge to know if maximum profits are made. They are happy as far as 'satisfactory' profits are being made. Thus the combination of organisational and market imperfections gives rise to the 'strategic conservatism' rather than 'strategic flexibility', in terms of Whittington, and thus 'firms can build sufficient 'organisational slack' to buffer themselves against the need for strategic change' (Whittington, 1993, p. 24). As a consequence, firms with differing performance outcomes continue to exist side by side.

Another way of approaching the problem of sustainability is to use one of the central analytical concepts in the behavioural construct: standard/administrative operating procedures, which play the same role in explaining firm differentials, and the persistency of differentials as routines do in Nelson and Winter's evolutionary theory. The firm is assumed to follow standard operating procedures, rules of thumb or heuristic devices from which the firm's actions proceed. These standard operating procedures are assumed to have been acquired through past searches or experience, and to govern decisions, and thereby performance. The standard operating procedures define the capabilities of the firm in much the same way as routines do in Nelson and Winter's model (1982). It is assumed that not all standard operating procedures are retained in the organisation's repertoire, that is, only successful ones are retained. The unsuccessful are discarded or restrained by greater caution if repetition of it seems desirable again on some future occasion. Therefore, over time the retained operating procedures have a certain element of stability, and so it can be assumed that they have a significant impact on long term performance. Moreover, it takes time for rivals to discover and develop operating procedures of successful firms because of bounded rationality and bargaining process.

## Hard Core Assumptions: Multiple-exit Situations

The behavioural theory of the firm is intended to apply to the most representative type of modern firm, as Cyert and March maintain: 'The theory outlined ... specifies an alternative framework and an alternative set of key relations [to the neoclassical theory of the firm] for dealing with the modern "representative firm" - the large, multi-product firm operating under uncertainty in an imperfect market' (Cyert and March, 1963, p. 115). To explain the behaviour of the firm, the theory is based on the following psychological, situational and cognitive hard core assumptions:

1. Decision makers are boundedly rational. Decision makers are cognitively limited (a) in their comprehension of problems, which makes it impossible to figure out all possible cause-effect relations; (b) in their knowing or imagining all possible solutions, which makes it impossible to make decisions with complete information; and (c) in their computational ability, which makes it impossible to map out the complete decision tree showing the paths to all possible solutions.
2. The environment in which the firm operates is uncertain. Uncertainty predominates in organisational decision making, in terms of Cyert and March:

   > To all appearances, at least, uncertainty is a feature of organisational decision making with which organisations must live. In the case of the business firm, there are uncertainties with respect to the behaviour of the market, the deliveries of suppliers, the attitudes of shareholders, the behaviour of competitors, the future actions of governmental agencies, and so on (Cyert and March, 1963, pp. 118-119).

   The future is inherently uncertain and unknowable, so that information as to what consequences are attached to which alternatives is not a 'given'.
3. The firm pursues multiple goals simultaneously: The firm is a coalition of conflicting interest groups, not a 'monobrain', and different parts of the organisation have different goals such as inventory, production, sales, market share and profit. The goals of a firm cannot be taken as given because they change according to who the participants in the firm are, and the process of bargaining between them. Which goal is dominant and continues to be in a dominant position depends upon the relative power position of a

group within the internal polity and its ability to preserve its rights over the power structure. It is likely that the interest of members of the coalition influences decisions over firm objectives, behaviour, and thereby outcomes.

4. Firms satisfice rather than maximise: In face of uncertainty, time pressure, disagreements over goals, cognitive limits of decision makers, etc., managers accept that an optimal solution cannot always be achieved. Therefore, they do not engage in long search for the 'best' solution, rather suffice with a satisfactory one by using simple rules of thumb or standard operating procedures. Thus, they set minimum performance standards and once achieved, stop searching for the ideal (maximising) solution.
5. Imperfections dominate the behaviour of markets and firms. In the neoclassical theory organisational slack is zero, at least at equilibrium. However, many interesting phenomena within the firm are assumed to occur because slack is typically not zero. Managers have discretionary powers, and organisational slack may exist in many forms. Managers, for example, may be provided with services and personal luxuries in excess of those required to keep them, prices that may be set lower than necessary to maintain labour are paid, subunits may be permitted to grow without real concern for the relation between additional payments and additional revenue, etc. Slack is not a problem provided 'satisfactory' profits are being made. Markets are not perfectly competitive, as is argued in the neoclassical perfect competition theory, but rather imperfectly competitive (oligopolistic markets), thereby allowing firms often enjoying market power and resultantly some kind of profits, even without maximum effort. Due to imperfections markets are quite 'tolerant' of underperformance, that is, even though a firm fails to fit into its environment, it may still continue to survive.

Latsis contends that the behavioural research programme defines multiple-exit situations 'where the actor's choice is *not* narrowly delimited by situational considerations' (Latsis, 1976, p. 16), and maintains that if we move away from single-exit situations it becomes difficult to account for action rationalistically. 'In multiple-exit situations the agent's internal environment, i.e., his decision and information-gathering rules, his psychological and social psychological characteristics etc. become central components in the explanation' (Latsis, 1976, p. 16). In other words, as Simon maintains,

> A basic contrast between these two programs is that the latter does, but the former does not, require as an essential component a psychological theory of rational choice. Both situational determinism and economic behaviouralism postulate behaviour that is, in a certain sense, rational, but the meaning of the term 'rational' is quite different for the two programs (Simon, 1976, p. 129).

Simply, the former assumes 'substantive', the latter assumes 'procedural' rationality, as Simon terms them. Procedural rationality pertains, not to the outcomes of actions, which Knudsen calls 'outcome rationality', as in standard neoclassical paradigm, but to the procedures or rules of actions (rationality as rule-following) (Knudsen, 1993a). As Knudsen argues, rationality as rule-following indicates an institutional behaviour since people are assumed to act according to (institutionalised) rules. They do not engage in case-by-case maximisation but rather behave similarly in similar situations, i.e. follow rules.

Is the behavioural theory of the firm a rival research programme to neoclassical?, asks Latsis. He arrives at the conclusion that

> the two approaches are, in my view, importantly different and mutually exclusive over an extensive area. The neoclassical view stresses the *situation* and turns the decision making agent into a cypher; the behavioural view focuses on the nature and characteristics of the *decision making agent* (emphasis in original) (Latsis, 1972, pp. 233-234).

Given the set of hard core assumptions, the assumption of 'satisficing' poses, in essence, an alternative explanation to neoclassical 'maximisation' explanations of the behaviour of the firm. The 'satisficing' theory, which, not being based on 'marginalist' or 'maximising/minimising' contention, seems to be highly useful in explaining the strategic behaviour of actual firms in the real world. Strategic decision makers do not fully understand the decision making situation, but, only are able to consider a number of alternatives. The best (i.e., optimal) strategy or set of strategic actions is neither known nor searched for; an overall *aspiration level* for the firm and various aspiration levels for departments are set and pursued. Hence, aspiration levels, rather than marginal or maximising/minimising behaviour, influence and govern the firm behaviour. Moreover, aspiration levels are subject to change, depending on feedback, learning and internal politics. Clearly, the contention of the process of setting aspiration levels as well as of the process of feedback, learning and internal power considerations seems to be highly illuminating in explaining strategy formation.

Behavioural theorists assume an intrinsic indeterminacy in all market situations. The looseness of the environmental constraints, to them, necessitates making real choices, rather than maximising or marginal adjustments. Nevertheless, like neoclassics (and unlike process theorists such as Nelson and Winter, Mises, and Penrose), they assume a closed system (no search for discovery or invention on the side of the firm). The firm faces a relatively stable market in which de-structuring and re-structuring do not take place, so that the firm follows 'standard' operating procedures.

Yet, contrary to the early work of Cyert and March (1963), the recent work of Simon (1993), the most prominent behavioural economists, assumes an open system in which firms 'seek continually (or invent) for new marketable products, new methods of marketing them, or even new ways of financing their activities' (Simon, 1993, p. 134). He argues that each firm makes its strategic decisions against the background of its history so that 'it is natural to view strategic questions within the framework of evolutionary theory' (Simon, 1993, p. 131). The evolutionary theory that he refers is the Nelson and Winter's kind. Like Nelson and Winter, he takes 'creative' and 'proactive', rather than 'standard' and 'reactive', view of decision making in competitive market situations:

> The most important skills required for survival and success in ... rapidly evolving world in which we live are (1) skill in anticipating the *shape* of an uncertain future, (2) skill in *generating alternatives* for operating effectively in changed environments, and (3) skill in *implementing new plans* rapidly and efficiently (emphasis in original) (Simon, 1993, p. 134).

Like other process-oriented theorists, he argues that a business firm's market 'niche' is typically transient and so that to continue to adapt to its uncertain outside world it needs to find 'new' sources of competitive advantage. Thus, behavioural theory substantiates the process-oriented resource-based view, rather than the structure-oriented positioning view of strategic management.

Apparent it must be hitherto that in the behavioural account it is recognised that firms seek for, and secure, if gained, competitive advantages. Boundedly rational decision makers follow rules under uncertain conditions to attend selectively to the environment in which they operate and information about it.

It should also be pointed out that, for behaviourists, strategies emerge in small steps of learning and compromise (political bargaining) rather than from a rational series of grand leaps forward (Wittington, 1993). Strategies are, therefore, path-dependent, emergent or processual, and encoded and followed in the form of 'standard operating procedures'. That is to say, strategies themselves are assumed to be programmed, and lead decisions into established paths. Firms are assumed to follow their existing strategies as long as they render acceptable-level of performance. Such procedures, like strategies, are employed to avoid uncertainty. The emergent or processual perspective has already been utilised by strategy theorists, most notably by Minzberg,[2] in furthering to understand the process of strategy making.

## Conclusions

The behavioural construct manifests an alternative view of the firm as a coalition of conflicting interest groups to the neoclassical theory of the firm as a production function run by a uni-brain. Condemning the neoclassical theory of the firm for ignoring the internal decision processes of business enterprises, it attempts to bring in *realism in process* of decision making, thus joining economic and behavioural constructs in the development of a theory of the firm. The subunits of the firm have different objectives in the form of aspiration levels to achieve. The firm does not, therefore, aim to maximise anything, instead, to achieve satisfactory levels of performance. Leaving aside the neoclassical view of profit maximisers or '*decision-makers without decision procedures*', in terms of Latsis (Latsis, 1976, p. 25), behavioural theorists also emphasise procedural/administrative rules (heuristic devices for dealing with risky situations) for decision selection.

This behavioural view of internal decision making processes seems highly useful in providing a framework for analysing how actual strategies are reached. It makes the investigation of strategy formulation/formation exciting in terms of the political bargaining involved in the process and the formation and guidance of standard operating procedures that influence and govern the behaviour of the firm. Each firm is assumed to be unique in terms of its organisational conditions, such as internal power structure, past performance, past strategies, standard operating procedures, the extent of organisational slack, etc. All these conditions have a significant impact on the internal working processes and outcomes of firms, and lead to the profit differentials between them. As in the case for routines in evolutionary theory, the ways of doing business (strategies, operating procedures, etc.) underlying initial success are retained and replicated by individual firms, and thereby they are specific and path-dependent. Thus, they are specific and path-dependent, and thereby difficult to be codify and imitate.

## Notes

1. See Cyert and March (1963), Chapter 3.
2. See H. Mintzberg (1978) Patterns in Strategy Formation, *Management Science*, Vol. 24, No. 9, pp. 934-948; (1987b) Crafting Strategy, *Harvard Business Review*, July-August, pp. 65-75.

Chapter 11

# Conclusions: Potential of Economics for its Foundational Service to Strategic Management Theory

## Introduction

In this remaining chapter, we try to assess the chief findings of the study, i.e. whether economic theories of the firm and of the market supply conceptual foundations on which strategy theory may rely to describe and predict its phenomena of inquiry, and what the study has achieved, i.e. what the study has contributed to existing knowledge. To this end the chapter is organised in three sections. In the first section we attempt to answer three interrelated questions: (1) do the economic theories provide theoretical foundations for strategic management theory to explain and predict strategic phenomena at firm and market levels of analyses, or, more specifically, do they meet the criteria set at the outset in order for them to be judged in this respect, (2) which theory offers the best foundational service for strategic theorising and research, and (3) in what respects do they supply conceptual foundations to strategy theory. In the second section, we assess the findings of the study with comparison to the debate over the legitimacy of the use of economics in furthering strategic thinking and research in strategy literature. There we attempt to identify the reasons for the increasing and intensifying debate and point out how the study may contribute to alleviate it. And, finally, in the third section, we point out the implications for further studies.

## Potential of Furthering Dialogue Between Economic and Strategy Fields of Inquiry

As we have been arguing, economic theories, like theories in any scientific discipline, are driven in large part by an agenda that reflects their proponents' shared sense of what problems are tractable, significant, and interesting (paradigm choice, problem dependency or ontological standpoint). Therefore, theories cannot be separated from the questions that they frame. As such it may not be possible to claim for the 'independence' of their content (in particular, conceptualisations of the market and of the firm) and heuristic or hard core assumptions from the questions that they frame. For the content, the meaning of propositions, conceptualisations of observed phenomena and heuristic devices are all paradigmatically conditioned. Hence, it may not be possible to regard them as supra-paradigmatical.

Given their paradigmatical settings, the study has examined the relationship between basic economic questions around which conceptions of the market and of the firm and heuristic devices are developed and those of strategy from the viewpoint of whether the former reflect the latter exactly, approximately, or not at all is ignored. The study demonstrated that many, if not most, of the problems on today's economic research agenda regarding the market and firm analyses reflect those of strategy theory.

In clearer terms, while each economic theory aims at the explanation of a critically important aspect of economic (market and firm) reality from economic profession viewpoint, they also shed light on a significant aspect of strategic phenomena each time. In other words, basic propositions or assumptions of strategic management theory are theoretically deducible from those of economic theories.

It is exactly this possibility of theoretical deductions of strategic propositions and assumptions from economic modes of theorising that lends a theoretical foundation to its neighbouring discipline (strategic management). Therefore, strategy researchers could build their thinking and research on theoretical foundations of economic conceptualisations of the market and of the firm to explain and predict strategic phenomena at market and firm levels of analyses.

In more concrete terms, the study demonstrated that, apart from the neoclassical theory (of perfect competition and of the firm), all the other economic theories of the firm and of the market that we examined seem to provide highly fruitful conceptual bases on which strategy theory may rely to explain its phenomena of inquiry, although they are not designed for that purpose. Neoclassical economic analysis of the firm and of the market has little, if anything substantive, to offer for furthering strategic thinking and research. In fact, the neoclassical analysis of the firm and of the market has thoroughly denied the very existence and importance of strategic phenomena (persistent profit differentials between firms). Thus, it obstructs a profitable dialogue between the two neighbouring fields.

Yet, the examination we carried out has demonstrated that later theorising movements on the economics of the market and of the firm have brought in new ways of looking at the firm and the market. Later analyses have begun to break away from the neoclassical theory, concerning with different questions (new problem areas). In order to answer the new questions they set for themselves, they disassociated themselves from highly abstract notions of the market and of the firm (the market as perfect competition and the firm as production function, which have merely notional or logical existence) and refuted each time at least one 'ideal' condition (hard core assumption, such as perfect information and complete certainty). In so doing, they have constructed alternative conceptions of the firm (such as the firm as a governance structure or as a bundle of resources) and of the market (such as the market as imperfectly working organisation or as a discovery process) which have created new possibilities to interrelate economics and strategic thinking in substantive ways.

In other words, the movements of breaking away from the neoclassical paradigm or research programme in economics have created an invaluable opportunity to bridge the two neighbouring fields of inquiry. The research findings have demonstrated that economics and strategic management disciplines exhibit surprisingly a large overlap in explaining strategic phenomena. More importantly, the overlap does appear to be, as we have been arguing, in essential respects. In clearer terms, the theories supply explanations about the very phenomena of strategic inquiry, that is, supply some kind of explanation for firm differentials in profitability, the reason or mechanism of their sustainability, as an outcome variable of strategy-following behaviour of the firm working under uncertainty and imperfect information, *as the following table shows.*

| Theories | Problem Area | Conception of Market/Firm | Source of Profit Differentials |
|---|---|---|---|
| Neoclassical Market theory | How scarce resources can be allocated efficiently? | Market as perfect competition | |
| Industrial Organisation<br>- The S-C-P Paradigm<br>- Chicago Schools<br>- Game Theory | What are the causes of supernormal profits? | Market as imperfectly working organisation | Market structure<br>Efficiency-building capabilities<br>Firm actions and dependencies |
| Austrian School | How a market economy function? | Market as a discovery process | Entrepreneurial knowledge |
| Evolutionary Theory | Whar are the dynamics of economic growth | Market as a process of search and selection | Firm routines |
| Neoclassical Firm Theory | How firms respond to market changes? | Firm as a production function | |
| Contractual Theories<br>- Transaction Cost Theory<br>- Agency Theory | Why firms exist? | Firm as a governance structure<br>Firm as a nexus of contracts | Ability of economising on costs (transaction and agency) |
| Growth Theory | What are the dynamics of the growth of the firm ? | Firm as a pool of resources | Productive managerial resources |
| Behavioural Theory | How decisions are made in firms? | Firm as a coalition of diverse interests | Operational procedures |

| Theories | Reason for the Persistency of Differentials | The Situation to which Theory is Constructed to Apply | Strategic Intent | Decision makers |
|---|---|---|---|---|
| Neoclassical Market theory | | Single-exit situational determinism (Environmental certainty) | Non-strategic maximising behaviour | Unboundedly rational |
| Industrial Organisation - The S-C-P Paradigm - Chicago Schools - Game Theory | Barriers to entry Barriers to imitation | Multiple-exit strategic situations (Environmental uncertainty) | Delibrate actions for creating conditions for high profits | Boundedly rational |
| Austrian School | Barriers to imitation | Multiple-exit strategic situations or Situational indeterminism (Environmental uncertainty) | Strategic intent as rule following behaviour | Boundedly rational |
| Evolutionary Theory | Barriers to imitation | Multiple-exit strategic situation (Environmental uncertainty) | Strategic intent as routine following behaviour | Boundedly rational |
| Neoclassical Firm Theory | | Single-exit situational determinism (Environmental certainty) | Non-strategic maximising behaviour | Unboundedly rational |
| Contractual Theories - Transaction Cost Theory - Agency Theory | Market failure or market sluggishness | Multiple-exit situations (Environmental uncertainty) | Strategic intent as institutional behaviour | Boundedly rational |
| Growth Theory | Barriers to imitation | Multiple-exit situation (Environmental uncertainty) | Strategic intent as managerial function | Boundedly rational |
| Behavioural Theory | Barriers to imitation | Multiple-exit situation (Environmental uncertainty) | Strategy intent as rule following behaviour | Boundedly rational |

Therefore, the research has made clear that apart from neoclassical theory of the firm and of the market, all other theories in question provide highly versatile conceptual foundations on which strategic theorising and research may be drawn to explain and predict its phenomena of inquiry at market and firm levels of analyses.

### *How to Construct Economic Foundation for Strategic Management Theory?*

The research findings suggest that the theories engender a wide variety of disparate explanations concerning the sources of differences among firms, the reasons of their persistency, strategic motivations, strategic situations and strategic decision makers. The various explanations rest on different problem areas and assumptions with varying degrees of abstraction, and sometimes rival but often complement each other. These findings imply that strategy theory and research can therefore be furthered in many directions, taking the existing body of knowledge generated within various market and firm theories in economics.

Yet, given the findings of the research, the question is, at this level of analysis, which theory offers the best foundational service for strategic theorising and research? Given the fact that, apart from orthodox neoclassical theory of the market and of the firm, all others satisfy our criteria of judging them for their foudational merits, the question simply amounts by indication to judging them on their relative merits in explaining strategic phenomena. In this respect, the question becomes much more complicated than it seems to be.

Apparent it must be from the research is that none of the theories captures all of the complexity of strategic phenomena concerning structural characteristics of market, market competition, dimensionality and intensity of competition, and market functioning and process; or, of firm existence, boundaries, structure, employee motivation, capabilities, internal workings, and decision making processes. Yet each has a unique perspective that sheds light on at least one major aspect of strategy phenomena from its problem-area and/or hard core assumptions viewpoint.

However, while each theory illuminates part of the complex reality (some aspects of market or firm) that conditions and determines strategic phenomena, it also shadows some other parts. In other words, each theory creates its own highlights (the elements of its problem area to which attention is naturally drawn) and shadows (the elements of complex reality that are overlooked, downplayed or ignored for the sake of model building or simplicity in order to focus on a particular problem) and hence different perspectives and recommendations.

Moreover, the research findings plainly show that strategy phenomena are variable-rich, multidimensional, and perhaps complex, and thereby imply that strategy theorising and research resists or is inappropriate to a reductionist approach. Therefore, it seems reasonable to argue in favour of the view that all theories together may lead to the development of various conceptions of strategy that shed more light on the multifaceted image of the nature of strategy phenomena, rather than of settling strategy theory and research on a narrow and limited set of conceptual boxes of a particular theory, especially in this developmental period of the discipline of strategic management. That is, it seems more appropriate, in this developmental period, to look for a comprehensive outlook, instead of choosing between them.

The reason for leaving the answer to the question at this vague level is that there is no generally accepted theoretical or empirical basis for preferring one explanation or variable to the others. From a theoretical point of view, if the variables are as important as their proponents claim in explaining sustainable firm differentials even on the basis of a particular problem, they must, by definition, be strategic, and hence potentially a legitimate part of the domain of strategic management. Apart from the criteria (an explanation about firm differentials, about sustainability, and compatibility of hard core assumptions-motivational, situational and cognitive-) set out at the outset for judging the theories for furthering strategic thinking and research, we do not have any other criteria to decide what makes one theoretical explanation, independent of its particular problem focus, more important than another. One possible criterion could be empirical findings, but we do not yet have such comprehensive as well as conclusive findings to probe which variables are *decisive* and which are *affective* in explaining persistent firm differentials. Hence it is difficult on the empirical basis as well to prioritise variables.

### *Potential of Economic Theories for Supplying Theoretical Bases to Strategic Management Theory*

Given the large overlaps between economic and strategic management fields in explaining strategic phenomena, now, the question is, 'how may economic theories of the firm and of the market supply theoretical foundations on which strategy researchers may rely to explain their phenomena of inquiry?' Arguably, they may provide theoretical foundations to strategy researchers to explain strategic phenomena from a grounded, systemic and more comprehensive perspective:

*1. Strategy researchers may explain their phenomena of inquiry from a grounded perspective*. By the grounded perspective it is meant that whether we can extract from economic theories inferential linkages that connect basic strategic explanations to economic ones. Two kinds of inferential linkages can be differentiated: positive and normative. Positive linkages are 'what is' strategic extractions from 'what is' explanations of economic theories, whereas normative linkages are 'what ought to be' strategic extractions from 'what is' economic explanations.

Economic theories may provide conceptual foundations to strategy researchers to investigate into strategic phenomena without wasting time each time to go back to basic explanations about the market and firm. For example, economists concern 'why markets are organised as they are', and strategy researchers may take economists' explanations for granted and then go a step further to make an inferential linkage from the strategic mode of thinking viewpoint, 'how the ways of markets are organised impact the strategic behaviour and performance of firms'. In the same respect, economists concern 'how decisions are made in firms', strategy researchers may be to find out 'how decision making process in firms impact their strategic behaviour and performance'; economists concern 'why firms are organised as they are', strategy researchers may attempt to find out 'how the ways of firms are organised impact the strategic behaviour and performance of them'; and son on. In this respect, economic analyses of the market and of the firm may provide a groundwork on which strategy researchers may rely as they build models or develop hypotheses for inquiry. This may speed the accumulation of scientific knowledge in the strategy sphere.

Also, economic theories of the firm and of the market seem to provide foundational service from which strategy scholars may proceed to get from 'what is' descriptions to 'what ought to be' prescriptions. As we have already argued, strategic concern shows a proactive, normative, practical and pragmatical orientation. However, this practical and pragmatical management concern should be based on some kind of 'justifiable foundations'. Economic theories of the firm and of the market seem to provide highly justifiable foundations to generate prescriptions for postscientific application to business world. A well-known example is that economists working within the S-C-P framework discovered the causal relationship between the way markets are organised and their performance level. This scientific discovery has given rise to the prescription regarding 'where firms ought to compete to earn high profits'.

In fact, theories often supply 'what is' descriptions not in terms of empirically discovered causal relationship, but in terms of theoretically justified causal relationships. They draw on theoretical grounds attention to the major interrelationships underlying a problem, as we have seen, and so that leads to informed insights into what ought to be done. In this respect, for example, evolutionary theory prescribes, in dealing with dynamics of economic change, businessmen to develop better information - embodying idiosyncratic routines to earn high profits or transaction cost economics prescribes, in dealing with the reason for the existence of the firm, economising (operational efficiency) as the best way to achieve sustainable competitive advantage.

*2. They may explain their phenomena of inquiry from a systemic perspective.* As we have argued in the first chapter, the subject of strategy analyses the firm's relationships with its environment. This requires a systemic perspective in the strategy sphere. In other words, a perspective of business strategy is meant to be systemic in the sense that it embraces the basic institutions of capitalist system, namely, both markets and firms in which strategic phenomena occur and so that it explains strategic phenomena with relation to them. Economic theories provide rich descriptions of the institutions of economic system. In this respect, strategy researchers may explain their phenomena of inquiry (persistent firm differentials in competitive markets) by connecting or relating them with economics insights about the nature of market competition, dimensionality and intensity of competition, the emergence and evolution of markets and market functioning, and about the nature of the firm, the reason for the existence of the firm, the determinants of its boundaries, its internal/external relational (agency) networks, its internal workings, and decision making processes.

As Part II and III explored, economic theories of the firm and of the market, in concerning with different aspects of the firm and of the market in their terms, raise the possibility of connecting or relating different aspects of strategic phenomena at market and firm level analyses. For example, game theory contributes strategy theory to grasping the dynamic interplay between competitors (succession of moves and countermoves) thereby illuminating strategic phenomena in a dynamic, interdependent competitive context. Or, the S-C-P paradigm is highly useful in explaining the multidirectional complex relationships between market structure, firm conduct and market performance. Evolutionary theory and Austrian theory focus on changes through time that transform the very environment as the result of individual firms' behaviour of seeking for competitive advantage, and thus they shed light on the 'formation' of market structures and historical competitive behaviour of the firm. They are highly illuminating in their explanations of the *emergence* and *formation* of markets in terms of individual firms' market creation activities (innovations and discoveries) and adaptation.

Together, while the structure-oriented theories (the S-C-P, Chicago School, and game theory) contribute strategic thinking and research to relating the existing state of market institution, that is, the organisation of the market, market forces at play in a specific period of time, interactions and other interdependencies between firms for understanding the *nature and structure* of ongoing competition in the *established* markets and how they affect behaviour of the firm for seeking and sustaining competitive advantage, the process-oriented theories of the market (evolutionary and Austrian schools of economics) relate strategic phenomena to the formation of the market institution, that is, how markets have become what they are and thus illuminate the dynamic nature of the market competition.

In the same respect, structure-oriented theories of the firm (transaction cost economics and agency theory) contribute respectively strategy theory to relating its phenomena of inquiry with firm internal structuring with regard to market structuring (the reason for organising an activity within the firm rather than leaving to markets), and the internal and external relational (agency) networking under the pressure of market institutions (labour markets, financial markets, etc.). The process oriented growth and behavioural theories of the firm contribute strategic theorising, respectively, to relating it to diversification behaviour of the firm in a competitive setting, and how decisions are actually made within the internal organisational polity to react/proact to the changes in the unique, uncertainty-prevailing, historical environments (internal and external).

As we have already seen, strategy scholars generally fail to recognise that strategic phenomena arise from the interactions and relationships, at system-wide, between markets and firms. Therefore, taking a systemic perspective may enable strategy researchers to see the set of variables that interact and influence one another in the economic system, and the world of business as an integrated whole.

*3. They may explain their phenomena of inquiry from a more comprehensive perspective*. As we argued, strategy theory does not address many key issues regarding the firm and the market. Yet, these may influence the firm's strategy in practice, and shed light on strategic modes of explanation in theory. Economic theories of the market and of the firm together draw attention to many ignored aspect of strategic phenomena, and supply theoretical lenses to see them.

By analogy with the old Hindu fable in which six blind men touch different parts of the elephant and come to different conclusions about its nature, and hence different perspectives and recommendations. An elephant may not *be* a trunk, but it certainly *has* a trunk, and it would be difficult to understand elephants without reference to trunks. Likewise, strategy may not be knowledge of particular time and spaces in terms of marketable opportunities, innovative routines, incentive schemes, managing conflicting interest groups within the organisational polity, etc. Yet they are certainly significant components of strategy (formulation/formation, implementation and outcomes), so that it would be difficult to understand strategic phenomena without reference to them. They are significant, as we have argued, since they can be transferred into sustainable competitive advantages. In this respect, economic theories of the firm and of the market supply conceptual bases for strategy researchers to see the variable-rich and multidimensional-facet of strategic phenomena, and so that prevent them from following a reductionist approach.

Economic theories of the firm and of the market may provide to strategy researchers with a broad as well as long-term perspective. The structure- and process-oriented theories shed light on many significant variables across firms and markets at a certain period of time and on significant dynamic variables causing what markets and firms have been over a long period of time. Thus, they might well provide strategy researchers with theoretical justifications to take into consideration more variables in their cross sectional and longitudinal studies. As such, they may help strategy researchers decompose the general categories of firm and market level effects into more detailed sub-categories. Decomposing the variance in profitability into more detailed categories may give them a way of assessing the relative importance of each variable in determining firm profitability but also a more complete or comprehensive picture of sustainable performance differentials.

## Contributions of the Study to the Debate Over Legitimising Strategic Management Theory Through Economics

The debate over which theory or theories in economics should be exploited in furthering strategy theory and research has hitherto demonstrated a number of significant disagreements rather than agreements over the role, legitimacy and methodology of economics in strategy thinking and research, as we have pointed out in the first chapter. From a 'legitimist' viewpoint, the debate turns on the arguments and counter-arguments regarding the 'kind' of economics, or, more clearly, regarding which economic theory offers the best theoretical foundation, on which strategy theory should be drawn. Given the debate, what has this study achieved? Before proceeding to answer the question, it seems, first, better to give some examples of the conflicting views to recognise their pattern and rationale.

*Which Kind of Economics to Substantiate Strategic Management Theory and Research?*

In the 1980s and 1990s ideas, tools, concepts or logic of economics were extensively exploited, in an eclectic or systematic fashion, to build or promote strategy theory. The two dominant approaches, namely positioning and resource-based, in the field of strategy, were based on economics in a way that did not allow ease of understanding without tracing back their economics' roots.

For example, Porter, the pioneer who made an explicit and systematic use of economics in developing a competitive theory of strategy, concluded, when assessing 'the contributions of industrial organisation to strategic management', that 'frontiers aside, there is gold to mine in applying IO [in particular the S-C-P paradigm] concepts to strategy formulation' (1981, p. 617). He aptly showed that the same information about the mechanisms of how exogenous structural features of a market govern the competitive behaviour of its buyers and sellers and affect economic performance are involved either in order to promote competition for economic welfare (IO) or to limit competition for individual firms to obtain competitive advantage (Caves, 1994).

On the other hand, criticising Porter for not paying due attention to alternative approaches or schools in IO, McWilliams and Smart argue that the application of the S-C-P paradigm in industrial organisation to strategic management has led to inappropriate or costly generalisations and predictions. In particular, they rationalise their argument on the grounds that the S-C-P paradigm and strategic management have different level of analysis (industry v firm), the kind of analysis (static v dynamic), and the determinants of persistent competitive advantage (industry level entry barriers v firm level idiosyncratic barriers). They suggest the Chicago School or the 'efficiency paradigm' in their terms, as an alternative paradigm base for strategy theory as against the S-C-P paradigm.

Another example in case is disagreement over the new IO or game-theoretic studies of behaviour and performance in imperfectly competitive markets for analysing business strategy. Shapiro confidently asserts that during the 1980s, 'game theory has emerged as the predominant methodology for analysing business strategy. ... At this time, game theory provides the only coherent way of logically analysing strategic behaviour' (1989, p. 125). He describes game-theoretical work in IO as the 'theory of business strategy', and argues that such strategic behaviours analysed in game-theoretic studies as the timing of strategic decisions, the ability of large firms to make commitments in investing in physical capital and intangible assets, contracting, strategic control of information (e.g. entry deterrence), and so forth are the key to understanding business strategy.

Against this provocative dismissal (the only way of analysing strategic behaviour) of others who have used other approaches when analysing strategic phenomena, Teece makes a counter-provocative claim in his review article, *Contributions and Impediments of Economic Analysis to the Study of Strategic Management*:

> ... game theorists almost always have at least one special theory to offer ... Consequently ..., it [game theory] has almost nothing to offer at this time to key issues in strategic management. By explaining everything, it explains nothing. I challenge proponents of game theory to demonstrate otherwise (Teece, 1990, p. 54).

He observes that the burgeoning class of special theories in the new IO is decidedly lacking in vigour and rarely exposed to the chill of empirical verification. Looking at its outcomes, he finds game theory as barren and pathetic at least in terms of its utility to students of the field of strategic management. Foss also argues, in the context of the likely contribution of the new IO to further the resource-based theory and research, that the new IO is unlikely to help satisfactorily in addressing such central issues as the creation, maintenance and renewal of competitive advantage in terms of the internal resources of firms. This is, he argues, because 'it is the *research style* and *assumptions* of the new IO, rather than the phenomena it highlights, that are not fully consistent with the competence [resource-based] perspective' (emphasis in origin) (Foss, 1996a, p. 195).

Another example in case is Jacobson's suggestion of the Austrian School of economics as the foundation for competitive strategy. He develops the 'Austrian School of strategy' as a rival strategy school to the then dominant IO variant strategic thinking and research, i.e. positioning approach, maintaining that IO largely ignores, despite their fundamental importance, change, uncertainty, and disequilibrium in the business environment. He maintains that 'though it has a number of different dimensions, the strategic implications from Austrian economics are closely related, if not saying the same thing' (1992, p. 803) since these fundamentals are the cornerstones of the school. However, Foss argues that 'Austrian economics may provide inspiration, but is too general' (1996a, p. 183) to be able to play a foundational role in the resource-based research. (Note that Foss makes this assertion only for the resource-based view, not the whole competitive strategy.) He asks, in his assessment of the Austrian School, 'Can strategy scholars get ... [such] benefits [as increasing the problem-solving ability of strategy thinking, making strategy theorising more susceptible to confrontation with empirical reality] from Austrian economics?'. Then he makes the assertion that 'the answer is largely in the negative' (Foss, 1996a, p. 188). Thus he gives a low profile to the Austrian economics and, instead, proposes evolutionary economics for the foundational role.

As to the theories of the firm, Williamson argues that transaction cost economics suggests the best foundation for strategic approach since it directs attention to the very basics: 'economy [economising on transaction costs] is the best strategy' (1991, p. 76). On the other hand, Donaldson (1990a) argues that organisational economics (transaction cost and agency theory) has inherent problems regarding its narrow model of human motivation and behaviour, its negative moral characterisation of managers, and its methodological individualist bias that it makes it highly difficult to be complementary to traditional management theory. By contrast, Barney (1990a) does not see these problems/differences substantial and unavoidable, and finds the debate between traditional management theory and organisational economics as intergroup conflict. In other words, to use the concepts of theories of history of science, Donaldson sees them alternative paradigms or research programmes, whereas Barney sees them within the same paradigm or research programme.

Out of many other examples, these are enough to show the current state of the debate over the economics and strategic management relationship in terms of finding a legitimate base for the strategic theorising and research. Apparently, the state of the debate shows no less than a state of 'legitimacy crisis'. Suffice it to say here that the legitimacy problem continues to grow and intensify, and the debates concerning it show no sign of abating.

### *Problems with the Debate on How to Support Strategic Management Theory by Economics*

Unfortunately, the growing and intensifying debate has been generating 'more heat than light' in the sense that rather than helping to resolve the legitimacy problem, it has been bringing about more perplexity. Why, has there not been hitherto found any 'legitimate' basis for strategy theory, and why has the debate been disseminating more heat than light? There seems to be a number of reasons:

1. Lack of Criteria for Judging the Economic Theories for Their Offerings: Though various and conflicting views may be seen as an indication of richness, reflecting various endeavours of furthering the field of management in different directions, it is, no doubt, also an indication of much subjectivism intruding into the debate.

Subjectivism originates in the lack of criteria for making objective judgements about whether a theory can play a foundational role for strategic management. As is shown above, one sees Austrian economics as a very sound basis for strategy research and may even claim the 'Austrian theory of strategy' as more explanatory (Jacobson, 1992) in comparison to IO-inspired strategy thinking (Porter, 1980, 1981), another sees evolutionary economics as more promising for the foundational role and gives a low profile to the Austrian economics.

2. Lack of a Comprehensive or Complete Examination of Economic Theories Available for their Potential Foundational Role: Researchers focus their attention on some economic theories for examination and ignore others. Little or no consideration given to competing paradigms in the economic discipline will induce incomplete conclusions and gives rise to further discussions. As our review of the debate demonstrates, for example, Porter (1981) examines the S-C-P paradigm only, McWilliams and Smart (1993) the S-C-P paradigm and efficiency paradigm (Chicago School), Jacobson (1990) Austrian School. While Foss (1996a) reviews game theory, Austrian School and evolutionary theory only.
3. Lack of a Paradigmatic View: The participants of the debate have chiefly reached their conclusion by taking a particular 'approach' point of view, for example, the positioning approach, the resource-based view of strategy or the Austrian School of strategic management, rather than from a 'disciplinary' or 'paradigmatic' point of view. Therefore, they see what they seek. The approach-based mindset have restricted the ability of strategy scholars to deal with many of the problems of the strategy paradigm. It has limited findings to the narrowness of its frame of reference, and ended up with rejecting those outside the limits of their approach. However, if we view strategic management as a paradigm or research programme, implications and conclusions may be quite different.

Arguably, of the three, the most important factor causing the conflict to grow and to dissipate more heat than light is the lack of criteria as a guide to examine, compare, relate and judge economic theories for their foundational services. The participants of the debate have chiefly disregarded the method of appraisal or the standard against which the theories are to be judged, and the justification of the standard or criteria. This study has remedied this deficiency by proposing and applying a rigorous standard for the examination of the economics and strategic management relationship. The thrust of the criteria lies in enabling us to go to the very core of the theories by looking at them from their *problem areas* and *hard core assumptional* viewpoint.

The study has also examined all the economic theories, both theories of the market and of the firm, which have been the subject matter for the debate mentioned or not mentioned above. This has enabled us to see the surprisingly large overlap between economics and strategy theory mentioned above, and the multiple strategic realities that the theories have indicated. Moreover, having taken a paradigmatic or research programme viewpoint, the study has saved us from losing ourselves in family intergroup quarrels (to look for support for an established view of strategy such as the positioning or resource-based approaches, rather than strategy theory as a paradigm), and enabled us to see the variable rich, multidimensional, and complex nature of strategic phenomena. Having a paradigmatic viewpoint seems particularly necessary, in particular, at this stage of the emerging discipline of strategic management.

By removing the inadequacies causing, increasing and intensifying the conflict over the economics and strategic management relationship, and by adopting a powerful method of resolving conflict, making a comprehensive examination of economics in terms of the theories of the market and of the firm, and approaching to the analysis of the relationship from a paradigmatic viewpoint, we believe that this research has helped moderate the debate and generated more light than heat.

On the contrary to the above mentioned arguments in favour of one theory or another in economics, the study has found that, apart from the neoclassical theory of perfect competition and of the firm, all the economic theories in case seem to provide relevant theoretical foundations on which strategy theory may be based, taking into consideration their character-forming problem areas and hard core assumptions. Moreover, as we have argued above, it is difficult to single out one or more of the theories as better for their foundational offerings than the others. It is because of difficulty in judging on which focal variables of any theory are more crucial in explaining strategic phenomena than others. For each of them is significant and can be considered as a source of sustainable competitive advantage, as the study has demonstrated.

## Concluding Remarks and Implications for Further Study

The study has exhibited that there are surprisingly large overlaps between economics and strategic modes of thought in explaining and predicting strategic phenomena. The utilisation of economics in the field of strategic management may raise the possibility of shedding more light on strategic phenomena from different but, arguably, complementary perspectives. It may possess greater explanatory and problem solving power than strategy theory may do in isolation.

It should also be admitted that there are undoubtedly 'sunk costs' and 'opportunity costs' of the use of economic modes of thought in the field of strategic management. One unavoidable consequence of utilising various explanatory apparatuses of economics seems to cause greater pluralism, rather than disciplinary purity in the strategy sphere. It may bring about the risk of exhibiting 'incredible eclecticism' or 'theoretical inconsistency' (Jackson, 1984) in the field. However, we do take the view that inter-theoretical linkages between economics and strategic management should be made in order to reap the benefits of scientific inquiry. At this stage of the development of the theory of strategic management pluralism can be tolerated in order to advance strategic thinking and research in many directions until the emergence of a unifying or a dominant paradigm of strategy.

This suggests that the dialogue should be increased between economics and strategic management for furthering strategic thinking and research. In fact, economic theories have already had a profound influence on thinking and research in the strategy field. Yet, we believe that further dialogue may help increase its problem-solving ability, straighten its explanatory power, and speed the accumulation of scientific knowledge within its frame of reference.

In this respect, further studies may explore yet unexploited or underdeveloped economic insights to further strategic mode of thinking in different respects. The present study generally ignored the question of what the yet unexploited or underdeveloped economic insights are and how they can be utilised to further strategic thinking and research, staying primarily within the limits of the question of whether the economic theories of the firm and of the market can be used to generate deductions or supports about strategic phenomena.

Since the answer is yes, and they are, then it is clear that these two fields are part of the cumulative knowledge process that is helping to refine, affirm and predict strategic phenomena. In this respect, a second, and ostensibly more informative continuation of the research may be to take a further step by asking a broader question: 'In what ways, and how can the dialogue between these two neighbouring fields be furthered?'. Such a study may generate new insights or ways regarding how the field of strategy may grow internally and stretch its boundaries.

This study used the method of refutation by theory, rather than refutation by observation (Wisdom, 1965), in order to find out the kind of economics on which strategy theory may rely to explain and predict strategic phenomena. For, arguably, the theories, as such, are not observation-refutable. Yet, the study has unearthed the focal variable of each theory. In this respect, as we have implied above, a further study may also be designed for empirical purpose to assess the relative merits of each focal variable of the economic theories, i.e., for instance, the relative effect of market structure, of innovative routines, of employee motivation, of productive managerial resources, or of operating procedures in accounting for the extent of strategic phenomena (sustainable firm differentials).

As Wisdom argues, 'the two [refutation by observation and refutation by theory] together seem ... to make up the corpus of science' (1965, p. 66). That is, an empirical study seems to a complementary endeavour to that theoretical one. An empirical study may help in two respects: to facilitate to choose the kind of economics on which strategy may rely and to give direction where strategy theory move to. As we have argued above, given the claim of each economic theory regarding the importance of the focal variable (such as market structure and transaction costs) on which all the theoretical explanation of it turns, it is impossible to make a choice of one over others. But, if we had knowledge regarding the relative merit of each focal variable in explaining the extent of strategic phenomena, then it would be easier to make such a choice. Secondly, such a knowledge may also give direction regarding where to focus when constructing strategy theories or models for refutation by observation.

# Bibliography


Agassi, J, 1979, The Legacy of Lakatos, *Philosophy of Social Sciences*, Vol. 9, pp. 316-326.

Alchian, A.A, 1950, Uncertainty, Evolution and Economic Theory, *Journal of Political Economy*, Vol. 58, pp. 211-221.

Alchian, A.A., 1965, Some Economics of Property Rights, *Il Politico*, Vol. 30, No. 4, pp. 816-829.

Alchian, A.A. and Demsetz, H., 1972, Production, Information Costs, and Economic Organisation, *American Economic Review*, Vol. 62, pp. 777-795.

Alchian, A.A. and Woodward, S., 1987, Reflections on the Theory of the Firm, *Journal of Institutional and Theoretical Economics*, Vol. 143, pp. 110-136.

Alchian, A.A. and Woodward, S., 1988, The Firm is Dead; Long Live the Firm. A Review of Oliver E. Williamson's The Economic Institutions of Capitalism, *Journal of Economic Literature*, Vol. 26, pp. 65-79.

Amit, R., and Schoemaker, P.J.H., 1993, Strategic Assets and Organisational Rent, *Strategic Management Journal*, Vol. 14, No. 1, pp. 33-46.

Ansoff, H.I., 1965, *Corporate Strategy*, New York: McGraw-Hill.

Ansoff, H.I., 1969 (first published in 1968, Economies et Societes, Vol. 2, No. 3), Toward a Strategic Theory of the Firm, in I. Ansoff (eds.) *Business Strategy*, London: Penguin, pp. 11-12.

Ansoff, H.I., 1980, Strategic Issue Management, *Strategic Management Journal*, Vol. 1, pp. 131-148.

Ansoff, H.I., 1991, Critique of Henry Mintzberg's 'The Design School: Reconsidering the Basic Premises of Strategic Management', *Strategic Management Journal*, Vol. 12, pp. 449-461.

Aoki, M., 1990, Knowledge: Its Acquisition, Sharing and/or Asymmetry, in M. Aoki, B. Gustafsson and O.E. Williamson (eds.) *The Firm as a Nexus of Treaties*, London: Sage Publications, pp. 26-52.

Archibald, G.C., 1979, Method and Appraisal in Economics, *Philosophy of Social Sciences*, Vol. 9, pp. 304-315.

Armentano, D.T., 1978, A Critique of Neoclassical and Austrian Monopoly Theory, in L.M. Spadaro (eds.) *New Directions in Austrian Economics*, Kansas: Sheed Andrews and McMeel, pp. 94-110.

Arrow, K., 1970, The Organisation of Economic Activity: Issues Pertinent to the Choice of Market Versus Nonmarket Allocation, in R.H. Haverman and J. Margolis (eds.) *Public Expenditure and Policy Analysis*, Chicago: Markham, pp. 67-81.

Arrow, K.J., 1983, *Collected Papers of Kenneth J. Arrow. General Equilibrium*, Vol. 2, Oxford: Basil Blackwell.

Auerbach, P., 1988, *Competition. The Economics of Industrial Change*, Oxford: Basil Blackwell.

Aumann, R.J., 1985, What is Game Theory Trying to Accomplish?, in K.J. Arrow and S. Honkapohja (eds.) *Frontiers of Economics*, Oxford: Basil Blackwell, pp. 28-76.

Aumann, R. and Hart, S., 1992, Preface, in R. Aumann and S. Hart (eds.) *Hand Book of Game Theory*, Amsterdam: North-Holland, pp. xi-xiv.

Awan, A.A., 1986, Marshallian and schumpeterian Theories of Economic Evolution: Gradualism Versus Punctualism, *Atlantic Economic Journal*, Vol. 14, pp. 37-49.

Backhouse, R., 1985, *A History of Modern Economic Analysis*, Oxford: Basil Blackwell.

Bailey, A. and Johnson, G., 1992, How Strategies Develop in Organisations, in D. Faulkner and G. Johnson (eds.) *The Challenge of Strategic Management*, London: Kogan Page, pp. 147-177.

Bain, J.S., 1952, *Price Theory*, New York: John Wiley & Sons.

Bain, J.S., 1956, *Barriers to New Competition*, Cambridge: Harvard University Press.

Bain, 1968, *Industrial Organisation*, 2nd ed. (1st ed., in 1959), New York: John Wiley and Sons.

Bass, F.B., 1974, Profit and A/S Ratio, *Journal of Advertising Research*, Vol. 14, No. 6, pp. 9-19.

Barney, J.B., 1985, Theory Z, Institutional Economics, and the Theory of Strategy, in P.R. Kleindorfer (eds.) *The Management of Productivity and Technology in Manufacturing*, New York: Plenum Press, pp. 229-237.

Barney, J.B., 1986a, Organisational Culture: Can It be a Source of Sustained Competitive Advantage?, *Academy of Management Review*, Vol. 11, pp. 656-665.

Barney, J.B., 1986b, Strategic Factor Markets: Expectations, Luck and Business Strategy, *Management Science*, Vol. 42, pp. 1231-1241.

Barney, J.B., 1986c, Types of Competition and the Theory of Strategy: Toward an Integrative Framework, *Academy of Management Review*, Vol. 11, No. 4, pp. 791-800.

Barney, J.B. and Ouchi, W.G., 1986, *Organisational Economics* (eds.), London: Jossey-Bass Publishers.

Barney, J.B. and Ouchi, W.G., 1986, Agency Theory: How Market Forces Affect the Management of a Firm, in J.B. Barney and W.G. Ouchi (eds.) *Organisational Economics*, London: Jossey-Bass Publishers, pp. 205-213.

Barney, J.B., 1990a, The Debate Between Traditional Management Theory and Organizational Economics: Substantive Differences or Intergroup Conflict?, *Academy of Management Review*, Vol. 15, No. 3, pp. 382-393.

Barney, J.B., 1990b, Strategic Groups: Untested Assertions and Research Proposal, *Managerial and Decision Economics*, Vol. 11, pp. 187-198.

Barney, J.B., 1991, Firm Resources and Sustainable Competitive Advantage, *Journal of Management*, Vol. 17, No. 1, pp. 99-120.

Barry, N.P., 1991, Austrian Economics: A Dissent From Orthodoxy, in D. Greenaway and I. Stewart (eds.) *Companion to Contemporary Economic Thought*, London: Routledge, pp. 68-67.

Bauerschmidt, A.D., 1996, Speaking of Strategy: A Comment on Inkpen and Choudhury (1995), *Strategic Management Journal,* Vol. 17, pp. 665-667.

Besanko, D., Dranove, D. and Shanley, M., 1996, *Economics of Strategy*, New York: John Wiley & Sons.

Best, M.H., 1990, *The New Competition. Institutions of Industrial Restructuring*, Oxford: Polity Press.

Bettis, R.A., 1991, Strategic Management and the Straightjacket: An Editorial Essay, *Organization Science*, Vol. 2, No. 3, pp. 315-319.

Baumol, W.J., 1959, *Business Behaviour, Value, and Growth, London: Macmillan.*

Baumol, W.J., Panzar, J., and Willing, R., 1982, *Contestable Markets and the Theory of Industry Structure*, New York: Harcout Brace Jovanovich.

Becker, G.S., 1993, Nobel Lecture: The Economic Way of Looking at Behaviour, *Journal of Political Economy*, Vol. 101, No. 3, pp. 385-409.

Becker, G.S., 1976, *The Economic Approach to Human Behaviour*, Chicago, Ill.: The University of Chicago Press.

Berle, A.A. and Means, G.C., 1932, *The Modern Corporation and Private Property*, London: Macmillan.

Bianchi, M. and Moulin, H., 1991, Strategic Interactions in Economics: The Game Theoretic Alternative, in N. Marchi and M. Blaug (eds.) *Appraising Economic Theories. Studies in the Methodology of Research Programs*, Hants: Edward Elgar, pp. 179-196.

Binger, B.R. and Hoffman, E., 1989, Institutional Persistence and Change: The Quest of Efficiency, *Journal of Institutional and Theoretical Economics*, Vol. 145, pp. 87-84.

Blaug, M., 1976, Kuhn versus Lakatos or Paradigms versus Research Programmes in the History of Economics, in S.J. Latsis (eds.) *Method and Appraisal in Economics*, Cambridge: Cambridge University Press, pp. 149-180.

Blaug, M., 1985, *Economic Theory in Retrospect*, (4th edition), Cambridge: Cambridge University Press.

Blaug, M., 1992 (First published in 1980), *The Methodology of Economics or How Economists Explain*, Cambridge: Cambridge University Press.

Bohm, S., 1989, Hayek on Knowledge, Equilibrium, and Prices: Context and Impact, *Wirtschaftspolitische Blatter*, Vol. 36, No. 2, pp. 201-213.

Boland, L.A., 1979, A Critique of Friedman's Critics, *Journal of Economic Literature*, Vol. 17, pp. 503-522.

Boland, L.A., 1984, On the State of Economic Methodology, in W.J. Samuels (eds.) *Research in the History of Economic Thought and Methodology*, Vol. 2, London: JAI Press, pp. 173-177.

Boland, L.A., 1986, *Methodology for a New Microeconomics. The Critical Foundations*, London: Allen & Unwin.

Boulding, K., 1950, *Reconstruction in Economics*, New York: Wiley.

Bourgeois, L.J., 1984, Strategic Management and Determinism, *Academy of Management Review*, Vol. 9, No. 4, pp. 586-596.

Bracker, J., 1980, The Historical Development of the Strategic Management Concept, *Academy of Management Review*, Vol. 5, No. 2, pp. 219-224.

Brandis, R., 1984, On the Current State of Methodology in Economics, in W.J. Samuels (eds.) *Research in the History of Economic Thought and Methodology*, Vol. 2, London: JAI Press, pp. 151-160.

Breeley, R. and Myers, S., 1988, *Principles of Corporate Finance,* New York: McGraw-Hill.

Brennan, T.J., 1984, Is Economics Methodologically Special?, in W.J. Samuels (eds.) *Research in the History of Economic Thought and Methodology*, Vol. 2, London: JAI Press, pp. 127-140.

Bronfenbrenner, M., 1971, The "Structure of Revolutions" in Economic Thought, *History of Political Economy*, Vol. 3, pp. 136-151.

Brozen, Y., 1971, Bain's Concentration and rates of Return Revisited, *Journal of Law and Economics*, Vol. 14, pp. 351-369.

Brozen, Y., The Antitrust Task Force Deconcentration Recommendation, *Journal of Law and Economics*, Vol. 13, pp. 279-292.

Buchanan, J.M., 1982, The Domain of Subjective Economics: Between Predictive Science and Moral Philosophy, in I.M. Kirzner (eds.) *Method, Process and Austrian Economics*, Lexington, Mass.: Heath and Company, pp. 7-20.

Buchanan, J.M. and Vanberg, V.J., 1991, The Market as a Creative Process, *Economics and Philosophy*, Vol. 7, pp. 167-186.

Buckley, P. and Michie, J., 1996, Introduction and Overview, in P.J. Buckley and J. Michie (eds.) *Firms, Organisations and Contracts*, Oxford: Oxford University Press, pp. 1-22.

Caldwell, B.J., 1980, A Critique of Friedman's Methodological Instrumentalism, *Southern Economic Journal*, Vol. 47, pp. 366-374.

Caldwell, B.J., 1983, The Neoclassical Maximisation Hypothesis: Commet, *American Economic Review*, Vol. 73, No. 4, pp. 824-830.

Caldwell, B.J., 1984, Economic Methodology in the Postpositivist Era, in W.J. Samuels (eds.) *Research in the History of Economic Thought and Methodology*, Vol. 2, London: JAI Press, pp. 195-205.

Caldwell, B.J., 1991, Clarifying Popper, *Journal of Economic Literature*, Vol. 29, pp. 1-33.

Caldwell, B.J., 1993, Economic Methodology: Rationale, Foundations, Prospects, in U. Maki, B. Gustafsson and C. Knudsen (eds.) *Rationality, Institutions and Economic Methodology*, London: Routledge, pp. 45-60.

Camerer, C., 1985, Redirecting Research in Business Policy and Strategy, *Strategic Management Journal*, Vol. 6, pp. 1-15.

Camerer, C., 1991, Does Strategy Research Need Game Theory?, *Strategic Management Journal*, Vol. 12, pp. 137-152.

Camillus, J.C., 1982, Reconciling Logical Incrementalism and Synoptic Formalism - An Integrated Approach to Designing Strategic Planning Processes, *Strategic Management Journal*, Vol. 3, pp. 277-283.

Campbell, A. and Yeung, S., 1991, Creating a Sense of Mission, *Long Range Planning*, Vol. 24, No. 4, pp. 10-20.

Capra, F., 1997, *The Web of Life. A New Synthesis of Mind and Matter*, London: HarperCollins.

Carrol, G.R. and Vogel, D., 1987, *Organizational Approaches to Strategy*, (eds.), Cambridge, M.A.: Ballinger.

Carrol, G.R., 1993, A Sociological View on Why Firms Differ, *Strategic Management Journal*, Vol. 14, pp. 237-249.

Caves, R.E., 1980, Industrial Organization, Corporate Strategy and Structure, *Journal of Economic Literature*, Vol. 18, pp. 64-92.

Caves, R.E., 1984a, Economic Analysis and the Quest for Competitive Advantage, *American Economic Review* (Papers and proceedings of Ninety-Sixth Annual Meeting of the American Association, San Francisco, California, December 28-30, 1983, ed. by J.G. Riley and W. St. John), pp. 127-132.

Caves, R.E., 1984b, Industrial Organization, Corporate Strategy and Structure, in R.B. Lamb (eds.) *Competitive Strategic Management*, Englewood Cliffs, NY: Prentice-Hall, pp. 134-170.

Caves, R.E. and Ghemawat, P., 1992, Identifying Mobility Barriers, *Strategic Management Journal*, Vol. 13, pp. 1-12.

Caves, R.E., 1994, Game Theory, Industrial Organisation, and Business Strategy, *Journal of the Economics of Business*, Vol. 1, No. 1, pp. 11-14.

Chaffee, E.E., 1985, Three Models of Strategy, *Academy of Management Review*, Vol. 10, No., 1, pp. 89-98.

Chamberlin, E.D., 1962 (First published in 1933), *Theory of Monopolistic Competition*, Cambridge, M.A.: Harvard University Press.

Chandler, A.D., 1962, *Strategy and Structure: Chapters in the History of the American Industrial Enterprise*, Cambridge, MA: MIT Press.

Chandler, A.D., 1977, *The Invisible Hand: The Managerial Revolution in American Business*, Cambridge: Harvard University Press.

Chandler, A.D., 1984, The Emergence of Managerial Capitalism, *Business History Review*, Vol. 58, No. 4, pp. 473-503.

Chandler, A.D., 1991, The Enduring Logic of Industrial Success, in C.A. Montgomery and M.E. Porter (eds.), *Strategy: Seeking and Securing Competitive Advantage*, Boston: Harvard Business School, pp. 257-275.

Chandler, A.D., Jr., 1992, What is a Firm? A Historical Perspective, *European Economic Review*, Vol. 36, No. 213, pp. 483-492.

Chi, T., 1994, Trading in Strategic Resources: Necessary Conditions, Transaction Cost Problems, and Choice of Exchange Structure, *Strategic Management Journal*, Vol. 15, pp. 271-290.

Child, J., 1972, Organizational Structure, Environment and Performance: The Role of Strategic Choice, *Sociology*, Vol. 6, pp. 1-22.

Clark, J.B., 1956 (First published in1899), *The Distribution of Wealth*, New York: Kelley and Millman.

Clarke, R. and McGuiness, T., 1987, *The Economics of the Firm*, (eds.), Oxford: Basil Blackwell.

Cleg, S.R., 1990, *Modern Organizations: Organization Studies in the Postmodern World*, London: Sage Publications.

Coase, R.H., 1937, The Nature of the Firm, *Economica*, Vol. 4, pp. 386-405.

Coase, R.H., 1960, The Problem of Social Cost, *The Journal of Law and Economics*, Vol. 3, pp. 1- 44.

Coats, A.W., 1969, Is There a "Structure of Scientific Revolutions" in Economics, *Kyklos*, Vol. 22, pp. 289-296.

Coats, A.W., The Methodology of Economics: Some Recent Contributions, *Kyklos*, Vol. 35, pp. 310-321.

Coats, A.W., 1984, The Sociology of Knowledge and the History of Economics, in W.J. Samuels (eds.) *Research in the History of Economic Thought and Methodology*, Vol. 2, London: JAI Press, pp. 211-234.

Coleman, J.S., 1988, Social Capital in the Creation of Human Capital, *American Journal of Sociology*, (Suppl.), Vol. 94, pp. 95-120.

Collis, D.J, 1994, Research Note: How Valuable are Organisational Capabilities?, *Strategic Management Journal*, Vol. 15, pp. 143-152.

Colman, A.M., 1995, *Game Theory and Its Applications in the Social and Biological Sciences*, (2nd ed.), Oxford: Butterwort-Heinemann.

Commons, J.R., 1950, *The Economics of Collective Action*, New York: MacMillan.

Commons, J.R., 1961, *Institutional Economics: Its Place in Political Economy*, Madison, Wis.: University of Wisconsin Press.

Conner, K.R., 1991, A Historical Comparison of resource-Based Theory and Five Schools of Thought Within Industrial Organisation Economics: Do We Have A New Theory of the Firm?, *Journal of Management*, Vol. 17, pp. 121-154.

Cox, W.E., Jr., 1977, Product portfolio Strategy, Market Structure, and Performance, in H.B. Thorelli, *Strategy+Structure=Performance. The Strategic Planning Imperative*, Bloomington: Indiana University Press, pp. 83-102.

Cowling, K. and Sugden, R., 1993, Control, Markets and Firms, in C. Pitelis (ed) *Transaction Costs, Markets and Hierarchies*, Oxford: Basil Blackwell, pp. 67-76.

Cubbin, J., and Geroski, P., 1987, The Convergence of profits in the Long Run: Inter-firm and Inter-Industry Comparisons, *Journal of Industrial Economics*, Vol. 35, pp. 427-442.

Currie, M. and Steedman, I., 1990, *Wrestling with Time. Problems in Economic Theory*, Ann Arbor: The University of Michigan Press.

Cyert, R. and March, J.G., 1963, *A Behavioural Theory of the Firm*, Englewood Cliffs, NJ: Prentice Hall.

Cyert, R.M. and Kamien, M.I., 1972, Behavioural Rules and the Theory of the Firm, in Readings in C.K. Rowley (eds.) *Industrial Economics*, Vol. I, London: MacMillan, pp. 91-102.

Cyert, R.M. and Hendrick, C.L., 1972, Theory of the Firm: Past, Present, and Future; An Interpretation, *Journal of Economic Literature*, Vol. 10, No. 2, pp. 398-412.

Daft, R.L. and Buenger, 1990, Hitching a Ride on a Fast Train to Nowhere. The Past and Future of Strategic Management Research, in J.W. Frederikson (ed) *Perspectives on Strategic Management*, London: Harper Business, pp. 81-103.

Dahmen, E., 1984, Schumpeterian Dynamics. Some Methodological Notes, *Journal of Economic Behavior and Organizations*, Vol. 5, pp. 25-34.

Dasgupta, A.K., 1985, *Epochs of Economic Theory*, Oxford, Basil Blackwell.

Davies, S. and Lyons, B., 1992 (1989 first edition), Introduction, in S. Davies, B. Lyons with H. Dixon and P. Geroski (eds.) *Economics of Industrial Organisation*, London: Longman.

Day, R.H., 1984, Disequilibrium Economic Dynamics. A Post-Schumpeterian Contribution, *Journal of Economic Behaviour and Organizations*, Vol. 5, pp. 57-76.

Dean, J.W. and Sharfman, M.P., 1993, Procedural Rationality in the Strategic Decision-Making Process, *Journal of Management Studies*, Vol. 30, No. 4, pp. 577-610.

Demsetz, H., 1967, Toward a Theory of Property Rights, *American Economic Review*, Vol. 57, No. 2, pp. 347-359.

Demsetz, 1968, Why Regulate Utilities?, *Journal of Law and Economics*, Vol. 11, pp. 55-65.

Demsetz, H., 1973, Industry Structure, Market Rivalry, and Public Policy, *Journal of Law and Economics*, Vol. 16, No. 1, pp. 1-9.

Demsetz, H., 1974, Two Systems of Belief About Monopoly, in H.J. Goldschmid, H.M. Mann and J.F. Weston, (eds.) *Industrial Concentration: The New Learning,* Boston: Little, Brown.

Demsetz, H., 1982, *Economic, Legal, and Political Dimensions of Competition,* Amsterdam: North-Holland Publishing Company.

Demsetz, H., 1983, The Structure of Ownership and the Theory of the Firm, *Journal of Law and Economics*, Vol. 26, No. 2, pp. 375-390.

Demsetz, H., 1988, The Theory of the Firm Revisited, *Journal of Law, Economics, and Organization*, Vol. 4, No., 1, pp. 141-161.

Demsetz, H., 1989, *Efficiency, Competition and Policy. The Organization of Economic Activity*, Vol. II, Oxford: Basil Blackwell.

Demsetz, H., 1997, The Intensity and Dimensionality of Competition, in H. Demsetz (eds.) *The Economics of the Business Firm*, Cambridge: Cambridge University Press, pp. 137-169.

Dess, G.G., Ireland, R.D. and Hitt, M.A., 1990, Industry Effects and Strategic Management Research, *Journal of Management*, Vol. 16, No. 1, pp. 7-27.

De Wit, B. and Meyer, R., 1994, *Strategy. Process, Content, Context*, New York: West Publishing Company. See pp. 214-217.

Dierickx, I. and Cool, K., 1989, Asset Stock Accumulation and Sustainability of Competitive Advantage, *Management Science*, Vol. 35, pp. 1504-1511.

Dolan, G., (ed.) 1976, *The Foundations of Modern Austrian Economics*, Kansas City, KS: Sheed & Ward.

Donaldson, L., 1990a, The Ethereal Hand: Organizational Economics and Management Theory, *Academy of Management Review*, Vol. 15, No. 3, pp. 369-381.

Donaldson, L., 1990b, A Rational Basis for Criticism of Organizational Economics: A Reply to Barney, *Academy of Management Review*, Vol. 15, No. 3, pp. 394-401.

Donaldson, L., 1991, Stewardship Theory or Agency Theory: CEO Governance and Shareholder Returns, *Austrian Journal of Management*, Vol. 16, No. 1, pp. 49-64.

Donaldson, L., 1992, The Weick Stuff: Managing Beyond Games, *Organization Science*, Vol. 3, No. 4, pp. 461-466.

Donaldson, L., 1995, *American Anti-Management Theories of Organization. A Critique of Paradigm Proliferation*, Cambridge: Cambridge University Press.

Dopfer, K., (ed.) 1976, *Economics in the Future*, London: Macmillan.

Dopfer, K., 1994, The Phenomenon of Economic Change: Neoclassical vs. Schumpeterian Approaches, in L. Magnusson (ed.) *Evolutionary and Neo-Schumpeterian Approaches to Economics*, Boston: Kluwer, pp. 125-171.

Dosi, G., 1990, Economic Change and Its Interpretation, or, Is There a "Schumpeterian Approach"?, in A. Heetje and M. Perlman (eds.) *Evolving Technology and Market Structure: Studies in Schumpeterian Economics*, Ann Arbor: The University of Michigan Press, pp. 335-341.

Dosi, G., 1991, Some Thoughts on the Promises, Challenges and Dangers of an "Evolutionary Perspective" in Economics, *Journal of Evolutionary Economics*, Vol. 1, pp. 5-7.

Dosi, G., Teece, D.J. and Winter, S., 1992, Towards a Theory of Corporate Coherence: Preliminary remarks' In G. Dosi, R. Gianetti and P.A. Toninelli (eds.) *Technology and Enterprise in a Historical Perspective*, Oxford: Oxford University Press.

Drucker, P.F., 1979, *Management*, London: Pan Books.

Edgeworth, F.Y., 1881, *Mathematical Psychics: An Assay on the Application of Mathematics to the Moral Sciences*, London: Kegan Paul.

Eisenhardt, K.M., 1989, Agency Theory: An Assessment and Review, *Academy of Management Review*, Vol. 14, No. 1, pp. 57-74.

Eisenhardt, K.M. and Zbaracki, M.J., 1992, Strategic Decision Making, *Strategic Managment Journal*, Vol. 13, pp. 17-37.

Eliasson, G., 1994, The Theory of the Firm and the Theory of Economic Change, in L. Magnusson (eds.) *Evolutionary and Neo-Schumpeterian Approaches to Economics*, Boston: Kluwer, pp. 173-201.

Encaoua, D., Geroski, P. and Jacquemin, A., 1986, Strategic Competition and the Persistence of Dominant firms: a Survey, in J.E. Stiglitz and G.F. Mathewson, 1986, *New Developments in the Analysis of Market Structure*, London: Macmillan, pp. 55-86.

Fama, E.F. and Jensen, M.C., 1983, Separation of Ownership and Control, *Journal of Law and Economics*, Vol. 26, pp. 301-326.

Faulkner, D. and Johnson, G., 1992, *The Challenge of Strategic Management*, (eds.), London: Kogan Page.

Ferguson, P.R. and Ferguson, G.J., 1994 (First published in1988), *Industrial Economics. Issues and Perspectives*, London: Macmillan.

Feyerabend, P., 1981, How to Defend Society Against Science, in I. Hacking (eds.) *Scientific Revolutions*, Oxford: Oxford University Press, pp. 156-167.

Forges, F., and Thisse, J.F., 1992, Game Theory and Industrial Economics: An Introduction, in G. Norman and M. La Manna (eds.) *The New Industrial Economics. Recent Developments in Industrial Organisation, Oligopoly and Game Theory*, Hants: Edward Elgar, pp. 12-46.

Foss, N.J., 1993, Theories of the Firm: Contractual and Competence Perspectives, *Journal of Evolutionary Economics*, Vol. 3, pp. 127-144.

Foss, N.J., 1994a, *The Austrian School and Modern Economics: Essays in Reassessment,* Copenhagen: Copenhagen Business School Press.

Foss, N.J., 1994b, The Theory of the Firm: The Austrians as Precursors and Critics of Contemporary Theory, *The Review of Austrian Economics,* Vol. 7, No. 1, pp. 31-65.

Foss, N.J., 1996a, Whither the Competence Perspective?, in N.J. Foss and C. Knudsen (eds.) *Towards a Competence Theory of the Firm*, London: Routledge, pp. 175-200.

Foss, N.J., 1996b, Research in Strategy, Economics, and Michael Porter, *Journal of Management Studies*, Vol. 33, No. 1, pp. 1-24.

Foss, N.J. and Knudsen, C., 1996, *Towards a Competence Theory of the Firm* (eds.), London: Routledge.

Foss, N.J., Knudsen, C. and Montgomery, C.A., 1995, An Exploration of Common Ground: Integrating Evolutionary and Strategic Theories of the Firm, in C.A. Montgomery (eds.) *Resource-Based and Evolutionary Theories of the Firm: Towards a Synthesis*, Boston: Kluwer Academic Publishers, pp. 1-17.

Fourie, F.C.v.N., 1989, The Nature of Frims and Markets: Do Transactions Approaches Help?, *South African Journal of Economics*, Vol. 157, pp. 142-160.

Fox, M.A. and Hamilton, R.T., 1994, Ownership and Diversification: Agency Theory or Stewardship Theory, *Journal of Management Studies,* Vol. 31, No. 1, pp. 69-81.

Frazer, W.J. and Boland, L.A., 1983, An Essay on the Foundations of Friedman's Methodology, *American Economic Review*, Vol. 73, pp. 129-144.

Friedman, M., 1953, The Methodology of Positive Economics, in M. Friedman (eds.) *Essays in Positive Economics*, Chicago: Chicago University Press.

Frisch, R., 1936, On the Notion of Equilibrium and Disequilibrium, *Review of Economic Studies*, Vol. 3, pp. 100-106.

Fulton, G., 1984, Research Programmes in Economics, *History of Political Economy*, Vol. 16, No. 2, pp. 187-205.

Gabel, H.D., 1984, The Microfoundations of Competitive Strategy, *Working Paper*, INSEAD.

Galbraith, J.K., 1991, Economics in the Century Ahead, *The Economic Journal*, Vol. 101, pp. 41-46.

Gale, B.T. and Branch, B.S., 1982, Concentration versus Market Share: Which Determines Performance and Why Does It Matter?, *The Antitrust Bulletin*, Spring, pp. 83-105.

Gardner, R., 1995, *Games for Business and Economics*, New York: John Wiley & Sons.

Garrat, B., 1995, *Developing Strategic Thought*, (eds.), London: HarperCollins.

Gee, J.M.A., 1990, The Neoclassical School, in D. Mair and A.G. Miller (eds.) *A Modern Guide to Economic Theory: An Introduction to Comparative Schools of Thought in Economics*, Hants: Edward Elgar, pp. 71-108.

Gee, J.M.A. and Norman, G., 1992, Introduction, in J.M.A. Gee and G. Norman (eds.) *Market Strategy and Structure*, London: Harvester Wheatsheaf, pp. 1-11.

Ghemawat, P., 1991, Sustainable Advantage, in C.A. Montgomery and M.E. Porter (eds.) *Seeking and Securing Competitive Advantage*, Boston: Harvard Business School, pp. 27-38.

Ghemewat, P., 1991, *Commitment. The Dynamic of Strategy*, New York: The Free Press.

Gilbert, C.L., 1991, Do Economists Test Theories? - Demand Analysis and Consumption Analysis as Tests of Theories of Economic Methodology, in N. Marchi and M. Balug (eds.) *Appraising Economic Theories. Studies in the Methodology of Research Programs*, Hants: Edward Elgar, pp. 137-168.

Godfrey, P.C. and Hill, C.W.L., 1995, The Problem of Unobservables in Strategic Management Research, *Strategic Management Research*, Vol. 16, pp. 519-533.

Goodwin, R.M., 1990, Walras and Schunpeter: The Vision Reaffirmed, in A. Heetje and M. Perlman (eds.) *Evolving Technology and Market Structure: Studies in Schumpeterian Economics*, Ann Arbor: The University of Michigan Press, pp. 39-49.

Grant, R.M., 1991, The Resource-Based Theory of Competitive Advantage: implications for Strategy Formulation, *California Management Review*, Vol. 33, No. 3, pp. 114-135.

Guthrie, W., 1984, Methodological Diversity: Recognition, Responses, and Implications, in W.J. Samuels (eds.) *Research in the History of Economic Thought and Methodology*, Vol. 2, London: JAI Press, pp. 141-149.

Hacking, I., 1981, *Scientific Revolutions*, (eds.), Oxford: Oxford University Press.

Hahn, F., 1973, *On the Notion of Equilibrium in Economics*, Cambridge: Cambridge University Press.

Hahn, F., 1984a, General Equilibrium Theory, in F. Hahn (eds.) *Equilibrium and Macroeconomics*, Oxford: Basil Blackwell, pp. 72-87.

Hahn, F., 1984b, Reflections on the Invisible Hand, in F.Hahn (eds.) *Equilibrium and Macroeconomics*, Oxford: Basil Blackwell, pp. 111-133, p. 117.

Hahn, F.H., 1989, Conjectural Equilibria, in J. Eatwell, M. Milgate and P. Newman (eds.) *The New Palgrave. General Equilibrium*, London: Macmillan, pp. 98-107.

Hahn, F., 1991, The Next Hundred Years, *The Economic Journal*, Vol. 101, pp. 47-50.

Hall, D.J. and Saias, M.A., 1980, Strategy Follows Structure!, *Strategic Management Journal*, Vol. 1, pp. 149-163.

Hambrick, D.C., 1990, The Adolescence of Strategic Management, 1980-1985. Critical Perceptions and Reality, in J.W. Frederikson (eds.) *Perspectives on Strategic Management*, London: Harper Business, pp. 237-261.

Hamel, G., 1991, Competition for Competence and Inter-Partner Learning Within International Strategic Alliances, *Strategic Management Journal*, Vol. 12, pp. 83-103.

Hamel, G., 1994, The Concept of Core Competence, in G. Hamel and A. Heene *Competence-Based Competition*, (eds.), New York: John Wiley & Sons, pp. 11-33.

Hamel, G. and Prahalad, C.K., 1993, Strategy as Stretch and Leverage, *Harvard Business Review*, March/April, pp. 75-84.

Hamel, G. and Heene, A., 1994, *Competence-Based Competition*, (eds.), New York: John Wiley & Sons.

Hamel, G. and Heene, A., 1994, Introduction: Competing Paradigms in Strategic Management, in G. Hamel and A. Heene *Competence-Based Competition*, (eds.), New York: John Wiley & Sons, pp. 1-7.

Hamilton, W.H., 1987, The Institutional Approach to Economic Theory, in R. Albelda, C. Gunn and W. Waller (eds.) *Alternatives to Economic Orthodoxy: A Reader in Political Economy*, Armonk, NY: M.E. Sharpe, pp. 204-212.

Hands, W.D., 1985, Second Thoughts on Lakatos, *History of Political Economy*, Vol. 17, No. 1, pp. 1-16.

Hands, W.D., 1991, The Problem of Excess Content: Economics, Novelty and a Long Popperian Tale, in N. Marchi and M. Blaug (eds.) *Appraising Economic Theories. Studies in the Methodology of Research Programs*, Hants: Edward Elgar, pp. 58-75.

Hands, D.W., 1993, Popper and Lakatos in Economic Methodology, in U. Maki, B. Gustafsson and C. Knudsen (eds.) *Rationality, Institutions and Economic Methodology*, London: Routledge, pp. 61-75.

Hansen, G.S. and Wernerfelt, B., 1989, Determinants of Firm Performance: The Relative Importance of Economic and Organizational Factors, *Strategic Management Journal*, Vol. 10, pp. 399-411.

Hanusch, H., 1988, *Evolutionary Economics. Applications of Schumpeter's Ideas*, (eds.), Cambridge: Cambridge University Press.

Hart, O., 1995, *Firms, Contracts and Financial Structure*, Oxford: Clarendon Press.

Hart, O., 1996, An Economist's Perspective on the Theory of the Firm, in P.J. Buckley and Michie (eds.) *Firms, Organisations and Contracts*, Oxford: Oxford University Press, pp. 199-218.

Hart, S. and Banbury, C., 1994, How Strategy-Making Processes Can Make a Difference, *Strategic Management Journal,* Vol. 15, pp. 251-269.

Hassard, J., 1994, Postmodern Organizational Analysis: Toward a Conceptual Framework, *Journal of Management Studies*, Vol. 31, No. 3, pp. 303-324.

Hassard, J. and Pym, D., 1990, *The Theory and Philosophy of Organisations*, (eds.), London: Routledge.

Hatten, K.J. and Hatten, M.L., 1987, Strategic Groups, Asymmetrical Mobility Barriers and Contestability, *Strategic Management Journal*, Vol. 8, pp. 329-342.

Hausman, D.M., 1989, Economic Methodology in a Nutshell, *Journal of Economic Perspectives*, Vol. 3, No. 2, pp. 115-127.

Hayek, F.A., 1937, Economics and Knowledge, in F.A. Hayek (1948) *Individualism and Economic Order*, Chicago: Chicago University Press, pp. 33-56.

Hayek, F.A., 1945, The Use of Knowledge in Society, in F.A. Hayek (1948) *Individualism and Economic Order*, Chicago: Chicago University Press, pp. 77-91.

Hayek, F.A., 1946, The Meaning of Competition, in F.A. Hayek (1948) *Individualism and Economic Order*, Chicago: Chicago University Press, pp. 92-106.

Hayek, F.A., 1948, *Individualism and Economic Order*, Chicago: Chicago University Press.

Hayek, F.A., 1955, *The Counter-revolution of Science: Studies on the Abuse of Reason*, Glencoe, Ill.: Free Press.

Hayek, F.A., 1964, Kinds of Order in Society, *New Individualist Review*, Vol. 3, No. 3, pp. 3-12.

Hayek, F.A., 1967a, Kinds of Rationality, in F.A. Hayek (eds.) *Studies in Philosophy, Politics and Economics*, London: Routledge & Kegan Paul, pp. 82-95.

Hayek, F.A., 1967b, *Studies in Philosophy, Politics, Economics and the History of Ideas*, Chicago: University of Chicago Press.

Hayek, F.A., 1968 (Reprinted in 1978), Competition As a Discovery Procedure, in F.A. Hayek (1978) *New Studies in Philosophy, Politics, Economics and the History of Ideas*, London: Routledge & Kegan Paul, pp. 179-190.

Hayek, F.A., 1973, Law, Legislation and Liberty, Vol. 1, *Rules and Order*, London: Routledge & Kegan Paul.

Hayek, F.A., 1976, Law, Legislation and Liberty, Vol. 2, *The Mirage of Social Justice*, London: Routledge & Kegan Paul.

Hayek, F.A., 1979, Law, Legislation and Liberty, Vol. 3, *The Political Order of a Free People*, London: Routledge & Kegan Paul.

Hayek, F.A., 1988, *The Fatal Conceit - The Errors of Socialism*, London: Routledge & Kegan Paul.

Heetje, A. and Perlman, M., 1990, *Evolving Technology and Market Structure: Studies in Schumpeterian Economics*, (eds.), Ann Arbor: The University of Michigan Press, pp. 335-341.

Heiner, R.A., 1983, The Origin of Predictable Behavior, *American Economic Review*, Vol. 75, pp. 560-595.

Henderson, B.D., 1984, On Corporate Strategy, in R.B. Lamb (eds.) *Competitive Strategic Management*, Englewood Cliffs, NJ: pp. 1-33.

Henderson, B.D., 1991, The Origin of Strategy, in C.A. Montgomery and M.E. Porter (eds.) *Seeking and Securing Competitive Advantage*, Boston: Harvard Business School, pp. 3-9.

Henderson, R. and Mitchell, W., 1997, The Interactions of Organizational and Competitive Influences on Strategy and Performance, *Strategic Manangement Journal*, Vol. 18 (Summer Special Issue), pp. 5-14.

Hendry, C., 1994, *Human Resource Strategies for International Growth*, London: Routledge.

Hendry, C. Johnson, G. and Newton, J., 1993, *Strategic Thinking. Leadership and the Management of Change*, New York: John Wiley & Sons.

Hesterly, W.S., Liebeskind, J. and Zenger, T.R., 1990, Organizational Economics: An Impending Revolution in Organizational Theory?, *Academy of Management Review*, Vol. 15, No. 3, pp. 402-420.

Hey, J.D., 1979, *Uncertainty in Microeconomics*, Oxford: Martin Robertson.

Hicks, J.R., 1939, *Value and Capital*, Oxford: Oxford University Press.

Hicks, J.R., 1976, Some Questions of Time in Economics, in A.M. Tang, F.M. Westfield and J.S. Worley (eds.) *Evolution, Welfare, and Time in Economics*, Toronto: Lexington Books, pp. 135-152.

Hill, C.W.L., 1985, Oliver Williamson and the M-Form Firm: A Critical Review, *Journal of Economic Issues*, Vol. 19, No. 3, pp. 731-751.

Hill, C.W.L., 1988, Differentiation Versus Low Cost or Differentiation and Low Cost: A Contingency Framework, *Academy of Management Review*, Vol. 13, No., 3, pp. 401-412.

Hill, C.W.L., 1990, Cooperation, Opportunism, and the Invisible Hand: Implications for Transaction Cost Theory, *Academy of Management*, Vol. 15, No. 3, pp. 500-513.

Hill, C.W.L., 1996, The Importance of Industry Structure for the Determination of Firm Profitability: A Neo-Austrian Perspective, *Journal of Management Studies*, Vol. 33, No. 4, pp. 429-451.

Hirsch, P.M., Friedman, R. and Koza, M.P., 1990, Collaboration or Paradigm Shift?: Caveat Emptor and the Risk of Romance with Economic Models for Strategy and Policy Research, *Organization Science*, Vol. 1, No. 1, pp. 87-97.

Hirshleifer, J., 1977, Economics From a Biological Viewpoint, *Journal of Law and Economics*, Vol. 20, No. 1, pp. 1-52.

Hodgson, G.M., 1988, *Economics and Institutions: A Manifesto for a Modern Institutional Economics*, Oxford: Polity Press.

Hodgson, G.M., 1989, Institutional Economic Theory: The Old versus the New, *Review of Political Economy*, Vol. 1, No. 3, pp. 249-269.

Hodgson, G.M., 1993, *Economics and Evolution: Bringing Life Back Into Economics*, Cambridge: Polity Press.

Hodgson, G.M., 1993, Evolution and Institutional Change: On the Nature of Selection in Biology and Economics, in U. Maki, B. Gustafsson and C. Knudsen (eds.) *Rationality, Institutions and Economic Methodology* (eds.), London: Routledge, pp. 222-241.

Holmstorm, B.R., 1989, The Theory of the Firm, in R. Schmalensee and R.D. Willing (eds.) *Handbook of Industrial Organization*, North-Holland: Elseiver Science Publishers B.V., pp. 61-133.

Houthoofd, N. and Heene, A., 1997, Strategic Groups as Subsets of Strategic Scope Groups in the Belgian Brewing Industry, *Strategic Management Journal*, Vol. 18, No. 8, pp. 653-666.

Howard, M., 1983, *Profits in Economic Theory*, London: MacMillan.

Hume, D., 1967 (1740), *A Treatise of Human Nature*, Edited by L.A. Selby-Bigge, Oxford: Clarendon Press.

Inkpen, A., 1996, The Seeking of Strategy Where It is Not: Towards a theory of Strategy Absence: a Reply to Bauerschmidt, *Strategic Management Journal*, Vol. 17, pp. 669-670.

Inkpen, A. and Choudhury, N., 1995, The Seeking of Strategy Where It is Not: Towards a Theory of Strategy Absence, *Strategic Management Journal*, Vol. 16, pp. 313-323.

Itami, H. with Roehl, T., 1987, *Mobilising Invisible Assets*, Cambridge, MA: Harvard University Press.

Iwai, K., 1984, Schumpeterian Dynamics, *Journal of Economic Behavior and Organizations*, Vol. 5, pp. 159-190.

Iwai, K., 1984, Schumpeterian Dynamics, Part II, *Journal of Economic Behavior and Organizations*, Vol. 5, pp. 321-351.

Jacobson, R., 1988, The Persistence of Abnormal Returns, *Strategic Management Journal*, Vol. 9, pp. 415-430.

Jacobson, R., 1992, The "Austrian" School of Strategy, *Academy of Management Review*, Vol. 17, No. 4, pp. 782-807.

Jaquemin, A., 1987, *The New Industrial Organisation: Market Forces and Strategic Behaviour*, Oxford: Clarendon Press.

Jensen, M.C. and Meckling, W.H., 1976, Theory of the Firm: Managerial Behaviour, Agency Costs and Ownership Structure, *Journal of Financial Economics*, Vol. 3, pp. 305-360.

Jensen M.C. and Meckling, W.H., 1976, Theory of the Firm: Managerial Behaior, Agency Costs and Ownershop Structure, *Journal of Financial Economics*, Vol. 3, pp. 305-360.

Jensen, M.C., 1983, Organisation Theory and Methodology, *Accounting Review*, Vol. 56, No. 2, pp. 319-339.

Jevons, W.S., 1957 (First published in 1871), *Theory of Political Economy*, New York: Kelley and Millman

Johnson, E.J. and Russo, J.E., 1997, Coevolution: Toward a Third Frame for Analysing Competitive Decision Making, in G.S. Day and D.J. Reibstein with R.E. Gunther (eds.) *Wharton on Dynamic Competitive Strategy*, New York: John Wiley & Sons, pp. 177-197.

Johnson, G., 1988, Rethinking Incrementalism, *Strategic Management Journal*, Vol. 9, pp. 75-91.

Jones, G.R. and Hill, C.W.L., 1988, Transaction Cost Analysis of Strategy-Structure Choice, *Strategic Management Journal*, Vol. 9, pp. 159-172.

Jones, R., 1976, *Supply in a Market Economy*, London: George Allen & Unwin.

Joskow, P.L., 1975, Firm Decision-Making Processes and Oligopoly Theory, *American Economic Review*, Papers and Proceedings, pp. 270-279.

Kaldor, N., 1934, The Equilibrium of the Firm, *Economic Journal*, Vol. 44, pp. 60-76.

Karlof, B., 1993, *Strategic Precision: Improving Performance Through Organisational Efficiency*, (Translated from German by A.J. Gilderson), Chichester: John Willey & Sons.

Kay, J., 1993a, *Foundations of Corporate Success*, Oxford: Oxford University Press.

Kay, J., 1993b, The Structure of Strategy, *Business Strategy Review*, Vol. 4, No. 2, pp. 17-37.

Kay, J.A., 1991a, Economics and Business, *The Economic Journal*, Vol. 101, pp. 57-63;

Kay, J.A., 1991b, Multinational Entreprise as Strategic Choice: Some Transaction Cost Perspectives, in C.N. Pitelis and R. Sugden (eds.) *The Nature of Transnational Firm*, London: Routledge, pp. 137-154.

Kay, N.M., 1982, *The Evolving Firm*, London: MacMillan.

Kay, N.M., 1984, *The Emergent Firm*, London: MacMillan.

Kirzner, I.M., 1973, *Competition and Entrepreneurship*, Chicago: The University of Chicago Press.

Kirzner, I.S., 1976, On the Method of Austrian Economics, in E.G. Dolan (eds.) *The Foundations of Modern Austrian Economics*, Kansas City, KS.: Sheed & Ward, pp. 40-51.

Kirzner, I.M., 1976, Equilibrium versus Market Process, in E.G. Dolan (eds) *The Foundations of Modern Austrian Economics*, Kansas City, KS.: Sheed & Ward, pp. 115-125.

Kirzner, I.M., 1978, Economics and Error, in L.M. Spadaro (eds.) *New Directions in Austrian Economics*, Kansas City, KS: Shhed Andrews and McMeel, pp. 57-76.

Kirzner, I.M., 1985, *Discovery and the Capitalist Process*, Chicago: The University of Chicago Press.

Knight, F., 1921, *Risk, Uncertainty and Profit*, Boston: Houghton Mifflin.

Knudsen, C., 1993a, Equilibrium, Perfect Rationality and the Problem of Self-Reference in Economics, in U. Maki, B. Gustafsson and C. Knudsen (eds.) *Rationality, Institutions and Economic Methodology*, London: Routledge, pp. 133-170.

Knudsen, C., 1993b, Modelling Rationality, Institutions and Processes in Economic Theory, in U. Maki, B. Gustafsson and C. Knudsen (eds.) *Rationality, Institutions and Economic Methodology*, London: Routledge, pp. 265-299.

Knudsen, C., 1996, The Competence Perspective: A Historical View, in N.J. Foss and C. Knudsen (eds.) *Towards a Competence Theory of the Firm*, London: Routledge, pp. 13-37.

Kogut, B. and Zander, U., 1992, Knowledge of the Firm, Combinative Capabilities, and the Replication of Technology, *Organization Science*, Vol. 3, No. 3, pp. 383-397.

Kornai, J., 1971, *Anti-Equilibrium. On Economic Systems Theory and the Tasks of Research*, Amsterdam: North-Holland Publishing.

Kosnik, R.D., 1987, Greenmail: A Study of Board Performance in Corporate Governance, *Administrative Science Quarterly*, Vol. 32, No. 2, pp. 163-185.

Koutsoyiannis, A., 1979 (First published in 1975) *Modern Microeconomics*, London: Macmillan.

Kreps, D.M., 1990, *Game Theory and Economic Modelling*, Oxford: Clarendon Press.

Kuhn, T.S., 1970 (Second and enlarged edition), *The Structure of Scientific Revolutions*, Chicago: Chicago University Press.

Kuttner, R., 1987, The Poverty of Economics, in R. Albelda, C. Gunn and W. Waller (eds.) *Alternatives to Economic Orthodoxy: A Reader in Political Economy*, Armonk, NY: M.E. Sharpe, pp. 18-34.

Lachmann, L.M., 1990, Austrian Economics: A Hermeneutic Approach, in D. Lavoie (eds.) *Economics and Hermeneutics*, London: Routledge, pp. 134-146.

Lakatos, I., 1970, Falsification and the Methodology of Scientific Research Programmes, in I. Lakatos and A. Musgrave (eds.) *Criticism and the Growth of Knowledge*, Cambridge: Cambridge University Press, pp. 91-196.

Lakatos, I., 1976, *The Methodology of Scientific Research Programmes*, Cambridge: Cambridge University Press.

Lakatos, I., 1977, Falsification and the Methodology of Scientific Research Programmes, in I. Lakatos and A. Musgrave (eds.) *Criticism and the Growth of Knowledge, Cambridge*, Cambridge University Press, pp. 91-196.

Lakatos, I., 1981, History of Science and Its Rational Reconstructions, in I. Hacking (eds.) Scientific Revolutions, Oxford: Oxford University Press, pp. 107-127, p. 116. (First published in R.C. Buck and R.S. Cohen (eds.) *Boston Studies in the Philosophy of Science*, Vol. 8, pp. 91-108.)

Langlois, R.N., 1982, Austrian Economics as Affirmative Science: Comment on Rizzo, in I.M. Kirzner (eds.) *Method, Process, and Austrian Economics. Essays in Honour of Ludwing von Mises*, Lexington, Mass.: D.C. Heath and Company, pp. 75-84.

Langlois, R.N., 1992, Transaction-cost Economics in Real Time, *Industrial and Corporate Change*, Vol. 1, No. 1, pp. 99-127.

Langlois, R.N. and Everett, M.J., 1994, What is Evolutionary Economics, in L. Magnusson (eds.) *Evolutionary and Neo-Schumpeterian Approaches to Economics*, Boston: Kluwer Academic Publishers, pp. 11-47.

Langlois, R.N. and Csontos, L., 1993, Optimization, Rule-Following, and the Methodology of Situational Analysis, in U. Maki, B. Gustafsson and C. Knudsen (eds.) *Rationality, Institutions and Economic Methodology*, London: Routledge, pp. 113-132.

Langlois, R.N. and Everett, 1994, What is Evolutionary Economics?, in L. Magnusson (eds.) *Evolutionary and Neo-Schumpeterian Approaches to Economics*, Boston: Kluwer, pp. 11-47.

Langlois, R.N. and Robertson, P. L., 1995, *Firms, Markets and Economic Change*, London: Routledge.

Latsis, S.J., 1972, Situational Determinism in Economics, *British Journal for the Philosophy of Science*, Vol. 23, pp. 207-245.

Latsis, S.J., 1976, A Research Programme in Economics, in S.J. Latsis (eds.) *Method and Appraisal in Economics*, Cambridge: Cambridge University Press, pp. 1-41.

Laudan, L., 1977, *Progress and Its Problems. Towards a Theory of Scientific Growth*, London: Routledge & Kegan Paul.

Lavoie, D., 1990, *Economics and Hermeneutics*, (eds.), London: Routledge.

Lawson, T., 1997, *Economics and Reality*, London: Routledge.

Levinthal, D., 1994, Surviving Schumpeterian Environment: An Evolutionary Perspective, in J.A.C. Baum and J.V. Singh (eds.) *Evolutionary Dynamics of Organisations*, Oxford: Oxford University Press, pp. 167-178.

Levinthal, D.A., 1996, Strategic Management and the Exploration of Diversity, in C.A. Montgomery (eds.) *Resource-Based and Evolutionary Theories of the Firm: Towards a Synthesis*, Boston: Kluwer Academic Publishers, pp. 19-42.

Levy, D., 1994, Chaos Theory and Strategy: Theory, Application, and Managerial Implications, *Strategic Management Journal*, Vol. 15, pp. 167-178.

Lippman, S.A. and Rumelt, R.P., 1982, Uncertain Imitability: An Analysis of Interfirm Differences in Efficiency Under Competition, *The Bell Journal of Economics*, Vol. 13, (Autumn), pp. 418-438.

Littlechild, S.C., 1982, Equilibrium and the Market Process, in I.M. Kirzner (eds.) *Method, Process, and Austrian Economics*, Lexington, Mass.: D.C. Heath and Company, pp. 85-100.

Loasby, B., 1971, Hypothesis and Paradigm in the Theory of the Firm, *The Economic Journal*, Vol. 81, pp. 863-885.

Loasby, B.J., 1981, Economics of Dispersed and Incomplete Knowledge, *Mimo*, Stirling University.

Loasby, B.J., 1991, *Equilibrium and Evolution. An Exploration of Connecting Principles in Economics*, Manchester: Manchester University Press.

Loasby, B.J., 1995, Running a Business: An Appraisal of Economics, Organization and Management by Paul Milgrom and John Roberts, *Industrial and Corporate Change*, Vol. 4, pp. 471-489.

Loasby, B.J., 1993, Institutional Stability and Change in Science and Economy, in U. Maki, B. Gustafsson and C. Knudsen (eds.) *Rationality, Institutions and Economic Methodology*, London: Routledge, pp. 203-221.

Lundy, O. and Cowling, A., 1996, *Strategic Human Resource Management*, London: Routledge.

MacCrimmon, K.R., 1993, Do Firm Strategies Exist?, *Strategic Management Journal*, Vol. 14, pp. 113-130.

Machlup, F., 1963, *Essays on Economic Semantics*, (ed. by M.H. Miller), Englewood Cliffs, N.J.: Prentice-Hall.

Machlup, F., 1963, Equilibrium and Disequilibrium: Misplaced Correctedness and Disguised Politics, in F. Machlup (eds. by M.H. Miller) *Essays on Economic Semantics*, pp. 43-72. (Printed Originally in *The Economic Journal*, Vol. LXVIII, March, 1958.)

Machlup, F., 1967, Theories of the Firm: Marginalist, Behavioural, Managerial, *American Economic Review*, Vol. 57, No. 1, pp. 1-33.

Maddock, R., 1984, Rational Expectations Macrotheory: A Lakatosian Case Study in Program Adjustment, *History of Political Economy*, Vol. 16, No. 2, pp. 291-309.

Mahoney, J.T. and Pandian, J.R., 1992, The Resource-based View within the Conversation of Strategic Management, *Strategic Management Journal*, Vol. 13, pp. 363-380.

Magnusson, L., 1994a, *Evolutionary and Neo-Schumpeterian Approaches to Economics*, (eds.), Boston: Kluwer.

Magnusson, L., 1994b, The Neo-Schumpeterian and Evolutionary Approach to Economics-An Introduction, in L. Magnusson (eds.) *Evolutionary and Neo-Schumpeterian Approaches to Economics*, Boston: Kluwer, pp. 1-8.

Mahoney, J.T., 1993, Strategic Management and Determinism: Sustaining the Conversation, *Journal of Management Studies*, Vol. 30, No. 1, pp. 173-191.

Mahoney, J.T. and Pandian, J.R., 1992, The Resource-Based View Within the Conversation of Strategic Management, *Strategic Management Journal*, Vol. 13, pp. 363-380.

Mair, D. and Miller, A.G., 1990, *A Modern Guide to Economic Theory: An Introduction to Comparative Schools of Thought in Economics*, (eds.), Hants: Edward Elgar.

Maki, U., 1988, How to Combine Rhetoric and Realism in the Methodology of Economics, *Economics and Philosophy*, Vol. 4, pp. 89-109.

Maki, U., Gustafsson, B. and Knudsen, C., 1993, *Rationality, Institutions and Economic Methodology* (eds.), London: Routledge.

Maki, U., 1993a, Social Theories of Science and the Fate of Institutionalism in Economics, in U. Maki, B. Gustafsson and C. Knudsen (eds.) *Rationality, Institutions and Economic Methodology* (eds.), London: Routledge, pp. 76-109.

Maki, U., 1993b, Economics with Institutions: Agenda for Methodological Enquiry, in U. Maki, B. Gustafsson and C. Knudsen (eds.) *Rationality, Institutions and Economic Methodology* (eds.), London: Routledge, pp. 3-42.

Malcomson, J.M., 1984, Efficient labour Organisation: Incentives, Power and the Transactions Costs Approach, in F.H. Stephen (eds.) *Firms, Organisation and Labour: Approaches to the Economics of Work Organisation*, London: Macmillan, pp. 119-126.

Man, A.-P. de, 1993, 1980, 1985, 1990, A Porter Exegesis, *Management Report Series* No. 166, Rotterdam School of Management, Erasmus Universiteit Rotterdam.

Marchi, N.D., 1988, *The Popperian Legacy in Economics*, (eds.), Cambridge: Cambridge University Press.

Markides, C.C. and Williamson, P.J., 1994, Related Diversification, Core Competences and Corporate Performance, *Strategic Management Journal*, Vol. 15, pp. 149-165.

Marris, R., 1963, A Model of the Managerial Entreprise, *Quarterly Journal of Economics*, Vol. 77, pp. 185-209.

Marris, R.L., 1964, *The Economic Theory of Managerial Capitalism*, London: Macmillan.

Marshall, A., 1919, *Industry and Trade*, London: Macmillan.

Marshall, A., 1961 (First published 1890) *Principles of Economics*, (ed. C.W. Guillebaud), London: Macmillan.

Mason, E.S., 1939, Price and Production Policies of Large-scale Enterprise, *American Economic Review*, Vol. 29, pp. 61-74.

Mason, E.S., 1982, The Harvard Department of Economics from the Beginning to World War II, *Quarterly Journal of Economics*, pp. 383-433.

Masterman, M., 1970, The Nature of a Paradigm, in I. Lakatos and A. Musgrave (eds.) *Criticism and the Growth of Knowledge*, Cambridge: Cambridge University Press, pp. 59-89.

McGahan, A.M. and Porter, M.E., 1997, How Much Does Industry Matter, Really?, *Strategic Management Journal*, Vol. 18 (Summer Special Issue), pp. 15-30.

McGee, J.S. and Thomas, H., 1986, Strategic Groups: Theory, Research and Taxonomy, *Strategic Management Journal*, Vol. 7, pp. 141-160.

McGee, J.S., 1988, *Industrial Organisation*, Englewood Cliffs, NJ: Prentice Hall.

McGuinness, T., 1987, Markets and Managerial Hierarchies, in R. Clarke and T. Mcguiness (eds.) *The Economics of the Firm*, Oxford: Basil Blackwell, pp. 42-61.

McKie, J.W., 1970, Market Structure and Function: Performance versus Behaviour, in J.W. Markham and G.F. Papanek (eds) *Industrial Organisation and Economic Development. In Honour of E.S. Mason*, New York: Houghton Mifflin, pp. 3-25.

McKiernan, P., 1996, *Historical Evolution of Strategic Management*, Vol. I and II, Hants: Darthmouth Publishing Company.

McNulty, P.J., 1984, On the Nature and Theory of Economic Organization: The Role of the Firm Reconsidered, *History of Political Economy*, Vol. 16, No. 2, pp. 233-253.

McWilliams, A. and Smart, D.L., 1993, Efficiency v. Structure-Conduct-Performance: Implications for Strategy Research and Practice, *Journal of Management*, Vol. 19, No. 1, pp. 63-78.

Menger, C. 1963, *Problems of Economics and Sociology*, 1883, Reprint, trans. F.J. Nock, ed. Louis Schneider, Urbana, Ill.: University of Illinois Press.

Milgrom, P. and Roberts, J., 1992, *Economics, Organisation and Management*, Englewood Cliffs, NJ: Prentice-Hall.

Mintzberg, H., 1978, Patterns in Strategy Formation, *Management Science*, Vol. 24, No. 9, pp. 934-948

Mintzberg, H., 1987a, The Strategy Concept II: Another Look at Why Organizations Need Strategies, in G.R. Carroll and D. Vogel (eds.) *Organizational Approaches to Strategy*, Cambridge, MA: Ballinger, pp. 21-28.

Mintzberg, H., 1987b, Crafting Strategy, *Harvard Business Review*, Vol. 65, No. 4, pp. 66-75.

Mintzberg, H., 1990, Strategy Formation: Schools of Thought, in J.W. Frederikson (eds.) *Perspectives on Strategic Management*, London, pp. 105-235.

Mintzberg, H, 1991, Learning 1, Planning 0. Reply to Igor Ansoff, *Strategic Management Journal*, Vol. 12, pp. 463-466.

Mintzberg, H., 1994, *The Rise and Fall of Strategic Planning*, New York: Prentice Hall.

Mintzberg, H. and Quinn, J.B., 1991, *Strategy Process. Concepts, Context, Cases*, (eds.), Englewood Cliffs, N.J.: Prentice-Hall.

Mintzberg, H., Raisinghani D., and Theoret, A., 1976, The Structure of "Unstructured" Decisions, *Administrative Science Quarterly*, Vol. 21, pp. 246-275.

Mintzberg, H. and Waters, J.A., 1985, Of Strategies, Deliberate and Emergent, *Strategic Management Journal*, Vol. 6, pp. 257-272.

Mirowski, P., 1990, The Phiolophical Bases of Institutionalist Economics, in D. Lavoie (eds.) *Economics and Hermeneutics*, London: Routledge, pp. 76-112.

Mises, L., 1966, *Human Action*, 3rd ed., Chicago: Henry Regnery and Co.

Mockler, R.J., 1995, Strategic Management: The Beginning of a New Era, in D.E. Hussey (eds.) *Rethinking Strategic Management: Ways to Improve Competitive Performance*, Chichester: John Wiley & Sons, pp. 1-41.

Montgomery, C.A., 1995, *Resource-Based and Evolutionary Theories of the Firm: Towards a Synthesis*, Boston: Kluwer Academic Publishers.

Montgomery, C.A. and Porter, M.E., 1991, Introduction, in C.A. Montgomery and M.E. Porter (eds.) *Strategy: Seeking and Securing Competitive Advantage*, Boston: Harvard Business School, pp. xi-xxiii.

Montgomery, C.A., Wernerfelt, B. and Balakrishnan, 1989, Strategy Content and Research Process; A Critique and Commentary, *Strategic Management Journal*, Vol. 10, pp. 189-197.

Morgan, G., Paradigm Diversity in Organisational Research, in J. Hassard and D. Pym (eds.) *The Theory and Philosophy of Organisations*, London: Routledge, pp. 13-29.

Morgenstern, O., 1972, Thirteen Critical Points in Contemporary Economic Theory: An Interpretation, *Journal of Economic Literature*, Vol. 10, pp. 1163-1189.

Morishima, M., 1991, General Equilibrium Theory in the Twenty-First Century, *The Economic Journal*, Vol. 101, pp. 69-74.

Moss, S.J, 1981, *An Economic Theory of Business Strategy*, Oxford: Martin Robertson.

Musgrave, A., 1981, Unreal Assumptions in Economic Theory: The F-Twist Untwisted, *Kyklos*, Vol. 34, No. 3, pp. 377-387

Nagel, E., 1963, Assumptions in Economic Theory, *American Economic Review*, Vol. 53, pp. 211-219.

Nayyer, P.R. and Kazanjian, 1993, Organizing to Attain Potential Benefits From Information Asymmetries and Economies of Scope in Related Diversified Firms, *Academy of Management Review*, Vol. 18, No. 4, pp. 735-759.

Needham, D., 1978, *The Economics of Industrial Structure, Conduct and Performance*, London: Holt, Reiehart and Winston.

Nelson, R.R., 1986, Evolutionary Modelling of Economic Change, in J.E. Stiglitz and G.F. Mathewson (eds.) *New Developments in the Analysis of Market Structure*, London: Macmillan, pp. 450-474, p. 466.

Nelson, R.R., 1991, Why Do Firms Differ, and How Does It Matter?, *Strategic Management Journal,* Vol. 12, pp. 61-74, pp. 61-62.

Nelson, R.R., 1994, The Role of Firm Differences in an Evolutionary Theory of Technical Advance, in L. Magnusson (eds.) *Evolutionary and Neo-Schumpeterian Approaches to Economics*, Boston: Kluwer, pp. 231-242, pp. 234-235.

Nelson, R.R. and Winter, S.G., 1982, *An Evolutionary Theory of Economic Change*, Cambridge, MA: Belknap Press.

Norman, G. and La Manna, M., 1992, *The New Industrial Economics*, (eds.), Aldershot: Edward Elgar.

North, D.C., 1993, Institutions and Economic Performance, in U. Maki, B. Gustafsson and C. Knudsen (eds.) *Rationality, Institutions and Economic Methodology*, London: Routledge, pp. 242-261.

O'Brien, D.P., 1976, The Longevity of Adam Smith's Vision: Paradigms, Research Programmes and Falsifiability in the History of Economic Thought, *Scottish Journal of Political Economy*, Vol. 23, No. 2, pp. 133-151

O'Brien, D.P., 1984, The Evolution of the Theory of the Firm, in F.H. Stephen (eds.) *Firms, Organisation and Labour: Approaches to the Economics of Work Organisation*, London: MacMillan, pp. 25-62.

Odigari, H. and Yamawaki, H., 1990, The Persistence of profits: International Comparison, in D.C. Mueller (eds) *The Dynamics of Company Profits*, Cambridge University Press.

O'Driscoll, G.P., Jr. and Rizzo, M.J., 1985, *The Economics of Time and Ignorance*, Oxford: Basil Blackwell.

Ohmea, K., 1991, Getting Back to Strategy, in C.A. Montgomery and M.E. Porter (eds.) *Strategy: Seeking and Securing Competitive Advantage*, Boston: Harvard Business School, pp. 61-74.

Oster, S.M., 1990, *Modern Competitive Analysis*, Oxford: Oxford University Press.

Ouchi, W.G., 1980, *Markets, Bureaucracies and Clans*, Administrative Science Quarterly, Vol. 25, pp. 129-141.

Penrose, E.T., 1952, Biological Analogies in the Theory of the Firm, *American Economic Review*, Vol. 52, pp. 804-819.

Penrose, E., 1959, *The Theory of the Growth of the Firm*, Oxford: Oxford University Press.

Penrose, E.T., 1971a (First published in 1960, The Business History Review, Vol. 34, No. 1, pp. 1-23), The Growth of the Firm. A Case Study: The Hercules Powder Company, in E.T. Penrose (eds.) *The Growth of Firms, Middle East Oil and Other Essays*, London: Frank Cass & Company, pp. 43-63.

Penrose, E.T., 1971b (First published in 1955, American Economic Review, Vol. XLV, No. 2), Limits to the Size and Growth of Firms, in E.T. Penrose (eds.) *The Growth of Firms, Middle East Oil and Other Essays*, London: Frank Cass & Co., pp. 30-42.

Peteraf, M.A., 1993, The Cornerstones of Competitive Advantage: A Resource-based View, *Strategic Management Journal*, Vol. 14, pp. 179-191.

Peters, T. J. and Waterman, R.H. Jr., 1982, *In Search of Excellence: Lessons from America's Best-Run Companies*, New York: Harper & Row.

Pettigrew, A.M., 1992, The Character and Significance of Strategy Process Research, *Strategic Management Journal*, Vol. 13, pp. 5-16.

Pickering, J.F., 1974, *Industrial Structure and Market Conduct*, London: Martin Robertson.

Pitelis, C., 1991, *Market and Non-Market Hierarchies. Theory of Institutional Failure*, Oxford: Basil Blackwell.

Pitelis, C., 1993, *Transaction Costs, Markets and Hierarchies*, (eds.), Oxford: Basil Blackwell.

Pitelis, C.N. and Sugden, R., 1991, *The Nature of the Transnational Firm*, (eds.), London: Routledge.

Pitt-Watson, D., 1992, Business Strategy and Economics, in D. Faulkner and G. Johnson (eds.) *The Challenge of Strategic Management*, London: Kogan Page, pp. 39-63.

Popper, K., 1978, *Conjectures and Refutations. The Growth of Scientific Knowledge*, London: Routledge and Kegan Paul.

Popper, K., 1981, The Rationality of Scientific Revolutions, in I. Hacking (eds.) *Scientific Revolutions*, Oxford: Oxford University Press.

Porter, M.E., 1980, *Competitive Strategy: Techniques for Analysing Industries and Competitors*, New York: The Free Press.

Porter, M.E., 1981, The Contributions of Industrial Organisation To Strategic Management, *Academy of Management Review*, Vol. 6, No. 4, pp. 609-620.

Porter, M.E., 1985, *Competitive Advantage*, New York: Free press.

Porter, M.E., 1991, Towards a Dynamic Theory of Strategy, *Strategic Management Journal*, Vol. 12, pp. 95-117.

Porter, M.E., 1996, What is Strategy?, *Harvard Business Review*, November-December, pp. 61-78.

Powell, T.C., 1996, How Much Does Industry Matter? An Alternative Empirical Test, *Strategic Management Journal*, Vol. 17, pp. 323-334.

Power, M., 1990, Modernism, Postmodernism and Organisation, in J. Hassard and D. Pym (eds.) *The Theory and Philosophy of Organisations*, London: Routledge, pp. 109-124.

Prahalad, C.K. and Hamel, G., 1990, The Core Competence of the Corporation, *Harvard Business Review*, Vol. 68, No. 3, pp. 79-91.

Pratt, J.W. and Zeckhauser, R.J., 1985, Principals and Agents: An Overview, in J.W. Pratt and R.J. Zeckhauser (eds.), *Principals and Agents: The Structure of Business*, Boston, Mass.: Harvard Business School Press.

Putterman, L., 1988, The Firm as Association Versus the firm as Commodity. Efficiency, Rights, and Ownership, *Economics and Philosophy*, Vol. 4, pp. 243-266.

Quinn, J.B., 1980, *Strategies for Change: Logical Incrementalism*, Homewood, IL: Richard D. Irwin.

Quinn, J.B., 1984, Managing Strategies Incrementally, in R.B. Lamb (eds.) *Competitive Strategic Management*, Englewood Cliffs, NY: Prentice-Hall, pp. 35-61.

Rajagopalan, N., Rasheed, A.M.A. and Datta, D.K., 1993, Strategic Decision Processes: Critical Review and Future Directions, *Journal of Management*, Vol. 19, No. 2, pp. 349-384.

Rasmusen, E., 1994, *Games and Information*, (2nd ed.), Oxford: Blackwell.

Rector, R.A., 1990, The Economics of Rationality and the Rationality of Economics, in D. Lavoie (eds.) *Economics and Hermeneutics*, London: Routledge, pp. 195-235.

Reed, M. and Hughes, M., 1992, *Rethinking Organization. New Directions in Organization Theory and Analysis*, (eds.), London: Sage Publications.

Reed, R. and DeFillipi, R.J., 1990, Causal Ambiguity, Barriers to Imitation, and Sustainable Competitive Advantage, *Academy of Management Review*, Vol. 15, No. 1, pp. 88-102.

Reekie, W.D., 1989, *Industrial Economics. A Critical Introduction to Corporate Enterprise in Europe and America*, Hants: Edward Elgar.

Remenyi, V.J., 1979, Core Demi-core Interaction: Toward a General Theory of Disciplinary and Subdisciplinary Growth, *History of Political Economy*, Vol. 11, No. 1, pp. 30-63.

Reve, T., 1990, The Firm as a Nexus of Internal and External Contracts, in M. Aoki, B. Gustafsson and O.E. Williamson (eds.) *The Firm as a Nexus of Treaties*, London: Sage Publications, pp. 133-161.

Ricketts, M., 1994 (First edition published in 1987), *The Economics of Business Enterprise*, London: Harvester Wheatsheaf.

Rizzo, M.J., 1982, Mises and Lakatos: A Reformulation of Austrian Methodology, in I.M. Kirzner (eds.) *Method, Process, and Austrian Economics. Essays in Honour of Ludwing von Mises*, Lexington, Mass.: D.C. Heath and Company, pp. 53-72.

Rizzo, M.J., 1985, Rules Versus Cost-Benefit Analysis in Common Law, *Cato Journal*, Vol. 4, pp. 865-884.

Robinson, J., 1969 (first published in 1933), *The Economics of Imperfect Competition*, London: Macmillan.

Robinson, J., 1977, What are the Questions, *Journal of Economic Literature*, Vol. 15, pp. 1318-1339.

Roquebert, J.A., Philips, R.L. and Westfall, P.A., 1996, Markets vs. Management: What 'Derives' Profitability?, *Strategic Management Journal*, Vol. 17, pp. 653-664.

Rothbard, M.N., 1976, Praxeology: The Methodology of Austrian Economics, in E.G. Dolan (eds.) *The Foundations of Modern Austrian Economics*, Kansas City: Sheed & Ward, pp. 19-39.

Rouleau, L. and Seguin, F., 1995, Strategy and Organization Theories: Common Forms of Discourse, *Journal of Management Studies*, Vol. 32, No. 1, pp. 101-117.

Rowlinson, M., 1997, *Organisations and Institutions. Perspectives in Economics and Sociology*, London: Macmillan.

Rumelt, R.P., 1981, Towards a Strategic Theory of the Firm, UCLA *Working Paper*.

Rumelt, R.P., 1984, Towards a Strategic Theory of the Firm, in R.B. Lamb (eds.) *Competitive Strategic Management*, Englewood Cliffs, NY: Prentice-Hall, pp. 556-570.

Rumelt, R.P, 1987, Theory, Strategy, and Entreprenurship, in D. Teece (eds.) *The Competitive Challenge*, Cambridge, M.A.: Balinger, pp. 137-158.

Rumelt, R.P., 1991, How Much Does Industry Matter?, *Strategic Management Journal*, Vol. 12, pp. 167-185.

Rumelt, R.P., 1994, Foreword, in G. Hamel and A. Heene (eds.) *Competence-Based Competition*, New York: John Wiley & Sons, pp. xv-xix.

Rumelt, R.P, Schendel, D. and Teece, D.J., 1991, Strategic Management and Economics, *Strategic Management Journal*, Vol. 12, pp. 5-29.

Rumelt, R.P., Schendel, D.E. and Teece, D.J., 1994, *Fundamental Issues in Strategy*, (eds.), Boston: Harvard Business School Press.

Rutherford, M., 1989, What is Wrong with the New Institutonal Economics (and What is Still Wrong with the Old)?, *Review of Political Economy*, Vol. 1, pp. 299-318.

Salanti, A., 1987, Falsificationism and Fallibilism as Epistemic Foundations of Economics: A Critical View, *Kyklos*, Vol. 40, pp. 368-392.

Saloner, G., 1991, Modelling, Game Theory, and Strategic Management, *Strategic Management Journal*, Vol. 12, pp. 119-136.

Salop, S., 1979, Strategic Entry Deterrence, *American Economic Review*, Vol. 69, pp. 335-338.

Samuels, W.J., 1984, *Research in the History of Economic Thought and Methodology*, (eds.), Vol. 2, London: JAI Press.

Samuelson, P.A., 1980, *Principles of Economics*, New York: McGraw Hill.

Sanchez, R., Heene, A. and Thomas, H., 1996, *Dynamics of Competence-Based Competition. Theory and Practice in the New Strategic Management*, (eds.), Oxford: Elseiver Science.

Saviotti, P.P. and Melcalfe, J.S., 1991, *Evolutionary Theories of Economic and Technological Change. Present Status and Future Prospects*, Chur: Harwood Academic Publishers.

Sawyer, M.C., 1979, *Theories of the Firm*, London: Weidenfeld and Nicolson, pp. 89-90.

Schelling, T.C., 1960, *The Strategy of Conflict*, Cambridge, Mass.: Harvard University Press.

Schendel, D., 1997, The Interactions of Organizational and Competitive Influences on Strategy and performance, *Strategic Management Journal*, Vol. 18, pp. 1-3.

Scherer, F.M., and Ross, D., 1990, *Industrial Market Structure and Economic Performance*, Third Edition, Boston: Houghton Mifflin Company.

Schmalensee, R., 1985, Do Markets Differ Much?, *American Economic Review*, Vol. 75, No. 3, pp. 341-351.

Schmalensee, R., 1988, Industrial Economics: an Overview, *The Economic Journal*, Vol. 98, pp. 643-681.

Schmalensee, R., 1989, Inter-Industry Studies of Structure and Performance, in R. Schmalensee and R.D. Willig (eds) *Handbook of Industrial Organisation*, Vol. II, Amsterdam: Elsevier Science Publishers B.V.

Schmalensee, R. and Willing, R.D., 1989, *Handbook of Industrial Organization*, Vol. I and II, (eds.), North-Holland: Elsevier Science Publishers B.V.

Schoemaker, P.J.H., 1993, Strategic Decisions in Organizations: Rational and Behavioural Views, *Journal of Management Studies*, Vol. 30, No. 1, pp. 107-129.

Schumpeter, J.A., 1934, *The Theory of Economic Development*, Cambridge, Mass. : Harvard University Press.

Schumpeter, J.A., 1947, The Creative Response in Economic History, *The Journal of Economic History*, Vol. 7, No. 2, pp. 149-159.

Schumpeter, J.A., 1950, *Capitalism, Socialism and Democracy*, London: George Allen & Unwin, p. 82.

Schumpeter, J.A., 1954, *History of Economic Analysis*, New York: Oxford University Press, p. 789

Schumpeter, J.A., 1997 (First published in 1952), *Ten Great Economists. From Marx to Keynes*, London: Routledge.

Scitovsky, T., 1943, A Note on Profit Maximisation, *Review of Economic Studies*, Vol. 11, No. 1, pp. 57-60.

Segal-Horn, S., 1998, The Resource-Based View of Strategy. Introduction, in S. Segal-Horn (eds.) *The Strategy Reader*, Oxford: Basil Blackwell, pp. 177-178.

Senge, P.M., 1997 (First bublished in 1990), *The Fifth Discipline. The Art and Practice of the Learning Organisation*, London: Century Business.

Seth, A. and Thomas, H., 1994, Theories of the Firm: Implications for Strategy Research, *Journal of Management Studies*, Vol. 31, No. 2, pp. 164-191.

Shapiro, C., 1989, The Theory of Business Strategy, *RAND Journal of Economics*, Vol. 20, No. 1, pp. 125-137.

Shepherd, W., 1984, "Contestability" vs. Competition, *The American Economic Review*, Vol. 74, No. 4, pp. 572-587.

Shrivastava, P., Huff, A.S. and Dutton, J.E., 1994, *Advances in Strategic Management. Resource-Based View of the Firm*, Vol. 10A, London: JAI Press.

Singleton, R.C., 1986, *Industrial Organisation and Antitrust: A Survey of Alternative Perspectives*, Columbus, Ohio: Publishing Horizons.

Simon, H.A., 1959, Theories of Decision-Making in Economics and Behavioural Science, *The American Economic Review*, Vol. 49, pp. 253-283.

Simon, H.A., 1976, From Substantive to Procedural Rationality, in S.J. Latsis (eds.) *Method and Appraisal in Economics*, Cambridge: Cambridge University Press, pp. 129-148.

Simon, H.A., 1993, Strategy and Organizational Evolution, *Strategic Management Journal*, Vol. 14, pp. 131-142.

Slater, M., 1980, Foreword, in E.T. Penrose, *The Theory of the Growth of the Firm*, (second edition), pp. vii-xxx.

Spinosa, C., Fernando, F. and Dreyfus, H.L, 1997, *Disclosing New Worlds. Entrepreneurship, Democratic Action, and the Cultivation of Solidarity*, Cambridge, Mass.: The MIT Press.

Spulber, D.F., 1993, Economic Analysis and Management Strategy: A Survey, *Journal of Economics & Management Strategy*, Vol. 1, No. 3, pp. 535-574.

Stephen, F.H., 1984, Economics and Work Organisation, in F.H. Stephen (eds.) *Firms and Labour: Approaches to the Economics of Work Organisation*, London: Macmillan, pp. 3-23, pp. 8-10.

Stewart, I.M.T., 1984, Views of Economic Ignorance, in W.J. Samuels (eds.) *Research in the History of Economic Thought and Methodology*, Vol. 2, London: JAI Press, pp. 161-172.

Stigler, G.J., 1957, Perfect Competition, Historically Contemplated, *The Journal of Political Economy*, Vol. 65, pp. 1-16.

Stigler, G.J., 1963, *Capital and Rates of Return in Manufacturing Industries*, Preston, N.J.: Princeton University Press.

Stigler, G.J., 1968, *The Organisation of Industry*, Homewood, Ill.: R.D. Irwin.

Strong, N. and Waterson, M., 1987, Principal, Agents and Information, in R. Clarke and T. McGuiness (eds.) *The Economics of the Firm*, Oxford: Basil Balckwell, pp. 18-41.

Sugden, R., 1991, Rational Choice: A Survey of Contributions From Economics and philosophy, *The Economic Journal*, Vol. 101, pp. 751-785.

Teece, D., 1980, Economics of Scope and the Scope of the Enterprise, *Journal of Economic Behaviour and Organisation*, Vol. 1, pp. 223-247.

Teece, D., 1982, Toward an Economic Theory of the Multiproduct Firm, *Journal of Economic Behaviour and Organisation*, Vol. 3, pp. 39-63.

Teece, D., 1981, The Multinational Enterprise: Market Failure and Market Powet Considerations, *Sloan Management Review*, Vol. 99, No. 3, pp. 3-17.

Teece, D.J., 1990, Contributions and Impediments of Economic Analysis to the Study of Strategic Management, in J.W. Frederickson (eds.) *Perspectives on Strategic Management*, pp. 39-79.

Teece, D.J., Pisano, G. and Shuen, A., 1990, Firm Capabilities, Resources and the Concept of Strategy, CCC *Working Paper* No. 90-8, University of California at Berkeley.

Teece, D.J., Rumelt, R., Dosi, G. and Winter, S., 1994, Understanding Corporate Coherence: Theory and Evidence, *Journal of Economic Behaviour and Organisation*, Vol. 23, pp. 1-30.

Thepot, J. and Thietart, R.-A., 1991, *Microeconomic Contributions to Strategic Management*, Amsterdam: Elsevier Science Publishers.

Thoben, H., 1982, Mechanistic and Organistic Analogies in Economics Reconsidered, *Kyklos*, Vol. 35, pp. 292-306.

Thorelli, H.B., 1977, *Strategy + Structure = Performance*, (eds.), Bloomington: Idiana University Press.

Thompson, S., 1988, Agency Costs of Internal Organisation, in S. Thompson and M. Wright (eds.) *Internal Organisation, Efficiency and Profit*, Oxford: Philip Allan, pp. 65-85.

Tirole, J., 1988, *The Theory of Industrial Organisation*, Cambridge: The MIT Press.

Tomlinson, J., 1986, Democracy Inside the Black Box? Neo-classical Theories of the Firm and Industrial Democracy, *Economy and Society*, Vol. 15, No. 2, pp. 220-250.

Torrance, T.S., 1990, The Philosophy and Methodology of Economics, in D. Mair and A.G. Miller (eds.) *A Modern Guide to Economic Theory: An Introduction to Comparative Schools of Thought in Economics*, Hants: Edward Elgar, pp. 21-39.

Towsend, H., 1995, *Foundations of Business Economics*, London: Routledge.

Tsoukas, H., 1994, What is Management? An Outline of a Metatheory, *British Journal of Management*, Vol. 5, pp. 289-301.

Tsoukas, H., 1994, Refining Common Sense: Types of Knowledge in Management Studies, *Journal of Management Studies*, Vol. 31, No. 6, pp. 761-780.

Utton, M.A., 1986, *Profits and Stability of Monopoly*, Cambridge: Cambridge University Press.

Vanberg, V.J., 1993, Rational Choice, Rule-Following and Institutions: An Evolutionary Perspective, in U. Maki, B. Gustafsson and C. Knudsen (eds.) *Rationality, Institutions and Economic Methodology*, London: Routledge, pp. 171-200.

Vanberg, V.J., 1994, *Rules & Choice in Economics*, London: Routledge.

Vaughn, K.I., 1982, Subjectivism, Predictability, and Creativity: Comment on Buchanan, in I.M. Kirzner (eds.) *Method, Process, and Austrian Economics. Essays in Honour of Ludwing von Mises*, Lexington, Mass.: D.C. Heath and Company, pp. 21-29.

Veblen, T.B., 1919 (1898), Why Is Economics Not An Evolutionary Science?, in *The Place of Science in Modern Civilisation and Other Essays*, New York: B.W. Huebsch, pp. 56-81.

Veblen, T.B., 1948, *The Portable Veblen*, edited by M. Lerner, New York: Viking Press.

Verdin, P.J. and Williamson, P.J., 1994, Core Competences, Competitive Advantage and Market Analysis: Forging the Links, in G. Hamel and A. Heene (eds.) *Competence-Based Competition*, Chichester: John Wiley & Sons, pp. 77-110.

Vernon, J.M., 1972, *Market Structure and Industrial Performance: A Review of Statistical Findings*, Boston: Allyn and Bacon.

Wagner, S.A., 2000, The Image of Man in Organisation Theory. On the Institutional Problem and the Potrayal of Human Behaviour in the Social Sciences, *Doctoral Dissertation*, Department of Management and Economics/Catholic University of Eichstaett at Ingolstadt, Germany.

Waterson, M., 1984, *Economic Theory of the Industry*, Cambridge: Cambridge University Press.

Weintraub, E.R., 1991, *Stabilizing Dynamics. Constructing Economic Knowledge*, Cambridge: Cambridge University Press.

Wensley, R., 1982, PIMS and BCG: New Horizons or False Dawn?, *Strategic Management Journal*, Vol. 3, pp. 147-158.

Wernerfelt, B., 1984, A Resource Based View of the Firm, *Strategic Management Journal,* Vol. 5, pp. 171-180.

Wernerfelt, B., 1995, The Resource-Based View of the Firm: Ten Years After, *Strategic Management Journal*, Vol. 16, pp. 171-174.

Wernerfelt, B. and Montgomery, C., 1988, Tobin's q and the Importance of Focus in Firm Performance, *American Economic Review*, Vol. 78, No. 1, pp. 246-251.

Whittington, R., 1993, *What is Strategy and Does It Matter?,* London: Routledge.

Wilber, C.K. and Hoksbergen, R., 1984, Current Thinking on the Role of Value Judgements in Economic Science: A Survey, in W.J. Samuels (eds.) *Research in the History of Economic Thought and Methodology*, Vol. 2, London: JAI Press, pp. 179-194.

Williamson, O.E. 1963, A Model of Rational Managerial Behaviour, in R.M. Cyert and J.G. March, *A Behavioural Theory of the Firm*, Englewood Cliffs, N.J.: Prentice-Hall, pp. 237-252.

Williamson, O.E., 1975, *Markets and Hierarchies: Analysis and Antitrust Implications: A Study in the Economics of Internal Organisation*, New York: Free Press.

Williamson, O.E., 1979, Transaction-Cost Economics: The Governance of Contractual Relations, *Journal of Law and Economics*, Vol. 22, No. 1, pp. 233-261.

Williamson, O.E., 1981, The Modern Corporation: Origins, Evolution, Attributes, *Journal of Economic Literature*, Vol. 19, pp. 1537-1568.

Williamson, O.E., 1985, *The Economic Institutions of Capitalism*, New York: Free Press.

Williamson, O.E., 1986, Vertical Integration and Related Variations on a Transaction-Cost Economics Theme, in J.E. Stiglitz and G.F. Mathewson (eds.) *New Developments in the Analysis of Market Structure*, London: Macmillan, pp. 149-174.

Williamson, O.E., 1988, Corporate Finance and Corporate Governance, *The Journal of Finance*, Vol. 43, No. 3, pp. 567-591.

Willimason, O.E., 1990, The Firm as a Nexus of Treaties: An Introduction, in M. Aoki, B. Gustasson, and O.E. Williamson (eds.) *The Firm as a Nexus of Treaties*, London: Sage Publications, pp. 1-25.

Williamson, O.E., 1991, Strategizing, Economizing, and Economic Organisation, *Strategic Management Journal*, Vol. 12, pp. 75-94.

Winter, S.G., 1982, An Essay on the Theory of Production, in S.H. Hymans (eds.) *Economics and the World Around It*, Ann Arbor: University of Michigan Press.

Winter, S.G., 1988, On Coase, Competence, and the Corporation, *Journal of Law, Economics, and Organization*, Vol. 4, No. 1, pp. 163-180.

Winter, S.G., 1995, Four Rs of Profitability: Rents, Resources, Routines, and Replication, in C.A. Montgomery (eds.) *Resource-Based and Evolutionary Theories of the Firm: Towards a Synthesis*, Boston: Kluwer, pp. 147-177.

Wisdom, J., 1965, Refutation by Observation and Refutation by Theory, in I. Lakatos and A. Musgrave (eds.) *Problems in the Philosophy of Science*, Vol. 3, Amsterdam: North-Holland Publishing Company, pp. 65-67.

Yamin, M., 1991, A Reassessment of Hymer's Contribution to the Theory of the Transactional Corporation, in C.N. Pitelis and R. Sugden (eds.) *The Nature of Transnational Firm*, London: Routledge, pp. 64-80.

Yao, D.A., 1988, Beyond the Reach of the Invisisble Hand: Impediments to Economic Activity, Market Failures, and Profitability, *Strategic Management Journal*, Vol. 9, pp. 59-70.

Zajac, E. and Olsen, C.P, 1993, From Transaction Cost to Transactional Value Analysis: Implications for the Study of Interorganizational Strategies, *Journal of Management Studies*, Vol. 30, No. 1, pp. 131-145.

# Index